P9-BAW-437

1817
THE
NORMAN WILLIAMS
PUBLIC LIBRARY.
WOODSTOCK · VERMONT
DISCARD
Norman Williams Public Library
Woodstock, VT
Date
AMERICAN BANK NOTE CO. NY

A Passion for Knitting

Step-by-Step Illustrated Techniques, Easy Contemporary Patterns, and Essential Resources for Becoming Part of the World of Knitting

NANCY J. THOMAS and ILANA RABINOWITZ

Foreword by Melanie Falick

A FIRESIDE BOOK
Published by Simon & Schuster
New York London Toronto Sydney Singapore

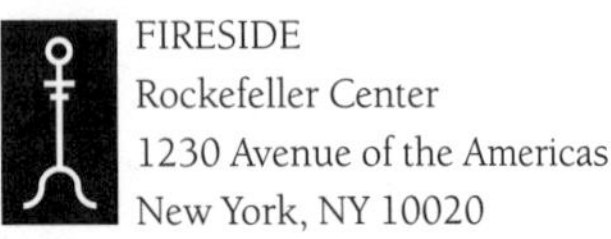

FIRESIDE
Rockefeller Center
1230 Avenue of the Americas
New York, NY 10020

Designed by Helene Berinsky

Manufactured in the United States of America

10 9 8 7 6 5 4 3 2

Library of Congress Cataloging-in-Publication Data

Thomas, Nancy J.
A passion for knitting: step-by-step illustrated techniques, easy contemporary patterns, and essential resources for becoming part of the world of knitting / Nancy J. Thomas and Ilana Rabinowitz ; foreword by Melanie Falick.
p. cm.
"A Fireside book."
Includes index.
1. Knitting. 2. Knitting—Patterns. I. Rabinowitz, Ilana. II. Title.

TT820.T473 2002
746.43'2—dc21 2002026884

ISBN 0-684-87069-X

Acknowledgments

We would like to thank the people whose help was so valuable to us. Lisa Considine, our editor at Simon and Schuster and fellow knitter, who with her assistant Anne Bartholomew shepherded this project through many stages; Harold Rabinowitz and the staff at The Reference Works, for their guidance and support; Alex Hoyt, our agent for finding a good home for this book; Charlotte Quiggle and Heather Fenby, who reviewed the countless facts and patterns as well as providing editorial assistance; the members of the KnitList, who graciously shared their suggestions, ideas and stories with us; Barbara Breiter, webmaster of the knitting site at About.com for her help with the chapter about Knitting on the Web; Adina Klein, who worked with the designers to develop easy, fashionable patterns; Jack Deutsch, our photographer, who made our designs look terrific, the Craft Yarn Council of America (CYCA) for their efforts to promote the craft of knitting through publicity and Knit Out events; and David Blumenthal of Lion Brand Yarn Company, who has done much for the growth and popularity of knitting in America and who has supported us so generously in the creation of this book. We also wish to acknowledge the knitters around the world and throughout history who have recorded, documented and authored books about the rich, vibrant, and creative legacy of knitting.

Contents

Foreword by Melanie Falick ix

Introduction xiii

PART I

The Craft of Knitting

1. *Tools* 3
2. *Learning the Knit Stitch* 30
3. *Learning the Purl Stitch* 38
4. *Learning the Rib Stitch* 41
5. *Help!!* 45
6. *Scarves* 49
7. *Increasing Your Knowledge* 57
8. *Glossary of Knitting Terms* 64
9. *Making Your First Sweater* 80
10. *Finishing and Sizing* 90
11. *Bells and Whistles* 107
12. *Branching Out* 130

PART II

The World of Knitting

13. *Knitting for Charity* 141

14. *Collecting and Storing Yarn* 156

15. *Knitting Traditions* 164

16. *Fashion Trends in Knitting* BY TRISHA MALCOLM 174

17. *Knitting on the Go—Events and Travel* 182

18. *Knitting on the Web* 189

19. *The Healing Power of Knitting* 204

20. *The Commerce of Knitting* 213

21. *The Chain of Knitting Instruction* 221

22. *Knitting Fellowship* 225

23. *Showing Off* 234

24. *The Literature of Knitting* 248

Resources 259

List of Patterns 262

Index 263

Foreword

BY MELANIE FALICK

I learned to knit as a child, but I became a knitter at twenty-five—that is, at twenty-five, I did more than cast on and knit a few rows before becoming distracted by something else. It was the late 1980s, and as I was to come to find out, the end of a mini knitting boom. Apparently, Perry Ellis had introduced oversized, bulky-knit sweaters in the early 1980s, and swarms of women bought yarn in order to reproduce them. Gradually those sweaters went out of fashion, many of those women lost interest, and, concurrently, the economics of the yarn business declined. Both yarn mills and knitting shops were closing at a record pace. But I didn't know any of that. I had simply met a new boyfriend in 1988 and decided to knit him a scarf for our first Valentine's Day together. I wanted to surprise him with something made with great care and love (though I dared not use that word too soon). Immediately, in fact within moments of walking into the yarn shop I had found in the yellow pages when I conceived of the gift, I realized that this scarf would be significant to me in a different way; even if my boyfriend and I didn't stay together (though we did and are now married), I knew I would continue to knit. Instantly I was drawn to the colors and textures of the yarn and soon after became intrigued by the culture of knitting, that is, the people around the world who knit and the role knitting plays in their lives.

I started to talk about my knitting with my friends and got a mixed response: Some recalled knitting in their past and pulled out old projects and joined me, some asked me to teach them how to knit, and some laughed and made comments about grandmothers or spinsters. My mother, a lapsed knitter, started knitting again. My father, a passionate appreciator of the work of the hand, bought me hand-spun yarn from a sheep farm he visited. Though I knew that knitting wasn't considered "cool," I didn't care at all. They're losers, I thought when people I met judged my new hobby as out of date or suitable only for those who had uninteresting lives. For me, the coolest thing to do was to follow my own creative path.

Today the situation has changed significantly. According to the mainstream media, knitting is "hot." Movie stars are knitting; high-powered financiers are knitting; college students are knitting; even men are knitting. While that is, in most ways, a positive development, it does make me slightly sad. Before, I felt as though I was part of a quiet underground movement, that I was the lucky member of a unique group of mostly women who had discovered the secret power of an age-old craft. By simply manipulating yarn on needles, we could explore our creativity, achieve a meditative-like calm, and express our love for others. We could bond with one another and, most important, with our female ancestors. As knitters of the late twentieth century, we could celebrate the stitches of the women who had come before us, and we could honor their work, most of which has gone unrecorded by history. By appreciating their knitting, we could acknowledge their artistry and the power they held in their hands when they knitted the sweaters, socks, hats, and scarves that kept the people in their lives protected, that let the recipients of their work know that they were cared for.

As we enter the twenty-first century, I am not at all surprised by the upswing in interest in knitting. With so much of our lives driven by high-tech influences, we are in need of "soft-tech," of the work of the hand rather than the work of machinery, of the one-of-a-kind rather than the mass-produced. We are in need of reasons to join others with similar interests and to share our passions. We are in need of the soothing rhythms of knit and purl, which can slow us down and ground us and remind us that what we most need is not always the newest, latest, and greatest.

Knitting's current vogue also reflects the evolution of the women's movement. Now that most women no longer feel compelled to reject that which is traditionally feminine in order to succeed in the professional world, they can safely re-evaluate the domestic and proudly reclaim that which they miss, be it frilly fashion, child care, cooking, or needlework. And this time they can get more respect for their endeavors. Though knitting still suffers from some sexist and ageist stereotyping, its image is, indeed, improving. Even in the famously snobbish art world, knitting is being reconsidered and the work of artists whose medium is knitting is being pursued. Most media coverage does still somewhat annoyingly begin with a headline like KNITTING ISN'T JUST FOR GRANDMA ANYMORE, but knitting is moving to the forefront—at least for a while—and that is drawing new knitters into the community, which I have to admit is a good thing on both an individual and societal level. I suspect I'll get my "underground movement" back again. But, for now, to the people who can't resist the stereotype of grandmothers knitting in rocking chairs, I always point out: Grandma may be knitting and she may be rocking, but it's not because she's old and has nothing better to do. It is because she is wise and knows what's important.

MELANIE FALICK is the editor in chief of *Interweave Knits* magazine, the coauthor of *Knitting for Baby* (Stewart, Tabori & Chang, 2002), and the author of *Kids Knitting* (Artisan, 1988) and *Knitting in America* (Artisan, 1985).

Introduction

This book is an introduction to both the craft and the world of knitting. Knitting embodies warmth, color, texture, companionship, relaxation, joy, and accomplishment. Knitters find that the activity builds self-confidence and provides opportunity for creative expression, for healing, and for giving. The basics of knitting are so easy that children as young as seven or eight can learn to knit in a half-hour. Once basic stitches are learned, the creative possibilities of needles and yarn are infinite.

In Part I: The Craft of Knitting we offer carefully illustrated, clear instructions so that anyone can learn to knit from this book, simply from the words and illustrations on the page. While everyone has his or her own way of learning, and some may prefer to be shown how in person, we have developed what we believe are simple, concise instructions for learning to knit without a teacher. Time and again, we have handed these instructions to people of all ages and sexes and they have succeeded without help. Once, at a photo-shoot for this book, the photographer asked whether he could borrow the instructions and a beginner's pattern for a hat on page 37. The next day he appeared with a nearly finished hat on his needles, the work of his own hands.

Once you know how to put stitches onto a needle (cast on) and how to make the knit stitch, the purl stitch, and to bind off, you have the basic apparatus for knitting. Beyond this, everything is a variation of the knit and purl stitches. You can create cables and intricate designs by changing the way you form those two basic stitches. Combine the basic stitch formula with the variety of existing yarns, and a world of unlimited design and creative possibilities is at your fingertips.

Because it is so easy to learn to knit, many people learn when they are children. Knitting teaches them the value of sitting quietly, paying attention, and maintaining focus. It teaches them that not everything in the world springs forth completely finished on a store shelf. They learn that it is possible to create something with their own two hands. And they enjoy a sense of accomplishment in creating something both practical and beautiful. With time, knitting may teach deeper lessons of patience, persistence, and the ability to deal with mistakes and move on. People who knit often use that time to think, sometimes without being totally aware they are thinking, reaping the joys and benefits of contemplation.

No matter when you learn to knit, if you have a teacher, you will have a special connection to that person. Often, the teacher is a family member, and the act of teaching becomes a thread that links the generations. One knitter, Diana, remembers teaching her brother how to knit when he was 21. He described such a sense of accomplishment after completing the first few rows that he told her he felt as if she had revealed a great treasure to him. "It was a defining moment for me as well—as bonding a moment as had ever taken place in the twenty years the two of us had coexisted on the planet," she said. "I was thrilled to be passing on a skill to my brother that had been taught to me by my sister, who had been taught by our mother, who had been taught by our grandmother, who had probably been taught by her mother. I began to see the yarn as a metaphor for the continuous thread that binds each of us to the members of our own family, as well as to our ancestors."

In Chapter 1 we introduce the basic tools of knitting—needles, and yarn—as well as additional accessories you may either need or want as your interest and abilities grow. Needles are available in a range of materials from metal to wood, in different colors and three types: straight, circular, and double-pointed. The different types of yarns on the market are even more varied, consisting of a virtually unlimited number of colors and combinations of natural and synthetic fibers. The same amount of yarn can sell for anywhere from a few to as much as hundreds of dollars, depending on the material. Whenever knitters congregate, they tend to debate and discuss their favorite needles—which type are the easiest and most comfortable to use—and their favorite yarns. Which ones make the best baby clothes, which make the fastest throws or the warmest sweaters. The tools you start out with, especially the yarn you choose, help determine what your knitting experience will be like and what the finished product will look like. Other elements that go into your project are less tangible, including everything from your skill level to your talent to your mood at the time. The beauty of knitting is how your inner world spills out into the knitted finished product through the stitched yarn.

From the time you learn to cast on, knit, and purl, you are not far from being able to complete an easy sweater pattern, a scarf, or a throw. Learning to read a pattern—the language of knitting—is the next step in exploring the realm of possibilities that knitting offers. There are knitters who are perfectly happy making unshaped scarves and throws year after year, and knitters who will not venture on to the next project unless it includes a new technique or a new approach. Both of these styles are valid. Both can be extremely rewarding. Where you go with knitting is a highly individual choice.

In Part II, we introduce you to the world—the culture—of knitting. Its many facets invite sustaining and meaningful participation. One powerful aspect of this world immediately connects knitters with others: knitting for charity. Perhaps since knitting for loved ones is already such a generous gift of time and self, it is a small step to move to knitting for those in need. Knitting charities (Chapter 13) abound on websites, in magazines, among knitting guilds and clubs, and wherever knitters gather.

Serious knitters often enjoy collecting yarn, knitting memorabilia, and knitting accessories. Knitters tend to have a love of fiber, texture, and color that compels them to collect yarn for its own sake—to look at it, to touch it, and, some say, even to smell it. In Chapter 14, you will meet people who collect not only yarn but every imaginable knitting-related item—messages from online knitting conversations, patterns (even of out-of-date styles designed with long-discontinued yarns), photos of cats playing with a ball of yarn, bags designed to carry yarn, and stuffed toys of animals whose wool is used for yarn, like sheep and alpacas. All of this collecting calls for organizing, storing, and sometimes (when a spouse is in the picture) hiding the fruits of this collection. This

Chapter, "Collecting and Storing Yarn," lets you peek into the homes of some of these avid savers of the regalia of knitting, and, perhaps, provides a glimpse of your own future.

It is also true of devoted knitters that they immediately feel a connection and camaraderie when meeting a fellow knitter. There is a sense of trust that opens a door into conversation and often leads to deep, long-lasting friendships. But knitters don't wait for the serendipity of finding one another on the street. They meet through the knitting guilds, college clubs, corporate office groups, knitting conventions, travel, and camps that cater to the need to commune with others who knit. In Chapter 22, we describe how the fellowship of knitters is like an extended family. It is one of the great benefits of knitting—and one of the more gratifying experiences of life.

In Chapter 18, we'll see how the Internet has forever changed the craft and influenced knitters in ways not previously possible. Knitters who were once isolated or had contact with no more than a handful of other knitters can now communicate with thousands of like-minded individuals every day. Through the Internet, we can immediately know how people are reacting to issues that affect the knitting community. We can all commiserate about the reactions we have gotten to knitting in public; we can become part of a fad to knit socks; we can create and donate a section of a memorial quilt to respond to a crisis. What we receive from being in instant touch with other knitters can be as practical as a solution to a knitting problem or an offer of a skein of yarn needed to complete a project, or as central to our well-being as support, validation, and comfort.

There are powerful emotional benefits available to those who become part of the universe of knitting. In Chapter 19 we share inspiring stories of how knitting has been a healing force in people's lives, providing a source of relaxation and solace in difficult times. Beyond the positive feelings of fellowship with others is the intrinsic quality of knitting to quiet a troubled mind and slow a racing heart during times of stress. Not everyone finds comfort in the same activities, but avid knitters receive a healing benefit that others describe getting from yoga, running, listening to beautiful music, or gardening. There's a sense of fulfillment that comes from completing a difficult project, improving one's self-esteem, and giving vent to creative expression that can provide a much-needed lift in challenging times.

Fashion and design (Chapter 16) are an exciting part of the world of knitting. Knitters eagerly anticipate the next issue of their favorite knitting magazine to see new designs that they might try for their own projects. They scan the pages of the fashion magazines looking for inspiration and ideas for unique sweaters. Anyone who has had to roll up the too-long sleeves of store-bought sweaters or who can't find a beautiful sweater in a size 2X can appreciate the ability to make one's own perfectly fitting sweater. Because design is such an important part of knitting, the top designers, authors, and teachers in the knitting world have become celebrities in their own right. People like Nicki Epstein, Lily Chin, Kaffe Fassett, Debbie Bliss, and Meg Swansen are invited to speak across the country about their approach to designing and knitting and to teach eager participants at guild meetings, knitting cruises, and knitting conventions.

This book will provide a door, a portal, into the exciting world of knitting. We believe that if you enter this world, at the very least you will learn a craft that you can enjoy for a lifetime and perhaps pass on to a child, a grandchild, a relative, or a friend. You may also discover things about yourself, both in the act of knitting and in the ruminative moments during which you build stitch upon stitch. Once you have started to knit, you may be motivated to journey further into this world—to talk to other knitters on the Internet, pick up a knitting magazine, start a knitting club at work, or attend a Knit-Out event in a nearby city. If it turns out that knitting entices you—that you have a passion for knitting—you will discover the deeper benefits of this ancient, continually evolving craft.

PART I

The Craft of Knitting

1

Tools

The most wonderful aspect of knitting is that your actual "needs" to begin knitting are minimal. Getting down to the bare bones, the only "must have's" are yarn and needles. All the other elements are designed to make your knitting more fun and enjoyable. As you become a more practiced knitter, your desire to refine your implements and add to your collection of gadgets and helpful tools will grow. No longer will just any needle do—you'll get fussy about your tools. A collection of knitting paraphernalia adds to your enjoyment of the knitting process. Eventually you will want to have a complete set of needles—and in some cases, more than one set.

Needles

When it comes to selecting needles, there is no right or wrong type to use. Beginners sometimes find that working with plastic or wooden needles is slightly easier than starting out with aluminum needles. Stitches tend to slip less on plastic or wooden needles. However, if your first knitting experience is with aluminum needles, you can still have the same results as someone who begins with other needles.

There are three common knitting-needle categories: straight, circular, and double-pointed. While some needles have specific uses, others can be used interchangeably. For example, you can make straight pieces on both straight and circular needles, and you can make circular pieces on both circular and double-pointed needles. The subtleties of when and how to use specific needles will be discussed within each section.

All three needle categories come in the same range of sizes. There are about 20 needle sizes based on the diameter of the needle. Some of these sizes may not be appropriate for your knitting needs, but it is good to be aware of the sizing difference. Note in our needle table that knitting needles have both an American size number and a metric measurement. Where there is no American size, it simply means that there is no equivalent number. You may find one or both numbers used on your needles. In future years, the metric system may become more widely used, as the millimeter size is the actual diameter of the needle shaft.

KNITTING NEEDLE CHART

U.S.	*Metric*
0	2 mm
1	2.25 mm
	2.5 mm
2	2.75 mm
3	3.25 mm
4	3.5 mm
5	3.75 mm
6	4 mm
7	4.5 mm
8	5 mm
9	5.5 mm
10	6 mm
10½	6.5 mm
	7 mm
	7.5 mm
11	8 mm
13	9 mm
15	10 mm
17	12.75 mm
19	16 mm
35	19 mm
50	25.5 mm

STRAIGHT NEEDLES

Straight needles are the most common and widely available. Almost any store or shop that sells yarn has some selection of straight needles. They are generally used for the learning-to-knit process. While they come in a variety of sizes, straight needles primarily come in two lengths: 10" (25 cm) and 14" (36 cm).

It's important to understand the correlation between the needle size and your knitting yarn. In photo at right, there is one larger pair of needles in a 14" length and one smaller pair in a 10" length. The larger pair would be used with a thick yarn and the smaller pair would be used with a thinner yarn. The longer needles can fit more stitches than the shorter needles. For example, you could make a scarf on shorter needles, but longer needles are more appropriate to make a sweater back.

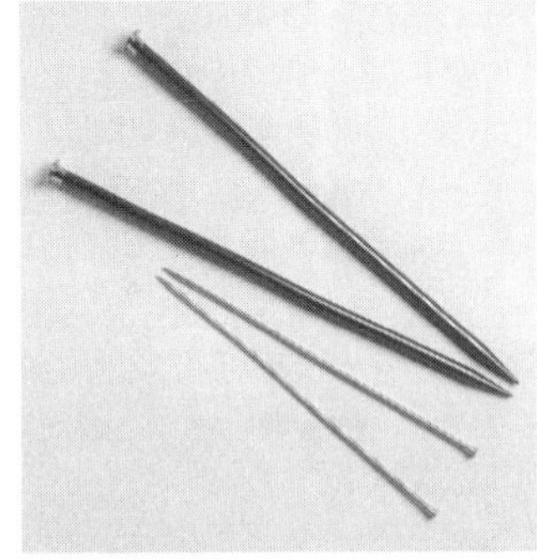

Needle size is an important consideration and should be paired with an appropriate-sized yarn.

Needles are made from aluminum (often shiny pearlized metallic colors), coated aluminum, plastic, hardwoods, and bamboo. The prices of the needles range from about $4 to $9 per pair depending on the material. Once you are an avid knitter, you might want to treat yourself to some very special luxury needles in ebony or ones with fancy tops. Needles are also available in a variety of sets. If you want a good starter set, buy sizes 6 through 13 and fill in as the need arises.

When selecting knitting needles, other than the size, length and material, you'll want to look at the needle tip. Some needles have a very pointy tip, and others are more rounded. If you are a novice, this may not seem important, but as you become a more practiced knitter, you'll notice that you enjoy knitting with some needles more than with other needles. The way the tip is formed may be one of the reasons that you do or don't enjoy the process.

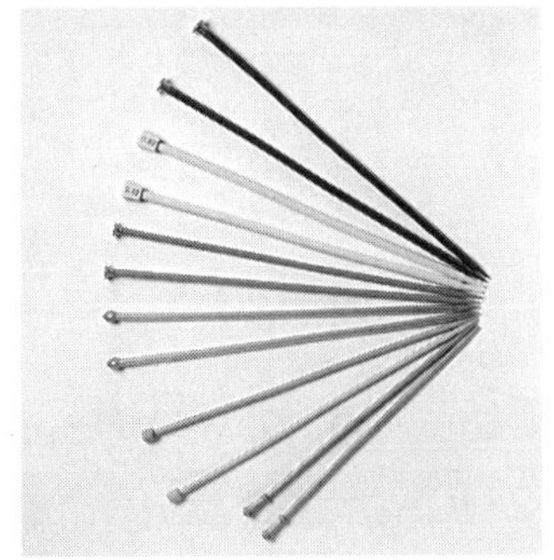

From top to bottom, pearlized aluminum needles, flexible plastic needles, plastic needles, cellulose acetate needles in hip pastel shades, bamboo needles, birch wooden needles.

CIRCULAR NEEDLES

A circular needle looks like two half needles united by a thin plastic cable. The main purpose of a circular needle is to work a joined, tubular piece that doesn't need seaming. The neckband of a sweater is a perfect example. In recent years, circular needles have risen in popularity, and some knitters use them exclusively for both straight and joined knitting projects. These circular advocates

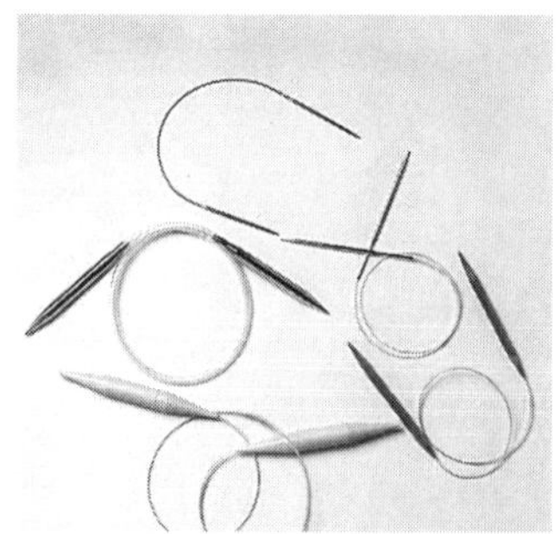

Large- and small-sized circular needles come in several lengths and materials.

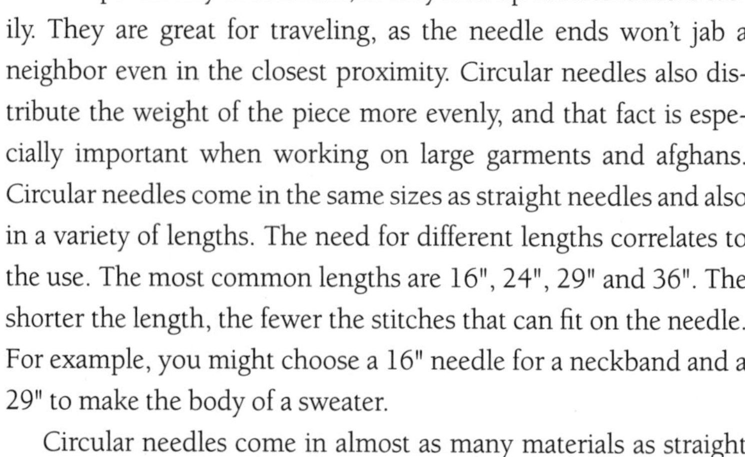

love the portability of circulars, as they fold up and store more easily. They are great for traveling, as the needle ends won't jab a neighbor even in the closest proximity. Circular needles also distribute the weight of the piece more evenly, and that fact is especially important when working on large garments and afghans. Circular needles come in the same sizes as straight needles and also in a variety of lengths. The need for different lengths correlates to the use. The most common lengths are 16", 24", 29" and 36". The shorter the length, the fewer the stitches that can fit on the needle. For example, you might choose a 16" needle for a neckband and a 29" to make the body of a sweater.

Circular needles come in almost as many materials as straight needles. The big difference is that metal- or wooden-tipped needles have plastic cables. They are sold singly or in interchangeable sets of needle points that can be screwed onto cables of different lengths.

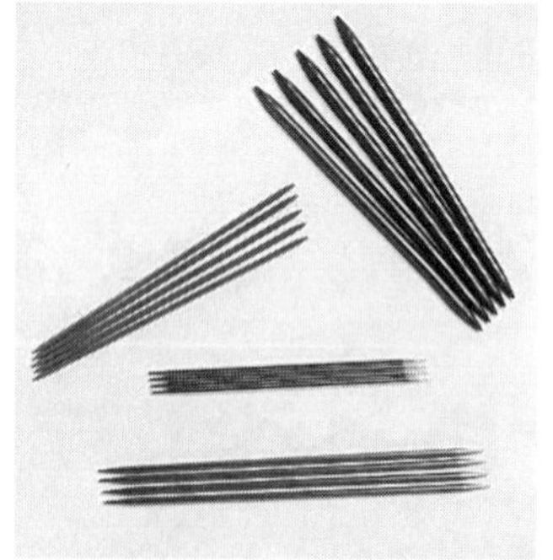

Doubled-pointed needles in aluminum and plastic in several lengths in sets of four and five needles.

DOUBLE-POINTED NEEDLES

Double-pointed needles are, as the name suggests, needles with points on both ends. They are sold in sets of four or five. When working with a set of four, you have stitches on three needles and knit with the last needle; with a set of five, you have stitches on four needles. The abbreviation for double-pointed needles is "dpn."

Double-pointed needles also come in aluminum, coated aluminum, plastic, bamboo, and hardwood. The most common lengths are 7", but you'll also find them in 6", 8", and 10" lengths. There are longer needles, but they are not as commonly used.

These needles are used to make circular items such as socks, mittens, and hats. You can also use them in conjunction with a circular needle. For example, if making a tubular hat, you may begin with a circular needle and decrease stitches as you work until you have too few stitches to fit comfortably around the circular needle. Transferring the stitches to double-pointed needles allows you to easily finish your hat.

ORGANIZING YOUR NEEDLES

Once you begin to collect needles, having a convenient way to store them becomes essential. There is a variety of options. A flat needle case that zips closed is one way to organize. There are different types of cases—some tie, roll, or snap closed. Some cases give space or compartments for storing other accessories. There are specific cases just for circular needles. You can also store your needles in devices not specifically for needles, such as a jar or box.

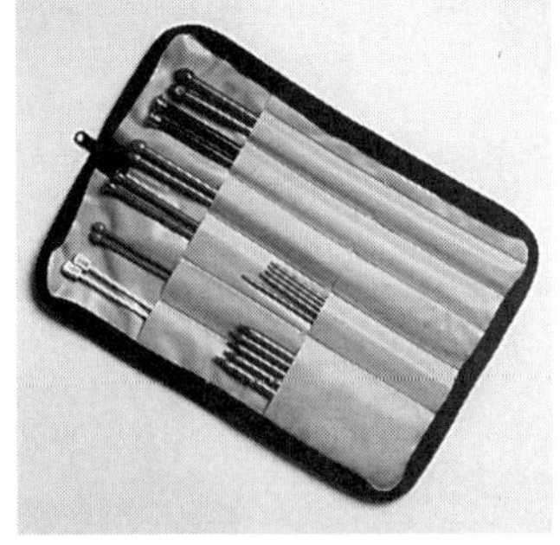

To keep your needles organized, finding a convenient storage method such as this flat, zippered case is essential.

Gadgets

With a clear understanding of knitting needles, the next logical step is to add accessories and gadgets that make your knitting easier. Some you will use frequently and others are simply nice to have. Our discussion will begin with the most essential and then cover items that are considered "frills." While you can purchase specific knitting gadgets, there are a number of everyday items that can be used.

STITCH GAUGE AND NEEDLE/HOOK SIZE TOOL

This handy device should be at the top of your must-have list. The L-shaped opening makes it easy to take a stitch and row gauge over 2" by laying the tool onto the knitted fabric. Usually, along the top and bottom edge is a metric and inch measurement (5", 14 cm). The circular holes are used to measure the size of knitting needles and crochet hooks (measure shaft to determine size for crochet hooks). While the sizes of straight needles are almost always clearly marked, circular and double-pointed needles rarely indicate their size. The needle-size area gives American, metric, and crochet-hook sizes. Some of these devices are metal, and others are plastic and all are relatively inexpensive.

MEASURING TAPE

Measuring tapes are endlessly useful for measuring widths and lengths of pieces and for taking your own measurements. You can also measure existing sweaters to guide you in size selection. Retractable tapes are easy to use and carry. Most tapes have both inches and metrics.

STITCH MARKERS

Stitch markers are used in several ways. Most often, they are used to set off a group of stitches currently in work on the needle. They can also be used to mark the placement of a particular area such as the beginning of an armhole. There are two basic types of markers—one that is a continuous ring (best used to set off stitches on a needle) and one that can be opened and closed in some manner (used to insert into pieces or to mark pieces on a needle). There is a variety of both kinds. They are inexpensive—try out a few different kinds to see which you like best. When you come to a stitch marker on your knitting needle as you are knitting, slip it from the left needle onto the right needle on every row. You can also use coilless pins, orthodontic rubber bands, contrasting yarn loops, paper clips, or rubber rings found at the hardware store.

STITCH HOLDERS

Stitch holders come in a wide variety of sizes and are used to keep stitches waiting for further action. They generally look like giant safety pins. The size of the holder has direct correlation to the number of stitches to be placed on hold. A large holder can hold all the stitches for the back of a sweater, while smaller ones are used to hold a few stitches such as for a front or back neck. In a pinch, a few safety pins or contrasting yarn looped through the stitches can be used for the same task.

SCISSORS OR SNIPS

A good small pair of scissors is an invaluable tool for a knitter. You may want several pairs so that you can include one in your traveling project. A pair of snips with a cover is even better for traveling, as it doesn't poke its way out through your knitting bag.

Keep your knitting scissors for exclusive yarn-cutting use to avoid having them become dull.

TAPESTRY OR LARGE-EYED YARN NEEDLES

Once you complete a project, the next step is to sew it together. Although finishing is covered in Chapter 10, you may want to be prepared with a few vital elements. Tapestry needles come in various sizes, are made from metal and plastic, have a large eye and a blunt, not sharp, point. The needle shown in the photo on page 10 here has a slight bend for easier insertion into the knitted fabric. A little needle case is very handy. Small plastic cases with a circular opening on the top can be threaded with string or yarn and attached to your needle case. Having needles ready and available when you need them is made easier when you keep them organized in a case.

PINS

Metal or plastic straight pins are used to tack pieces in place for easier seaming and for pinning pieces in place to block. It's best to use T-pins specially designed for this purpose rather than the shorter pins used by sewers. When using metal pins, make sure that they are rustproof.

CABLE NEEDLES

Learning to make cables is a natural progression in knitting basics. Cable needles are fundamental to the cabling process. They hold stitches in place as you complete your cable. They are short needles that are available in metal, plastic, and wood. Cable needles come in different thicknesses and, just as with your knitting needles, should be paired with the appropriate-sized yarn. Some cable needles have a slight curve in the center to keep the stitches on hold in place. Other cable needles are slightly thicker on each end, which also keeps the stitches from slipping off. They often come in sets of two or three in different sizes. If you get stuck without a cable needle, a double-pointed needle works nicely. You can actually use anything thin and straight such as toothpicks, curler sticks, or bobby pins.

ROW COUNTERS

Counting rows isn't always essential, but when you do need to keep track of rows, some sort of device is helpful. Basically all counters should click off rows as they are completed. Some are handheld, and others slip onto a knitting needle. There's even one that has a ring to fit onto a circular needle. If you don't have a counter, paper or Post-it notes and a pencil work equally well.

CROCHET HOOKS

While not absolutely necessary, crochet hooks often come in handy. They can be used for seaming or for hooking up a dropped stitch. Simple crocheted edges work very well on knitted pieces.

POINT PROTECTORS

To keep the stitches on your needles in place when not knitting, place a point protector on the needle tip. This will also keep the needle tip from injuring you or others. These protectors come in several sizes and are paired to the size knitting needle being used. Rubber bands wrapped around a needle will do if you find yourself without a protector.

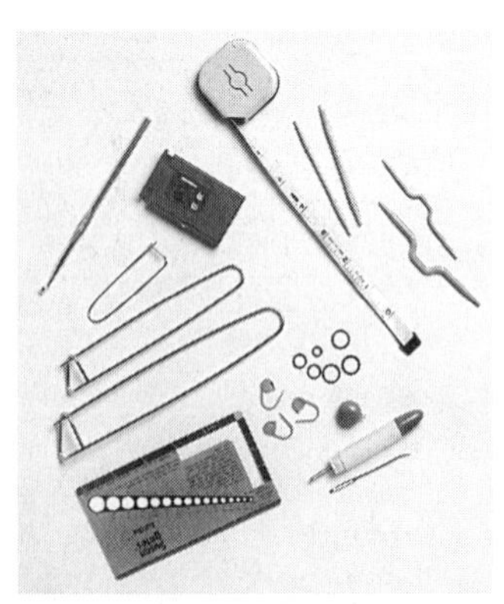

Clockwise from upper left: crochet hook, row counter, tape measure, wooden cable needles, two plastic cable needles, tapestry needles and case, two types of stitch markers, stitch gauge and needle/hook tool, and three stitch holders.

TOTES

Carrying a knitting project or just having a place to keep it is made easier with a tote bag or bag stand specially designed for needlecrafts. They often have inner and outer pockets to keep your tools and pattern from straying. Once you become a multi-project knitter, you'll find having several totes or storage carriers very valuable. Totes vary in price and material. You can find very lovely, luxury totes with exquisite details and quality fabrics, but simple bags work just as well.

You can also store needles, gadgets, and projects in ziplock bags (available in sandwich, quart, one gallon, two gallon), pencil cases, or tackle boxes. As you acquire more knitting-related items, you'll want to find ways to organize them.

Reading a Yarn Label

The yarn label, also called a ball band, includes a great deal of valuable information. Yarn companies include these details in different formats and in different places on the band, but once you are familiar with how to decipher the material, you will easily be able to find the important information.

Note that the design of the labeling varies as does the way the yarn is packaged. You may find yarn in wound pull-skeins, balls, or hanks. The size of each of these also differs widely.

COMPANY NAME AND YARN NAME

If you are looking for a specific yarn, this will be valuable information. Keep in mind that occasionally you may find a pattern that gives two company names and only find one of those names on the yarn label. This generally means that the second company is the distributor of the yarn named on the band.

YARN WEIGHT

Yarn weight doesn't relate to physical weight, but rather to the thickness of the yarn strand. It is a key element in the process of selecting the proper yarn for your project, especially if you are trying to make a yarn substitution. If you are not familiar with yarn weights, turn to the next page to review the weights.

PATTERN ON THE LABEL

A few manufacturers offer a pattern on the reverse side of their yarn label. The label gives the actual number of yarn skeins or balls needed and the appropriate-sized knitting needles required for the pattern. Even if you aren't interested in making that project, you can use the photo to get an idea of how an actual completed garment or project looks in the yarn.

CARE INSTRUCTIONS

This information may be found either in words or symbols. Generally yarn companies give the most conservative information to keep it foolproof for the consumer. If you have any doubts, wash and dry a swatch before you actually launder your finished garment. Look carefully at instructions to machine- or hand-wash. Some yarns can be washed by machine, but not dried by machine. Occasionally the yarn company will include more specific care instructions on the front or back of the label.

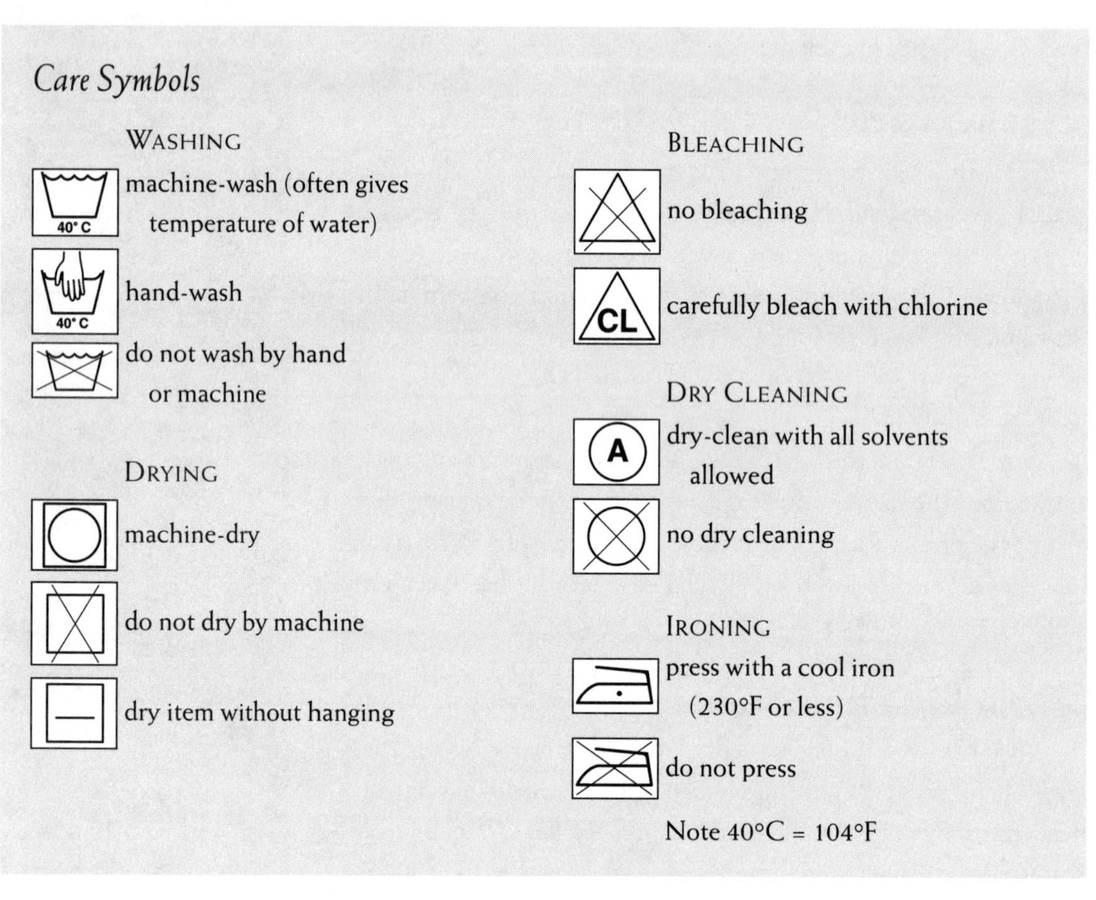

Care Symbols
WASHING
40° C
machine-wash (often gives temperature of water)
40° C
hand-wash
do not wash by hand or machine
DRYING
machine-dry
do not dry by machine
dry item without hanging
BLEACHING
no bleaching
CL
carefully bleach with chlorine
DRY CLEANING
A
dry-clean with all solvents allowed
no dry cleaning
IRONING
press with a cool iron (230°F or less)
do not press
Note 40°C = 104°F

FIBER CONTENT

This is the place to find out the exact fiber content. Fibers such as wool and cotton are fairly easy to identify, but you'll find a variety of synthetic fibers. Acrylic, polyester, nylon, or microfiber are the most common synthetics. Blends combine two or more fibers and often enhance the properties of both yarns. For the consumer, the fiber-content data often relate to care of the finished project.

WEIGHT AND YARDAGE

Weights and yardages are often given in both the American standards of inches and yards as well as metrics in grams and meters. In some cases you may find only metrics. For easy conversion, remember that 28 grams equals approximately one ounce and meters are about 10 percent less than yards. While the ounce weight is somewhat important, for substitution from one yarn to another, the yardage is essential.

GAUGES

This information isn't always available on the yarn label, but when it is, it is a very helpful guideline. The label may include a gauge for knitters and crocheters. For knitters, the format is most likely given with a number of stitches and rows over a certain stitch pattern (usually stockinette stitch—knit on right side and purl on wrong side) on a suggested needle size. This doesn't mean that you necessarily will use that specific needle size or even get this gauge. Your particular knitting pattern may give another suggestion. The manufacturer has added this detail to give the consumer guidance.

COLOR NAME AND NUMBER

This gives the manufacturer's item number and its name for the color. Magazines and books may use a generic color name rather than using the yarn company's specific color name. This information is especially helpful when you need several balls of a color. Always check the name and number to make sure that you have picked up the correct color.

LOT, OR DYE-LOT, NUMBER

This piece of data is very important when buying more than one ball of yarn for a project. Yarns are dyed in batches that are given dye-lot numbers. Even though the same formulas are used for each batch, there may be a slight difference from one lot to the next. This affects your project if you mix yarn from more than one dye lot—you might get one section where the color is obviously different from that of the rest of your project.

It's always best to purchase all the required yarn at one time to enable you to find the same lot number. When in doubt, get an additional ball of yarn just to make sure. If you need to buy two different lots, stagger the yarn by working a few rows from one lot and then a few from the second lot through the piece. You are then assured of a more consistent look to the piece.

YARN SUBSTITUTION

If you can use the exact yarn called for in a pattern, the results you achieve are optimum, but this is not always possible or desirable. For many reasons, you may prefer a different fiber and thus choose a different yarn. Being able to read and understand a yarn label will help you make a more informed selection.

Choose a yarn weight closest to the original weight. See page 15 for more on yarn-weight classifications.

Select a fiber type that closely matches the original yarn. For example, if the model sweater is designed with a hairy, thick mohair, your sweater in a flat cotton/acrylic blend won't resemble the original.

If you have doubts concerning your selection, purchase one ball of yarn and make a swatch. Be sure the gauge of your new yarn matches that of the pattern. More information on the gauging process is on page 25.

When choosing colors, keep in mind that dark and highly variegated shades tend not to show off detailed patterning. A sweater with a great deal of stitch pattern is best worked in a lighter shade.

To calculate the amount of yarn you'll need, multiply the yardage of the original yarn by the number of required balls. This will give you a good idea of the total yardage. Compare this to the yarn you plan to use. For example, if the pattern's yarn has 200 yards per ball and you need 6 balls, that is 1200 yards in total. If the yarn you plan to use has 300 yards per ball, you can purchase 4 balls and still have the needed 1200 yards.

Yarns

Yarn makes knitting exciting, enticing, and ultimately, enjoyable. Understanding yarn and yarn types will make you a more skilled and knowledgeable knitter and guide you into making the correct yarn choices. While whole books have been written on yarns and their properties, the following is designed to give you a general overview and introduction to a variety of yarns.

YARN WEIGHTS

In standard flat yarns, there are five or six different weight categories. Novelty yarns and yarns that aren't considered plain yarns also fall into these categories, but are best described in relationship to the gauges that they achieve. Here we will discuss weights in terms of the thickness of the yarn and not a specific fiber or weight (as in ounces). Keep in mind that a jumbo yarn in a lofty, lightweight fiber can make a garment that isn't "heavy"; it simply has larger stitches and uses a larger needle to knit.

1. Super Bulky or Jumbo

This category contains the thickest yarns and is good for beginners, as it is worked on large needles and creates big stitches that are easy to see. Although they are used for sweaters, jumbo yarns

Yarn weights

are generally best used for outerwear, hats, and accessories such as scarves and thick boot socks.

Gauge: 2–3 stitches per inch.

2. Chunky or Bulky

A chunky yarn is also easy to use and is a versatile weight that can be used for a number of projects including garments, accessories, and home décor.

Gauge: 3½–4½ stitches per inch.

3. Worsted Weight or Standard Weight

Worsted weight is the most widely available weight of yarn in both acrylic and wool. For many years, the terms yarn or wool referred to worsted-weight yarn. This weight is used exclusively by many knitters and is extremely versatile. It can be used for many types of projects. It is sometimes used with two strands together to create a thicker, chunky-weight yarn.

Gauge: 5 stitches per inch.

4. Double Knitting and Sportweight

The term double knitting (DK) came to the United States from Britain and refers to a weight of yarn that is between a worsted and a sportweight. Its finer weight makes it good for lighter sweaters, and it is ideal for children's wear. The same is true of sportweight. These yarns are especially suited to accessories such as socks and hats. Yarns in this category are not ideal for home-decor items such as afghans, partly because of the time required to make such a large piece on a fine yarn and smaller needles.

Gauge: 5½–6 stitches per inch.

5. Baby, Fingering, or Sock Weight

This fine weight is wonderful for infant wear. It also makes lovely shawls. Fingering weight is an older term that is less commonly used. You may find this weight of yarn also referred to as sock yarn.

Gauge: 7–8 stitches per inch.

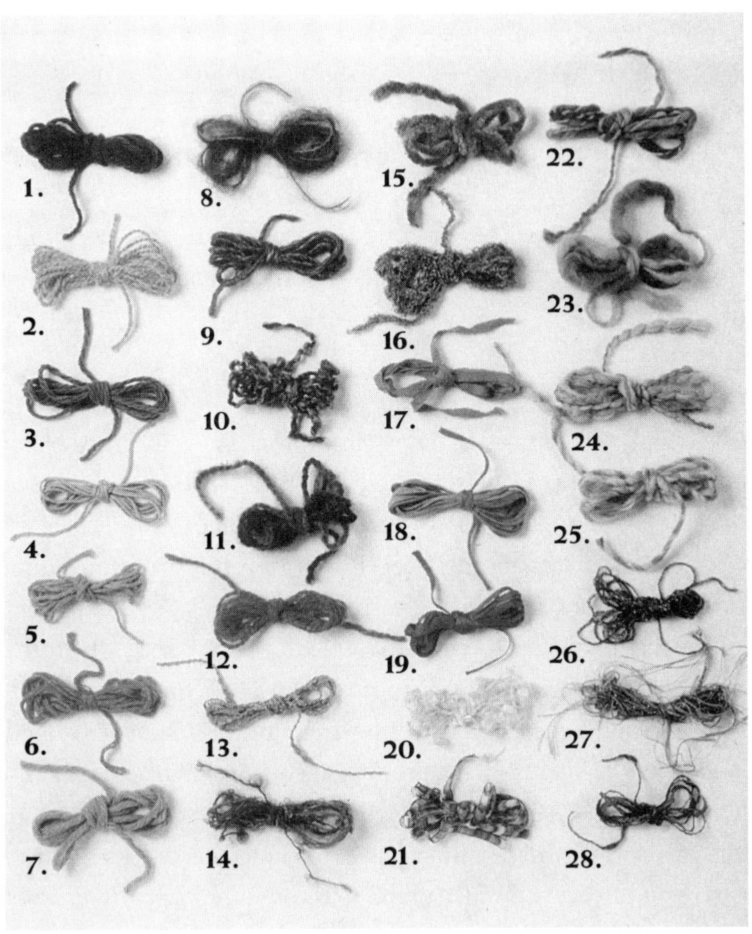

Twenty-eight of the numerous varieties of available yarns

1 Worsted-Weight Wool 2 Wool/Angora-Blend Tweed 3 Cotton/Acrylic Blend 4 Mercerized Cotton 5 Matte Cotton 6 Microfiber Acrylic 7 Wool/Acrylic Blend 8 Variegated Mohair/Wool Blend 9 Silk/Wool-Blend Tweed 10 Multicolor Textured Acrylic 11 Variegated Brushed Acrylic 12 Wool Tweed 13 Slubbed Cotton 14 Wool/Mohair Bouclé 15 Extra Chunky Acrylic Chenille 16 Rayon Novelty Chenille 17 Cotton Ribbon 18 Variegated Cotton Ribbon 19 Rayon Ribbon 20 Novelty Yarn with Multi-Fibers 21 Variegated Novelty Ribbon 22 Variegated Thick-and-Thin Wool 23 Variegated Thick-and-Thin Roving Wool 24 Thick-and-Thin Wool 25 Wool with Ragg Treatment 26 Metallic 27 Eyelash Yarn with Metallic 28 Thin, Variegated, Slubbed Cotton-Blend Yarn

ANIMAL FIBERS

Although there are a number of other animal fibers used for yarn, wool is the best known. What they all have in common is their warmth and durability. Care should be taken in cleaning, as most animal fibers will felt when they are agitated in hot water or placed in a dryer. The exception is yarns that are specifically treated, such as superwash wools or yarns blended with acrylic fibers.

Wool

Sheep's wool comes in many yarn forms and is the chameleon of the yarn world. It can be twisted, brushed, blended, and spun so that there are a multitude of end results. Some people consider wool the ultimate knitting fiber. It is warm, but wicks moisture; garments from wool will last for years. The quality of wool varies and is mainly determined by the breed of sheep from which the fiber comes. Merino sheep are noted for their fine-grade wool. Lamb's wool comes from the first shearing of a lamb. Shetland wool refers to fiber from the sheep that come from the Shetland Islands in the North Sea off Scotland. They have durable coats formed by an extreme climate. By touching the ball or skein of yarn, you can get some idea of the softness of the yarn. Virgin wool means wool that is being used for the first time and has not been recycled.

Wool is often relatively easy to work, especially for beginners, as unevenness in gauge can be blocked out in the finishing process.

Mohair

Mohair fiber is derived from the Angora goat, which is known for its long, lustrous, lightweight hair. This is one of the warmest available fibers and dyes easily. Mohair is most often found blended with wool or spun with a nylon binder. Kid mohair is the finest quality of mohair.

Angora

The hair of the Angora rabbit is remarkably soft. Angora is best blended with wool and other fibers, as on its own it is extremely dense. The short fibers of the Angora rabbit cause it to shed. The best-quality angora comes from rabbit hair that is plucked rather than shorn. As these rabbits are small and produce little fiber, angora tends to be expensive. Yarn blends that include angora have its soft quality but are less costly.

Alpaca

The alpaca is a small animal from the camel family with a soft, lush coat. While South America is the main exporter of alpaca fiber, the animals are now being raised in the United States. The fiber produced by these animals is extremely soft and warm. It doesn't have the resiliency of wool, so it tends to be drapy. Natural alpaca also comes in more shades than any other fiber-producing animal, including gray, black, brown, and dark brown shades. Overdyed non-white shades produce beautiful muted tones. The combination of wool with alpaca creates a yarn that has the advantages of both fibers.

Llama and Vicuna

Similar to an alpaca, the llama is better known than the almost-extinct vicuna. Neither animal produces fiber imported to the United States. Yarn that is labeled "llama" is actually a lower-grade alpaca.

Cashmere

Cashmere is most well known as an expensive yarn, and with good reason. The breed of goats that produce this fiber live in high, mountainous areas. The soft, luxuriant underhair of these goats is not shorn but combed, giving only a small amount of fiber each year. To keep the costs lower but retain the extremely soft nature of cashmere, the fiber is often mixed with wool to create yarn.

Camel

This fiber, from the undercoat of camels, is not widely available and is almost always found mixed with wool. It doesn't take dyes well, so it is usually available only in natural shades.

Silk

Silk fibers come from a filament produced by the silkworm. While 100 percent silk is costly and lacks resiliency, the fibers are lustrous and soft. They are best used in combination with cotton, wool, and other fibers.

Other Animal Fibers

In your search for yarn you are likely to encounter exotic fibers such as qiviut (the underbelly of the muskox), yak, and possum. There are knitters and hand spinners that turn dog hair into yarn. These are often expensive and not as readily available.

PLANT FIBERS

Next to wool and acrylics, cotton is the most recognized and widely available fiber used to make yarn. Other plant fibers are much less used and accessible, but are worth mentioning.

Cotton

Americans love cotton clothing and household items, so knitting with cotton yarn is a natural. The plus side of cotton is that it is easy to wash and wear and can be used to make garments for the whole family as well as for home accessories. The downside of this fiber is that it lacks the resiliency of wool and can become quite heavy if not mixed with wool or acrylic. Nevertheless, it continues to be a very popular yarn and has improved greatly.

Cotton is found in both mercerized and matte forms. Mercerization is a process that gives cotton a shiny appearance and makes it incredibly durable. Mercerized cottons are dyed into beautiful, rich shades. Matte cotton yarns are, as the name indicates, matte in appearance. In dyed shades, matte cottons have a slightly duller look. However, matte cottons are more absorbent than mercerized cottons and are best used for utilitarian items such as washcloths and towels.

Linen

Linen, made from the flax plant, is known for its use in woven fabrics. It has a slightly harder finish that is less appealing for knitted garments. It is best used in blends with cotton and acrylic. This fiber makes lovely shawls, home-decorating pieces and sweaters, and 100 percent linen does soften with washing and wearing.

Other Plant Fibers

Other plant-based fibers that you'll encounter are hemp and raffia. These are coarser than linen and cotton and are often used for accessories and home décor. There are even some novelty yarns formed from paper products.

SYNTHETICS

Synthetic fibers were originally made to simulate animal and plant fibers, but in recent years have come into their own as viable alternatives to natural fibers. All synthetic fibers are made in a chemical process. Newer synthetic-making processes have been created to manufacture incredibly soft yarns. They are all similar in that they are easy to care for, cost less than many natural fibers, and are widely available in chain shops. Microfiber is a newer generation of synthetic that has all of the attributes of acrylic, nylon, and polyester. When finishing projects using yarns made from any of these fibers, it is best to avoid the direct heat of an iron or extremely hot steam.

Acrylic

This man-made fiber is generally the one most common in the United States and is often combined with wool and cotton as well as nylon and polyester. Added softness and luster have been recent advents in the manufacture of acrylic fibers and have greatly enhanced their use. These fibers are used to create simple, flat yarns as well as a wide variety of novelty and textural yarns. Acrylic fibers can be used for the whole family as well as for home use as long as they do not come in direct contact with extreme heat.

Nylon

Nylon is sometimes called polyamide or polyamid, especially on yarn labels from foreign countries. This fiber was a very early entry into the synthetic-fiber market and was originally designed to simulate silk. It is very durable and is often an addition to blended yarns. Sometimes a fine nylon strand is used to wrap another yarn or as the core of a novelty yarn.

Polyester

Another synthetic fiber most often found in combination with acrylic and natural fibers. Polyester adds strength, but it is not absorbent.

Rayon

Not a true synthetic, rayon is actually derived from wood chips. It is known for its shiny look and ability to drape; the origin of rayon was an attempt to create a silk look-alike. Sometimes the terms viscose and rayon are used interchangeably, although they are created by slightly different methods. To avoid a very slippery fiber, rayon is often mixed with cotton.

Metallic, Lamé, Lurex

Metallic yarns are created with pliable metals, plastic film, or an extruded synthetic that is flattened and treated. Some newer processes, designed specially for knitting and crochet, have made these yarns quite soft. Metallics add shine and are often mixed with other yarns to make novelty yarns. These specialty fibers are used for both garments (in softer forms) as well as accessories such as bags (in stiffer forms).

YARN TERMS AND TREATMENTS

Bouclé

Bouclé yarn is a combination of at least three strands. The main loopy, yarn randomly wraps a thin core, and these two are bound together by the third. When knitted, the loops give the yarn a pile-like texture.

Chenille

Chenille yarns come in cotton, rayon, acrylic, silk, and wool varieties and are made by a spinning process that simulates weaving—two vertical warp core yarns catch the horizontal weft yarn as they are spinning. The horizontal yarn is immediately cut, thereby creating the pile effect. When knitted, chenille resembles velour or velvet. Certain chenille yarns have a tendency to "worm," or pull out in loops. If this occurs, work the yarn at a tighter gauge than normal.

Eyelash

An eyelash treatment consists of short strands that stick out of a core strand. When knitted, these yarn types have a slightly hairy or furry appearance. As many eyelash yarns are thin, they are often worked as a carry-along yarn with another yarn or incorporated into a novelty yarn.

Heather

A heathered yarn is usually considered a solid color, but actually has strands of several complementary colors spun together to create one tone. Some heathers have added flecks that give them a tweeded appearance.

Homespun or Hand Spun

Any yarn that is spun by hand fits into this category. These yarns often have a rustic appearance and may be slightly uneven in places. They are available only from hand spinners or in shops that specialize in such yarn, and are often expensive. Less costly yarns are created by machine to simulate hand-spun looks.

Ombré

Ombré is a term used to describe a method of variegation with long lengths of each color. Sometimes one color fades into the next color, creating another tone.

Ply

Yarns are very often made from several strands of yarn that are spun together. Thus, you will hear terms such as 2-ply, 3-ply or 4-ply yarn. For many years, worsted-weight acrylic yarn was called 4-ply acrylic, but is increasingly known as worsted, because a 4-ply yarn might not be worsted weight if the four plies used to create it are not the size required to make that your weight. Conversely, a 2-ply yarn can be thicker than a 4-ply if two very thick plies are spun together.

Printed Yarn

In this yarn, one main color is predominant throughout and short areas have other colors printed onto the yarn. Baby prints are the most common example.

Ragg

This yarn is made by combining two distinctly different-colored plies (such as cream and gray or black and white) to make a yarn that has an allover tweedy look. This is different from a space-dyed or variegated yarn, in which complete sections are dyed different colors.

Roving

Unlike a tightly twisted yarn, a roving yarn is loosely spun or even unspun. The look achieved with this type of yarn is more rustic. Although some roving yarns must be knitted with care to avoid having them fray as they are worked, they are very stable once knitted.

Thick and Thin

These yarns are formed on machines that twist certain sections tighter than others to give a thick-and-thin appearance. When knitted, such yarns have texture and dimension. They are best used for simple patterning.

Tweed

Tweed yarns are made by randomly adding flecks of contrasting-colored yarn to the fiber before it is spun.

Variegated

Variegation (sometimes known as space dying) is a method of creating a yarn in several colors that self-patterns. This process can be done by hand or machine. Hand-dyed yarns are more expensive than the machine-dyed yarns.

What Is Gauge?

When you knit, you'll be making fabric of stitches (horizontally) and rows (vertically). Gauge is a measurement of those stitches and rows, given in a per-inch/cm number (most often over 4", or 10 cm).

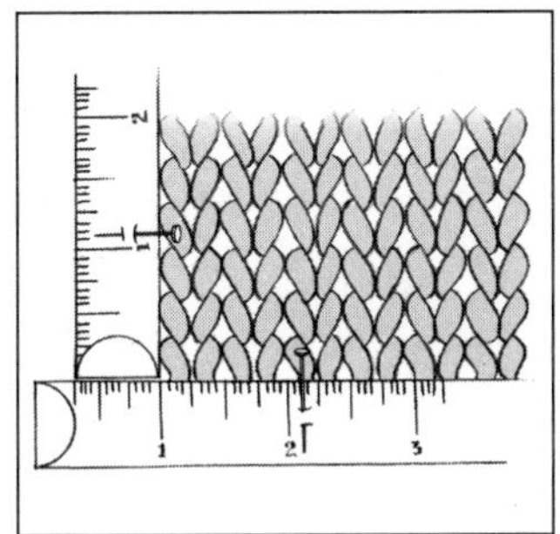

Measure the gauge to determine the number of stitches and rows per inch.

When you sew, you *cut* fabric to a certain dimension. In knitting you are *making* your fabric and need a way to ensure that it is the correct size. Your gauge determines your fabric's finished size, so it's essential to accurately determine your gauge before you begin a knitting project.

Gauge (sometimes called tension) varies between knitters, so you can't always assume that if you use the yarn and needles given in the pattern you'll achieve the desired gauge. You should always knit a piece (at least 4" square) called a swatch to check your gauge.

Begin with the suggested needle size and cast on stitches. Work in the pattern stitch suggested in the instructions, for example, stockinette stitch or garter stitch. (You'll find more about these two stitch patterns in the next two chapters.) Work at least 4" and bind off the stitches or just take your stitches off the needle.

Without stretching the fabric, place a tape measure on your work and gently pin where the tape measure reads one inch. Count your stitches and multiply the one-inch stitch or row number by four to compare to the gauge in your pattern. Don't cheat! Make sure to count even a half or quarter of a stitch and include that in your gauge. You may want to measure in a couple of places if you're not quite sure, or if the stitches seem uneven in one spot. While we talk about gauge in one-inch increments, a more accurate gauge should be measured over 2" (5 cm) using a stitch gauge or over 4" (10 cm) using a tape measure or ruler.

If you have more stitches per inch than the gauge suggests, that means you are knitting too tightly and should try another swatch on a larger needle. If you have fewer stitches than the suggested gauge, your stitches are too loose, so you should try a smaller needle.

The stitch-gauge tool is an easy way to measure your gauge. It will give you the stitches and rows over 2 inches. Multiply these numbers by two to get your four-inch gauge number.

For a beginning knitter, it's almost always easiest to take a gauge over a flat yarn in stockinette stitch where the stitches and rows are clearly identifiable. As your gauge can change from stitch pattern to stitch pattern, be sure to make swatches of each pattern before proceeding with your project.

When taking a gauge in garter stitch, remember that each ridge equals two rows of knitting.

When working with a yarn that obliterates the stitch and row definition, it may be necessary to count each row as you work your swatch. For example, it is difficult to see stitches and rows in the finished fabric when using a yarn like bouclé.

After you are a seasoned knitter, you'll have some idea of whether you are a loose or a tight knitter. This information can save you time when you make your gauge swatches. If you know that you tend to knit loosely, you may want to work your first swatch with needles one or two sizes smaller than those called for in the pattern.

Keep in mind that all the information so far about gauge assumes that you are using the yarn called for in the instructions. If you are opting to change the yarn, it becomes even more important to check your gauge. For the best results, always try to find a yarn similar to the one originally used.

MAKING AN EASY-TO-MEASURE GAUGE SWATCH

To work your swatch, cast on at least 4" worth of stitches and add 4 stitches to that number for borders. Use a non-rolling border stitch such as garter stitch for the edges of your swatch. Knit every row for 4 rows for a lower border and then change to stockinette stitch for the main body of the swatch. At the beginning and end of every purl row, knit 2 stitches. Knit for 4" above the garter-stitch edge and then finish your swatch with 4 rows of garter stitch. You can easily measure across the stitches that should be 4" and see whether you are on target or not.

You may want to wash your swatch and allow it to dry so that you can see how it will react and if it will change after washing. Recheck the measurements.

Gauge What-If's

- *You get your stitch gauge, but can't get the row gauge.*

Row gauge does have importance, but is not always essential. Row gauge does matter when portions of your pattern give specific row increments for the depth of a neck or shaping on a sleeve. But when these measurements are given in inches/cm, rather than as rows, you can relax about not getting your row gauge.

- *You've worked and measured a gauge swatch, but the measurements change when you knit your sweater.*

The phenomenon of a changing gauge will occasionally happen

when working on a larger piece rather than your smaller gauge swatch. It's always best to measure your first piece after working a few inches to make sure you are on the right track before you get too far along in the project.

• *What if my pattern doesn't give a specific pattern stitch for the gauge?*

If not given, assume that the gauge is in stockinette stitch. Take care to read your gauge information—it may say "in pattern stitch." This could be something other than stockinette or garter stitch and should be used to take your gauge.

• *My pattern says gauge over a cable. How do I measure a cable in a gauge?*

If you have to take a gauge over a cable, you can assume that there will be other stitches along with the cable such as purl stitches on either side of the cable. Include them in your swatch. The trick with cables is that they are wider and narrower in places. Be sure to measure the cable over the widest point and not on a cable twist row, where the cable pulls in.

• *What if the pattern says to take the gauge over all patterns?*

If your design features several pattern stitches such as an Aran pattern, you may need to work the gauge swatch over all the patterns. For example, if there are three separate patterns used at the same time totaling 30 stitches (e.g. a cable with 10 stitches, stockinette stitch over 5 stitches, another cable pattern of 15 stitches), cast on the 30 stitches plus 4 border stitches for a total of 34 and work your swatch. Measure the full width of the piece and divide 30 by that measurement to find out the number of stitches in an inch.

• *Can I make anything without worrying about the gauge?*

If you are making an item that doesn't have to fit, such as a scarf or an item for home decorating, gauge is not critical. It's always good practice to make a gauge swatch; it helps you create a fabric that is proper for the yarn you are using.

• *Should I rip out my swatch once I get the correct gauge?*

You might want to keep the swatch as a record of your project—perhaps even start a scrapbook of items you have knitted. If you want to use up the yarn, wait until you are at the end of the project in case you need to refer to the swatch as you work on the project.

• *If the pattern is done circularly, how do I make my gauge?*

You should actually work a round piece, as your knitting tension can change when working on circular pieces. Cast on enough stitches to join your work and knit for at least 4" (10 cm). You may need to use a shorter circular needle, or double-pointed needles, for this process.

2

Learning the Knit Stitch

Learning to knit will give you a lifetime of pleasure and relaxation. This is a skill that, once learned, will remain with you the rest of your life. From just two simple stitches, you can come up with an unlimited number of variations that will help you to make special handmade items for yourself and people you love.

Relax as you begin and review the steps before you start. As with any new skill, learning to knit requires equal measures of patience and perseverance. Remember that you should have fun with your knitting. If you get stuck, take a deep breath, but keep at it.

Before You Cast On

To knit, you need to have stitches on one needle. "Casting on" is the term for making the foundation row of stitches. Your first stitch is actually a slipknot, shown in steps 1 and 2.

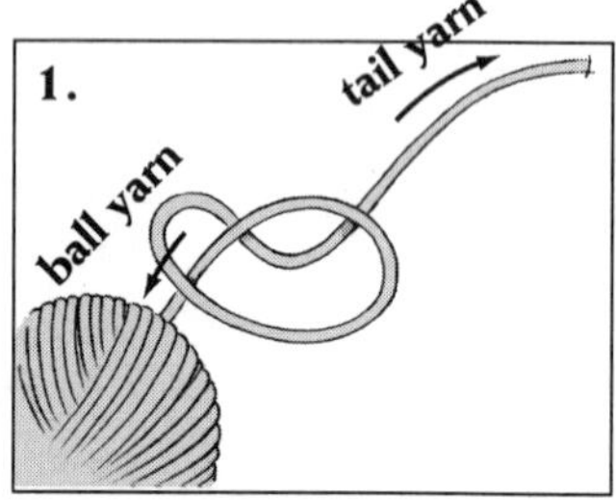

1. Make a loop about 5" to 6" from the end (called the tail) by placing the tail in front of the ball yarn, then letting the rest of the tail yarn fall slightly behind the loop as illustrated.

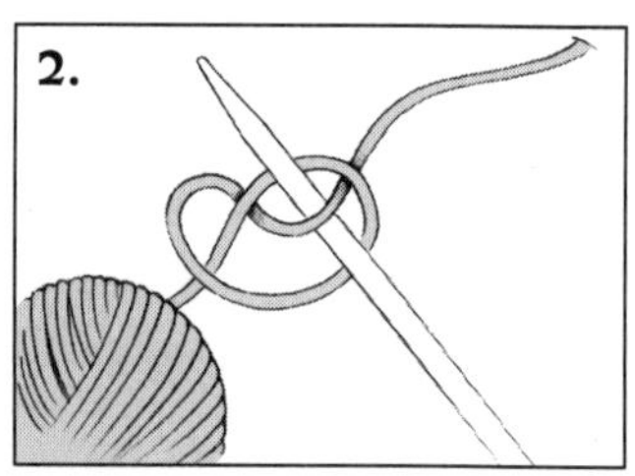

2. Insert the needle into the loop as shown. Scoop up the yarn in the back of the loop with the tip of the needle. Pull the yarn through the front of the loop. Gently pull the tail yarn to tighten the loop around the needle. The loop can be made to fit any size needle. This is the first stitch.

Casting On

This cast-on is called the knitted-on cast-on. It's the easiest one to learn for beginners. There are numerous other cast-on methods. The second cast-on you may learn is called the long-tail cast-on. A description and detailed steps on working this cast-on are shown in a number of all-purpose reference books. Look at page 248 in Chapter 24 for a list of books that will include more cast-ons.

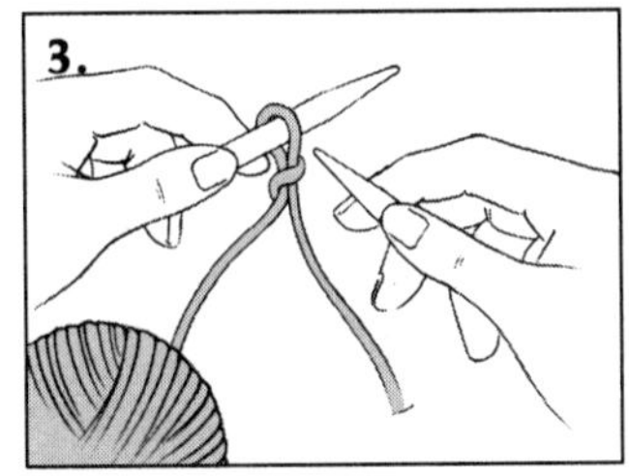

3. With the yarn from the ball in back of your needles, hold your hands as shown. You may want to tie the tail yarn into a bow so as not to confuse it with the ball yarn. You will work from the ball yarn as you continue to add new stitches.

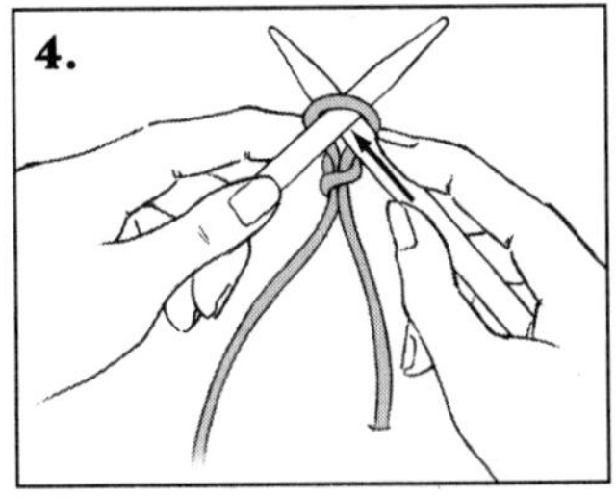

4. Insert the tip of the right (empty) needles, from the front to the back (from the left side of the stitch to the right) into the loop on the left needle.

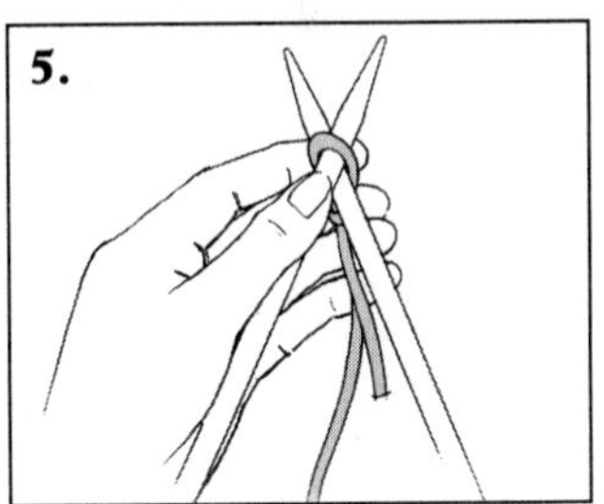

5. Adjust your thumb so that you are gently gripping both needles between the thumb and forefinger of your left hand. Keep the stitch close to the points and don't be too concerned about how you are holding the needles. Your technique will smooth out once you become comfortable with the process.

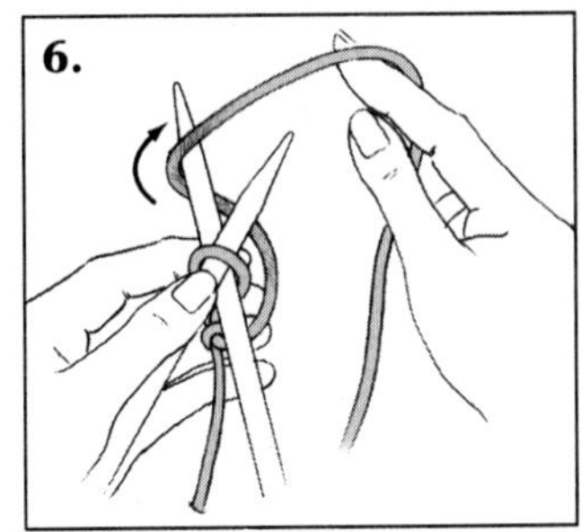

6. Holding the yarn with your right hand, wrap the yarn around the tip of the right needle in a clockwise motion as shown.

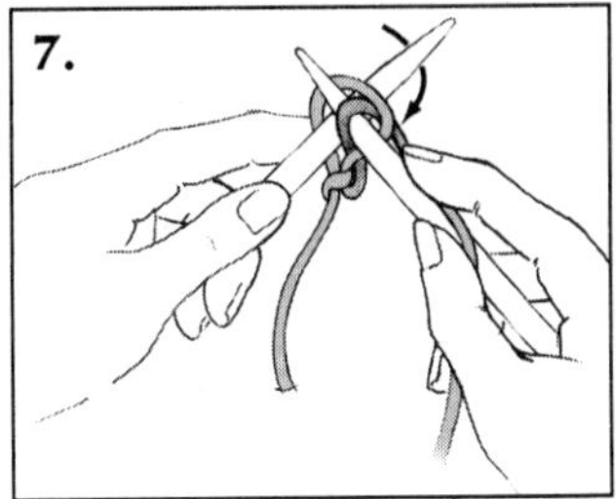

7. Hold the loop you have just made with your right index finger. Pull the tip of the right needle toward you, below the left needle through the center of the stitch. This is the one step that often causes knitters to stumble. Try it once or twice before you move on. The tips of your needles now cross with the right one on top and the left one below.

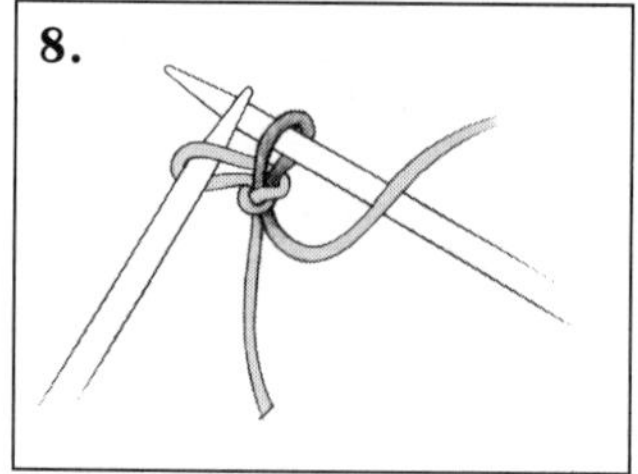

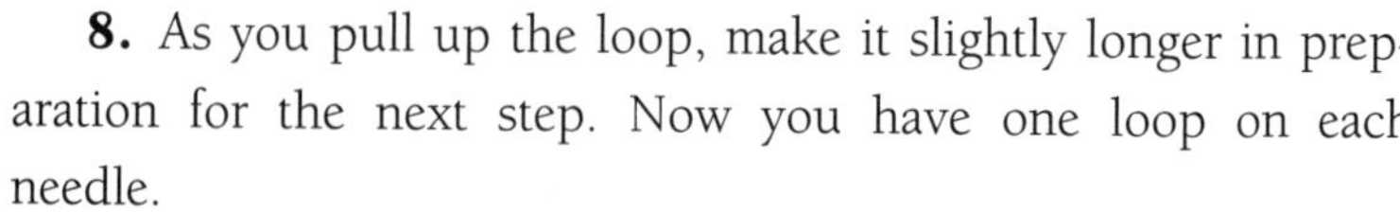

8. As you pull up the loop, make it slightly longer in preparation for the next step. Now you have one loop on each needle.

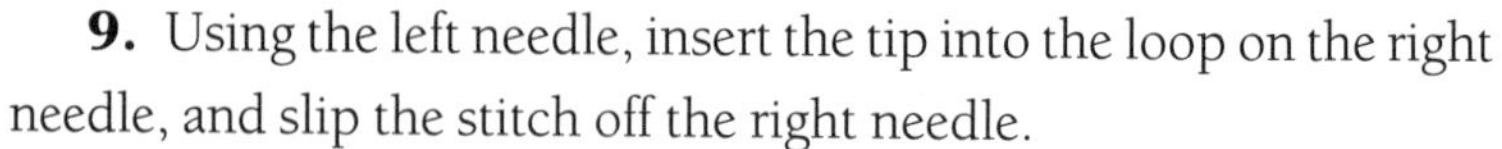

9. Using the left needle, insert the tip into the loop on the right needle, and slip the stitch off the right needle.

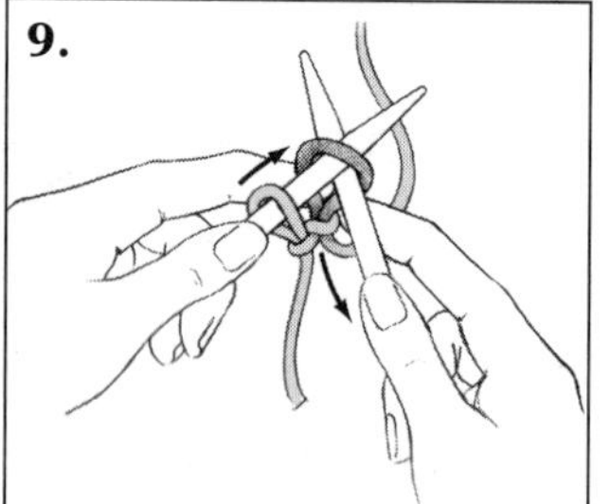

10. You now have two loops on your left needle—the original slipknot and the new stitch just made. Repeat steps 4 through 9 until you have the desired number of stitches on one needle. You are now ready to knit your first row.

Making the Knit Stitch

There are two methods of knitting. The one shown here is called the American or British technique. You can also knit using the Continental method. The basic difference is that when knitting in the American way, the yarn is held in the right hand. In the Continental way, it's held in the left hand. A good reference book will show you how to accomplish the Continental method. If you want to work color patterns, being able to use both methods more or less at the same time is helpful.

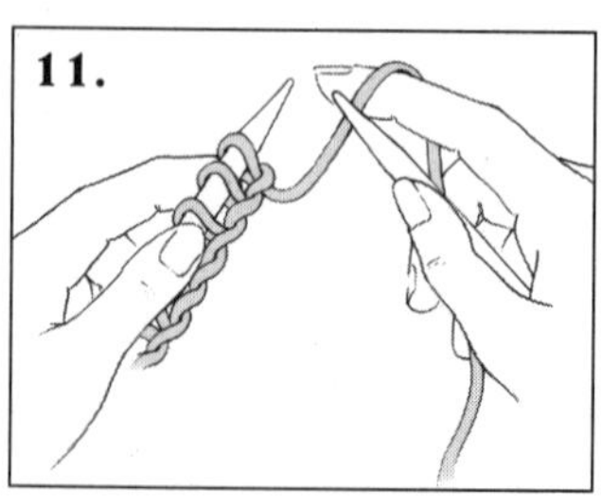

11. In a comfortable manner, hold the needle with the stitches on it in your left hand. The first stitch is approximately an inch from the tip as shown. The empty needle is in your right hand. Loop the yarn over a finger or let it hang down. Your yarn-holding technique is not important for this step.

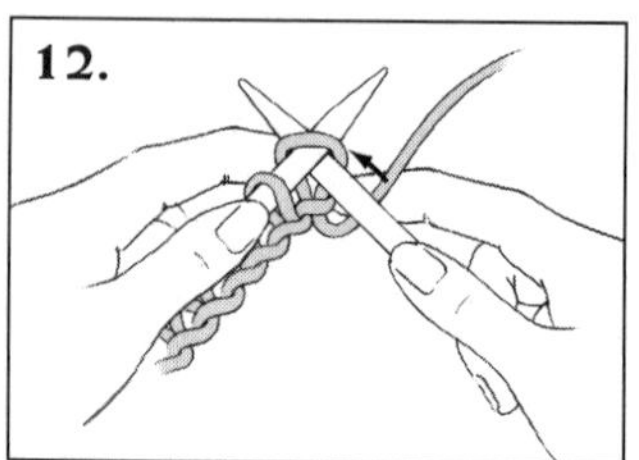

12. Just as you did in step 4 in casting on, insert the tip into the stitch closest to the tip of the left needle (from front to back). The needles are crossed forming an **X**.

13. Secure the two needles in your left hand between your thumb and your forefinger. Pick up the yarn with your right hand

and wrap it in a clockwise motion from under to over the tip of the right needle. This is the same as you did in step 6.

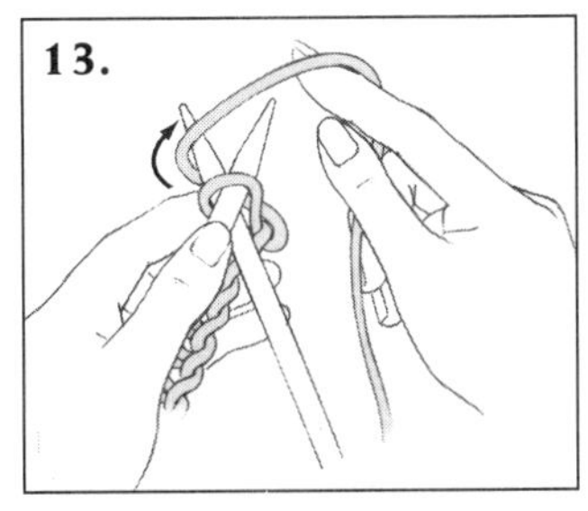
13.

14a, 14b. Slide the right needle (with the loop of yarn on it) down and toward you, drawing a loop through the center of the stitch just as you did in step 7.

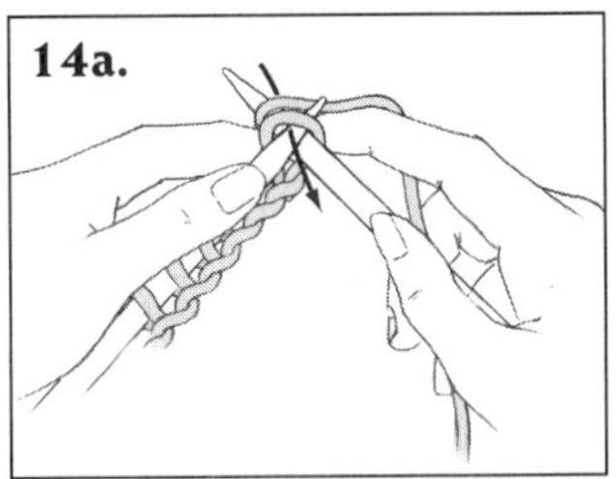
14a.

14b.

15. Now, instead of keeping the new loops on the left needle, slip the new stitch completely off the tip of the left needle. You now have one stitch on your right needle.

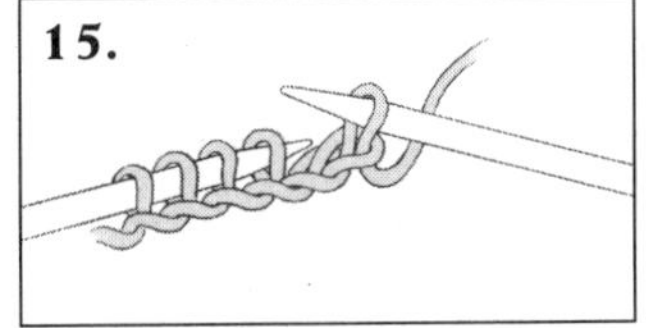
15.

Tips on Making the Knit Stitch

You have just knitted your first stitch! To complete your first row, continue repeating steps 12 through 15 until you have knitted all the stitches off your left needle. When you reach the last stitch, don't panic. Just knit the stitch. You have now completed the first row. Exchange the empty needle in your left hand with the full needle on your right and begin the steps over again.

Just remember that knitting is a four-step process:

1. Insert the needle
2. Wrap the yarn clockwise
3. Pull through the loop
4. Pull off the newly formed stitch

Garter Stitch

After you have knitted several rows, the fabric you have made should look like this. This is called garter stitch and is made by knitting every row. Note that one ridge in this fabric is created by two rows of knitting.

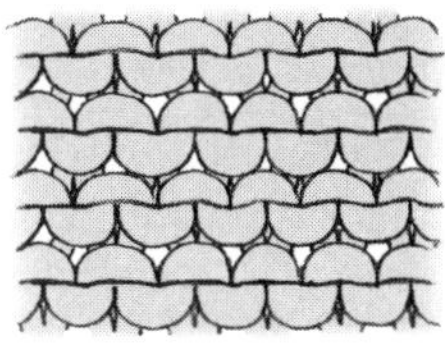

Look at Your Knitted Stitches

While you may not want to think about having one of these newly formed stitches slide off your needle, as a practical matter it will happen. Look at your stitches on the needle. The yarn that makes up the stitch should be coming from the front of the stitch. If it is twisted on the needle, it will appear to come from the back of the stitch. See the diagram on page 59 in Chapter 7 for a clearer picture of a stitch on the needle.

Left-Handed Knitters

Even if you are a left-hander, you can learn to knit as easily as a right-hander. Don't be concerned, as all knitters are awkward at first. As you practice, it will become clear to you that knitting is a two-handed skill in which neither hand is a dominant player. Once you learn, your dexterity improves greatly regardless of which hand you use. Keep in mind that to knit left-handed, you essentially work with your needles in opposite hands and in the opposite direction (basically, backward). Left-handed knitters may find the Continental knitting method somewhat easier, as the yarn is manipulated with the left hand rather than the right.

Binding Off

Once you know how to cast on stitches and knit, the next step is to bind off your stitches so that you can finish your piece. There are a number of ways to bind off, but here is the simplest method, which can be used effectively most of the time.

Make sure that your bind-off is smooth and even. It's better to work looser than tighter. Some knitters find that they achieve a looser bind-off by using a larger-sized needle to bind off the stitches on the needle. This is something you'll find by practicing. If your bind-off isn't satisfactory, undo the stitches before you fasten off your last stitch. Put them back onto the needle and do it again.

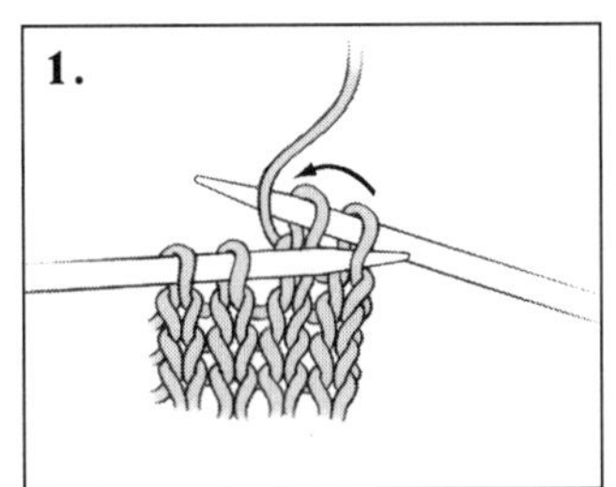

1. Knit two stitches. Insert the tip of the left needle into the first stitch on the right needle as shown. Lift the stitch over the last stitch you knitted and over the tip of the right needle.

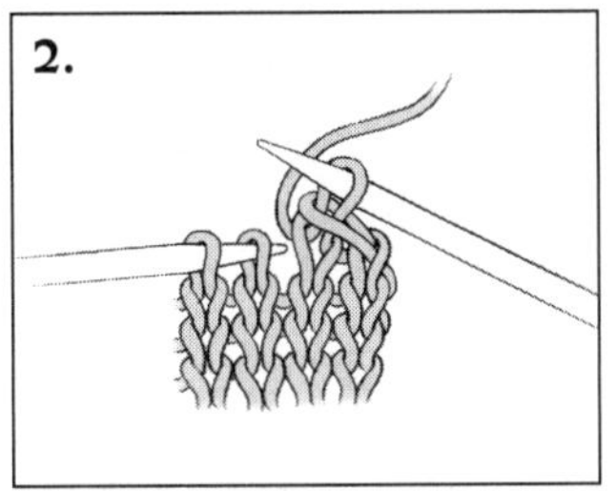

2. One stitch remains on the right needle. Knit another stitch. Again use the left needle to lift that stitch over the stitch just knitted.

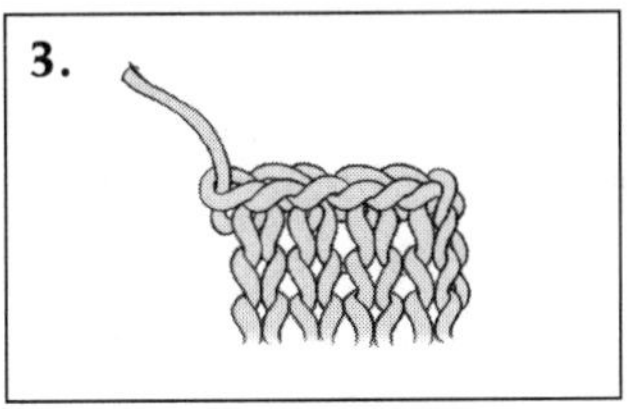

3. Continue in this way until one loop remains. Cut the yarn, leaving a tail of 4 or 5 inches, and draw the end through the last stitch. This is called fastening off. Your stitches will not unravel after you fasten off the last stitch.

Joining a New Strand of Yarn

Unless you always make projects that take one ball of yarn or less, you are going to have to learn how to add a new ball of yarn. It's very easy!

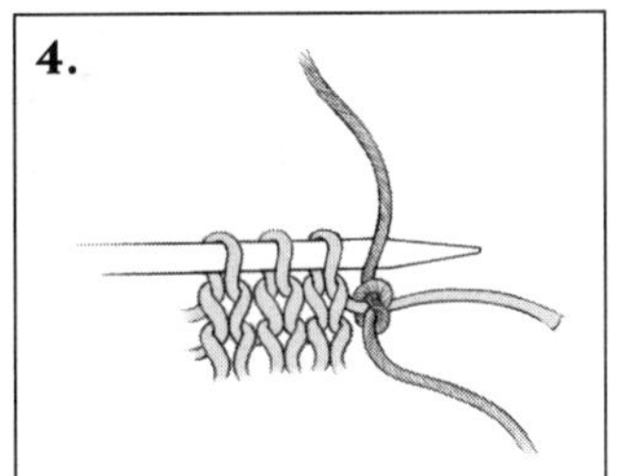

4. It is always better to add a new ball of yarn at the beginning of a row. If you are in doubt about whether you have enough yarn to work another row—don't work it, because you probably don't have enough yarn. It's time to join the next ball of yarn.

Loosely tie a knot with the new yarn around the old yarn, leaving a tail of at least 4 inches. Slide the knot up the tail of the old yarn as close as possible to your work. Leave both strands until the piece is complete. (To learn how to weave in ends, see page 101 in Chapter 10.)

If your first ball has more than a long end remaining, you may want to cut off all but 4" (10 cm) so that it doesn't get tangled as you continue your work. Set the yarn aside—you can use it for seaming.

Cell Phone Holder

SIZE

3" wide x 6½" long

MATERIALS

- 1 ball Lion Brand *Wool-Ease® Thick & Quick* #149 Charcoal (6 oz, 106 yds; 80% acrylic, 20% wool)
- Size 11 (8 mm) knitting needles, 14" long
- Large-eyed yarn needle

HOLDER

Cast on 16 stitches. Knit every row for 5". Bind off all stitches, leaving the last stitch on the needle.

STRAP

Using the last stitch, cast on 80 stitches. Bind off all stitches. Fasten off.

FINISHING

Fold holder lengthwise. Sew side seam and bottom of holder. Sew end of strap to opposite top of holder. Work in ends.

A color photo of this item can be found in the color insert, photo number 1

Tie Hat

FINISHED MEASUREMENTS
Circumference 20"

MATERIALS
- 1 ball each Lion Brand *Wool-Ease® Chunky* #107 Bluebell, (5 oz, 153 yds; 80% acrylic, 20% wool)
- Size 11 (8 mm) knitting needles or size to get gauge

GAUGE
12 stitches and 24 rows = 4" (10 cm) with size 11 needles in garter stitch (knit every row). *Be sure to check your gauge.*

NOTE
Hat is made from side to side, not bottom to top.

HAT
Cast on 36 stitches. Work in garter stitch for 20". Bind off all stitches.

FINISHING
Sew cast-on and bound-off edges together.

CORD
Cast on 80 stitches. Bind off all stitches loosely. Tie cord tightly approximately 2" down from top opening. Fold up lower edge to wear.

A color photo of this item can be found in the color insert, photo number 2

3

Learning the Purl Stitch

Once you are comfortable with the knit stitch, you should move on to the purl stitch. These two stitches are the foundation of knitting. From these two basic stitches, you can create everything else you'll ever want to knit including cables, color patterns, and lace stitches.

To make a purl stitch, you do the same four steps that you do to make a knit stitch, but use slightly different motions.

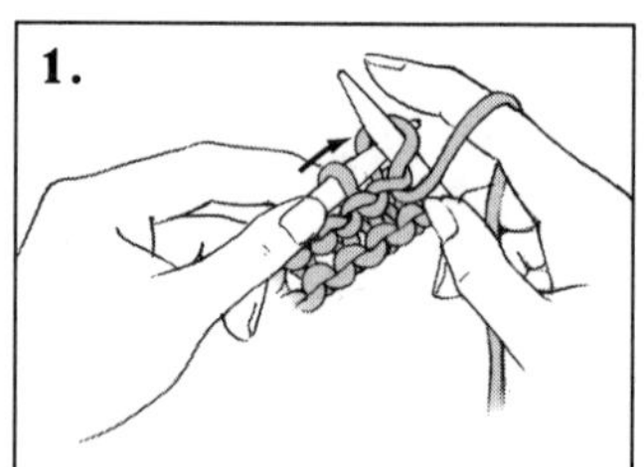

1. Begin your purl row by holding the needles as if to knit. Place the yarn *in front* of the needle. Insert the right needle from *back to front* (right to left) into the first stitch on the left needle as shown.

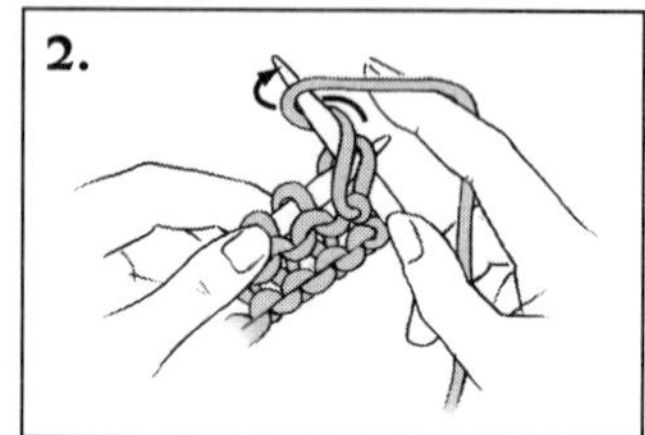

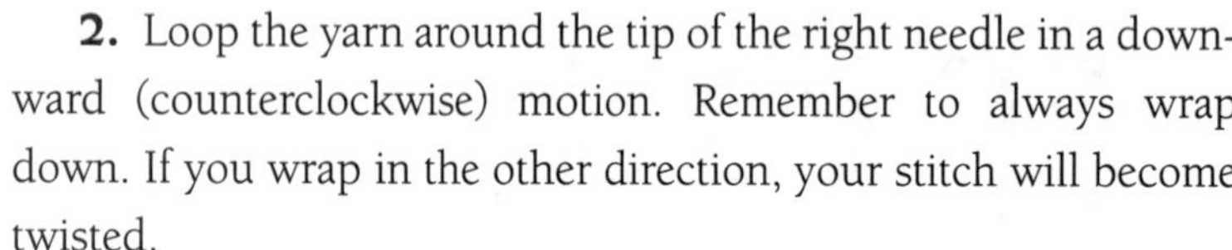

2. Loop the yarn around the tip of the right needle in a downward (counterclockwise) motion. Remember to always wrap down. If you wrap in the other direction, your stitch will become twisted.

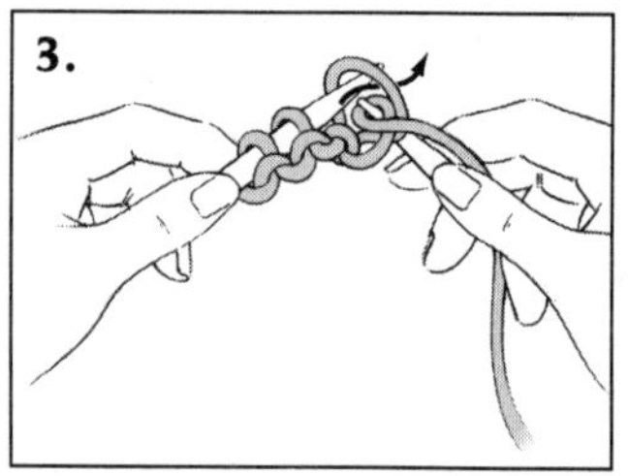

3. To make sure you don't lose the loop, place your right thumb over the yarn and against the needle. Slide the tip of the right needle, from the front to the back (away from you), and through the center of the stitch on the left needle.

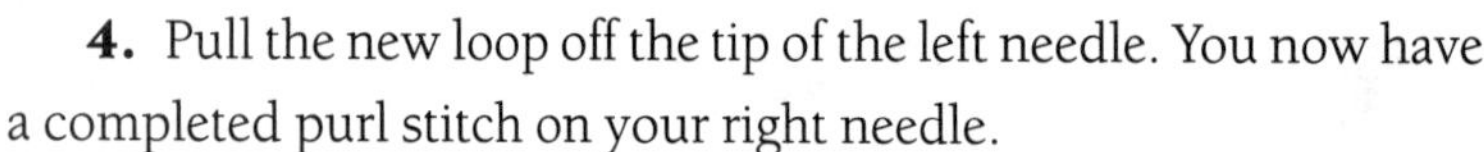

4. Pull the new loop off the tip of the left needle. You now have a completed purl stitch on your right needle.

Repeat steps 1 through 4 to complete the row. Purling, like

knitting, is a bit awkward at first, but with practice you'll soon be purling as easily as knitting.

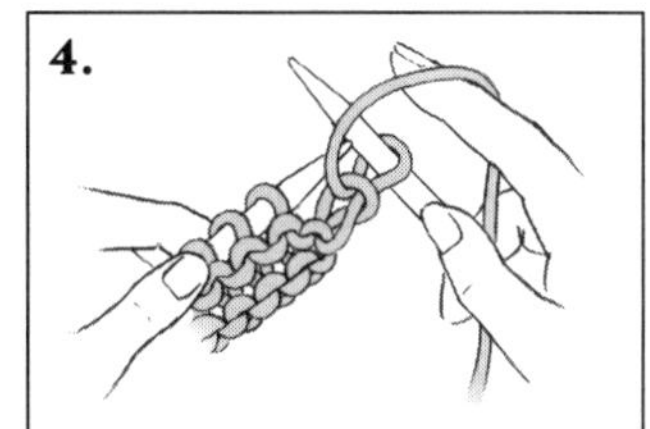

Stockinette Stitch

Once you know how to do both the knit and purl stitch, you can create a new fabric called stockinette stitch (also sometimes known as jersey or stocking stitch). It is worked by alternating rows of knit stitches and rows of purl stitches.

When you have finished your first purl row, turn the work (place the full needle in your left hand and the empty needle in your right hand) and *knit* the next row. After that, *purl* the next row. Continue working, alternating each knit row with a purl row. This is all it takes to create stockinette stitch.

Look at your work. One side of your fabric looks like it's cov-

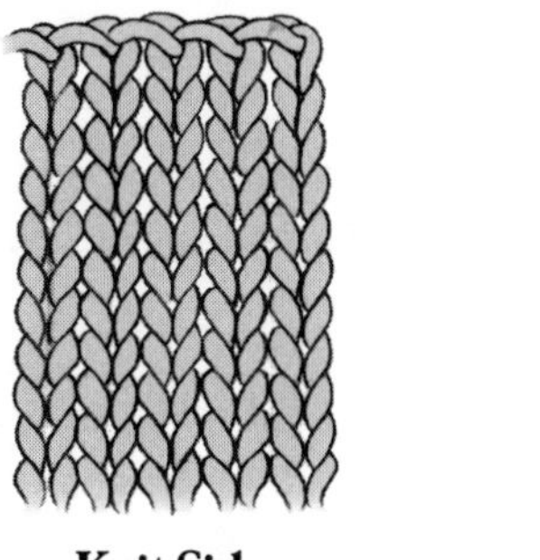

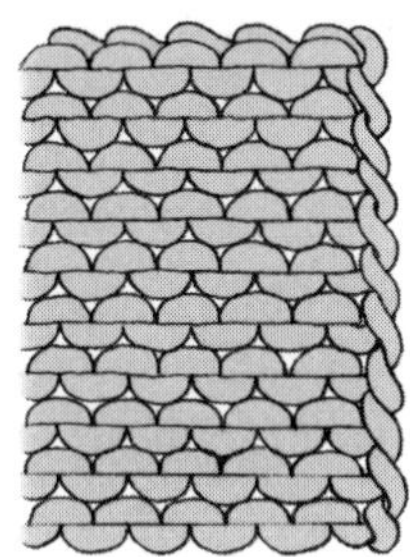

Knit Side

Purl Side

ered with **V**'s. That's the knit side. The other side looks like it's covered with bumps. That's the purl side.

As you alternate rows of knit and purl, you are likely to forget which row you completed last. To figure out whether you should be knitting the row or purling the row, put your work in your left hand, with the yarn coming from the right side ready to work. Which side is facing you? *If the **V**'s are facing you, you are on the knit side and should knit the row; if the bumps are facing you, you are on the purl side, so purl the row.*

Striped Stocking Cap

SIZE

Fits child's head 2–6 years old

FINISHED MEASUREMENTS

Circumference 17"

MATERIALS

• 1 skein each Lion Brand *Wool-Ease® Sportweight* #109 Royal Blue (A) and #099 Fisherman (B) (5 oz, 435 yds; 80% acrylic, 20% wool)

• Size 7 (4.5 mm) knitting needles or size to get gauge

GAUGE

18 stitches and 26 rows = 4" (10 cm) with size 7 (4.5 mm) needles in stockinette stitch (knit on right side, purl on wrong side).

Be sure to check your gauge.

NOTE

1. See abbreviations on page 71.
2. The edge of the hat rolls naturally.
3. For more information on changing colors, turn to page 117 in Chapter 11.

STRIPE PATTERN

2 rows B, 4 rows A.
2 rows B, 6 rows A.
2 rows B, 8 rows A.
2 rows B, 4 rows A.
2 rows B, 4 rows A.
2 rows B. Continue with A only to end of cap.

CAP

With A, cast on 77 stitches. Work in stockinette stitch for 2½". Begin stripe pattern and work even until piece measures 6" from beginning. Continuing in stripe pattern, work decreases as follows: **Dec row** *Knit 5, k2tog; repeat from * to end—66 stitches. Work 5 rows in stockinette stitch. **Dec row** *Knit 4, k2tog; repeat from * to end—55 stitches. Work 5 rows in stockinette stitch. **Dec row** *Knit 3, k2tog; repeat from * to end—44 stitches. Work 3 rows in stockinette stitch. **Dec row** *Knit 2, k2tog; repeat from * to end—33 stitches. Work 3 rows in stockinette stitch. **Dec row** *Knit 1, k2tog; repeat from * to end—22 stitches. Work 3 rows in stockinette stitch. **Dec row** *K2tog; repeat from * to end—11 stitches. Work 3 rows in stockinette stitch. **Dec row** *K2tog; repeat from * to end—6 stitches. Work 3 rows in stockinette stitch. **Dec row** *K2tog; repeat from * to end—3 stitches. Next row, purl 3 together. Fasten off. Sew side of hat and weave in ends. Knot top of hat.

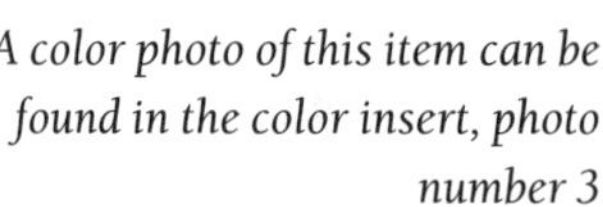

A color photo of this item can be found in the color insert, photo number 3

4

Learning the Rib Stitch

Ribbing is an elastic, flexible, reversible stitch that is commonly used on the neckbands, cuffs, and lower edges of sweaters. Ribbing is also used to make sock, mitten, and glove cuffs. It is used because it produces a stretchy fabric and prevents knitted fabric from rolling. Ribbing can also be used to make complete sweaters and other garments such as scarves.

Ribbing is sometimes worked on a needle size one or two sizes smaller than that used for the body of a sweater. Additionally, sometimes fewer stitches are worked in the ribbing and increased for the body. As the current styles dictate a softer, less drawn-in look, you may prefer to make a slightly looser edge. This can be achieved by working the ribbing on the needle size used for the body.

Ribbing is made with a combination of knit stitches and purl stitches. The most common ribbings are made of a stitch combination of knit 1, purl 1 or knit 2, purl 2. There are many other variations of common ribbings. Illustrated here is the technique for making a knit 2, purl 2 ribbing. This ribbing is softer, but pulls in slightly more than knit one, purl one ribbing.

1. On the right side of your piece, knit 2 stitches. Bring the yarn from the back of your work *between the needles* to the front. Now purl two stitches. Bring the yarn to the back of your work between the needles and knit the next two stitches.

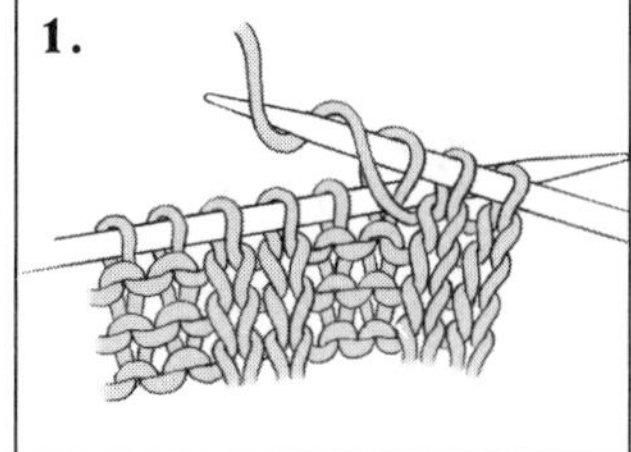

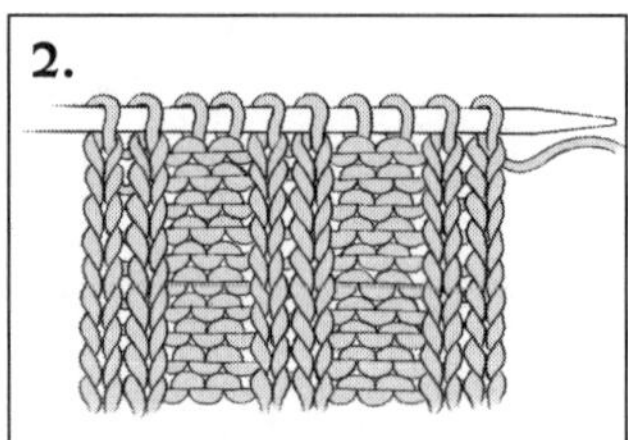
2.

2. As you continue to work rows, be sure to knit the knit stitches (**V** stitches) and purl the purl stitches (bump stitches). Remember to have the working yarn in *back* when you knit and in *front* when you purl.

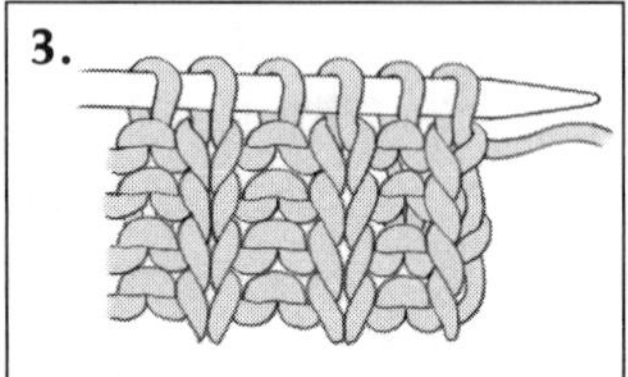
3.

3. A knit 1, purl 1 ribbing is also sometimes called 1 x 1 ribbing. Take care to line up your stitches correctly or you will end up with another simple stitch called seed stitch, in which the knits and purls are worked opposite to the ones below them.

For easier seaming, work knit 1, purl 1 ribbing over an uneven number of stitches so that you begin with 2 knit stitches and end with a knit 1 stitch. When sewing, if you sew the beginning and ending knit stitches into the seam together, there is a continuous, unbroken line.

Binding Off in Ribbing

Rather than knitting all the stitches as you bind them off, you knit the knit stitches and purl the purl stitches as you come to them on the needle. (This is referred to as binding off in pattern.) By working in this way, you'll give your ribbing a more flexible bind-off. When working a front band, where you might need more firmness, you may want to bind off in the regular way by knitting each stitch to be bound off.

Easy Bright Ribbed Pullover

SIZES

S (M, L, XL)

FINISHED MEASUREMENTS

Chest at underarm 38 (43, 48, 53)" Length from shoulder 19 (20, 21, 22)"

MATERIALS

- 7 (8, 9, 10) balls Colinette/Unique Kolours *Point Five* #134 Jamboree (3½ oz, 55 yds; 100% wool)
- Size 17 (12.75 mm) knitting needles, or size to get gauge
- Two stitch holders

GAUGE

8 sts and 10 rows = 4" (10 cm) in rib pattern.

Be sure to check your gauge.

NOTE

1. See abbreviations on page 71.
2. As hand-dyed colors may be inconsistent from ball to ball, for the best look, work with two balls of yarn at the same time and alternate them every other row. Do not cut yarns, but carry them up the side of your piece.

STOCKINETTE STITCH (St st)

Knit on right side (RS); purl on wrong side (WS).

RIB PATTERN

Row 1 (RS) K3, p2; repeat across to last 3 sts. k3. **Row 2 (WS)** P3, k2; repeat across to last 3 sts, p3. Repeat rows 1–2 for rib pattern.

BACK

With smaller needles, cast on 38 (43, 48, 53) sts. Work in rib pattern until piece measures 10½ (11, 11½, 12)" from beginning, ending with a wrong-side row.

Shape Armholes

Bind off 3 sts at beg on next 2 rows—32 (37, 42, 47) sts. Dec 1 st on each side of next 4 rows—24 (29, 34, 39) sts. Dec 1 st on each side of every other row until 22 (25, 28, 29) sts remain and work in St st until armhole measures 8½ (9, 9½, 10)".

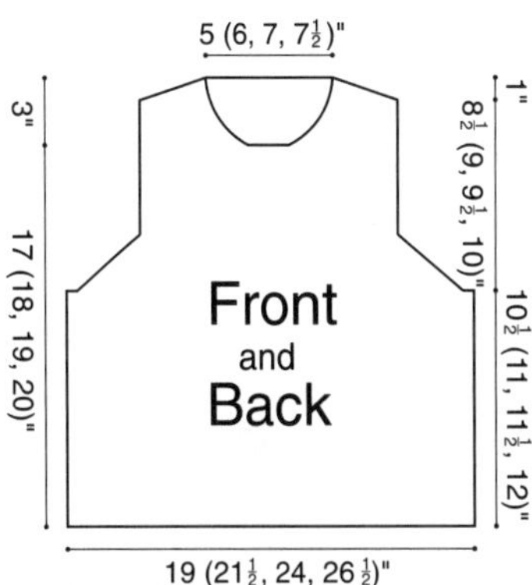

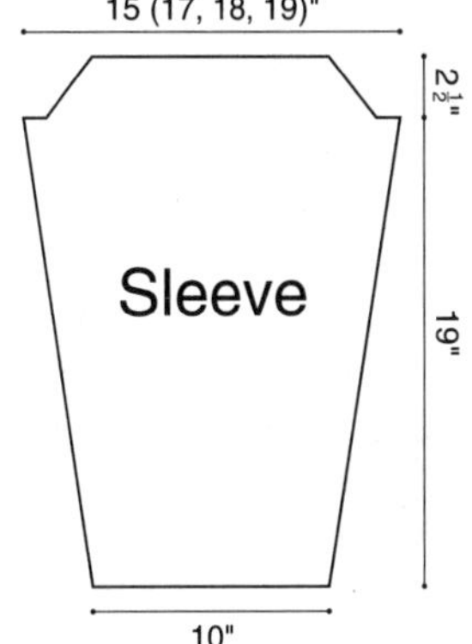

Easy Bright Ribbed Pullover (continued)

Shape Shoulders

Bind off 6 (6, 7, 7) sts at beginning of next 2 rows. Place remaining 10 (13, 14, 15) sts on a holder.

FRONT

Cast on and work rib pattern and armhole, shaping as for back until piece measures 17 (18, 19, 20)", ending with a wrong-side row.

Shape Neck

Mark center 6 (7, 6, 7) sts. **Next row (RS)** Work across to marked sts, place 6 (7, 6, 7) sts on a holder, join a new ball of yarn, and work to end. Working both sides at the same time, dec 1 st from each neck edge 4 (6, 4, 4) times. Work even until same length as back to shoulder, ending with a wrong-side row.

Shape Shoulders

Bind off 6 (6, 7, 7) sts at beginning of next 2 rows.

SLEEVE

NOTE

As you increase stitches, work them into the ribbed pattern on each side. For example, the first increased stitch at the beginning of the row will be a purl stitch and the last stitch a knit stitch.

Cast on 20 (20, 25, 25) sts. **Row 1 (RS)** K3, p2; repeat across to end of row. **Row 2 (WS)** K2, p3; repeat across to end of row. Repeat rows 1 and 2 three times more. **Inc row (RS)** K1, inc 1 st in next st, k1, p2, *k3, p2; repeat from * to last 2 sts, inc 1 st in next st, k1. Repeat last row every 8th row 4 (6, 5, 6) times more—30 (34, 37, 39) sts. Work even until piece measures 19" from beg.

Shape Sleeve Cap

Working in St st, bind off 3 sts at beg of next 2 rows—24 (28, 31, 33) sts. Dec 1 st each side of every row 4 times—16 (20, 23, 25) sts. Bind off all sts.

A color photo of this item can be found in the color insert, photo number 4

FINISHING

Block pieces. Sew right shoulder seam.

Neckband

With right side facing and beginning at left shoulder, pick up and knit 7 sts along left side of neck, knit 6 (7, 6, 7) sts from front neck holder, pick up and knit 7 stitches along right side of neck, knit 10 (13, 14, 15) sts from back neck holder—30 (34, 34, 36) sts. Knit 1 row. Bind off all sts loosely. Sew left shoulder and neckband seam. Sew in sleeves. Sew sleeve and side seams.

5

Help!!

Encountering problems and errors as you knit isn't unusual—everyone comes upon them. Even experts have ripped out their knitting. Part of the fun of experimenting is that you know that you can always do it over again. Practice and experience are sometimes all it takes to be able to work out your problems.

The key to solving knitting dilemmas is not to get flustered, but to work out the problems and find solutions. Whether it's a simple matter of dropping a stitch or just not understanding an instruction, you can find an adequate solution.

Dropping a Stitch

At some point you'll drop a stitch as you knit. Be on the lookout for dropped stitches as you work. You'll need a crochet hook to get your dropped stitch back in place. The hook size should be about the same as your knitting needle, but this is not essential. For example, if you were knitting with size 10 (6 mm) knitting needles, the best-sized crochet hook would be a J-10 (6 mm) hook. You could use a hook that is 3 or 4 sizes smaller or larger. You just have to be able to insert the hook comfortably into a stitch and pull the yarn through as shown in the illustrations.

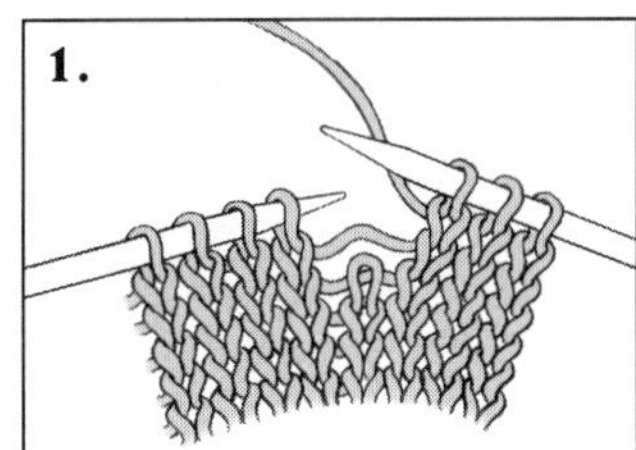

1. Once you encounter a dropped stitch, it's important to deal with the stitch before you move on with your knitting. What you will see is that a stitch has fallen off your needle and unraveled for several rows beneath the row you are working, as shown.

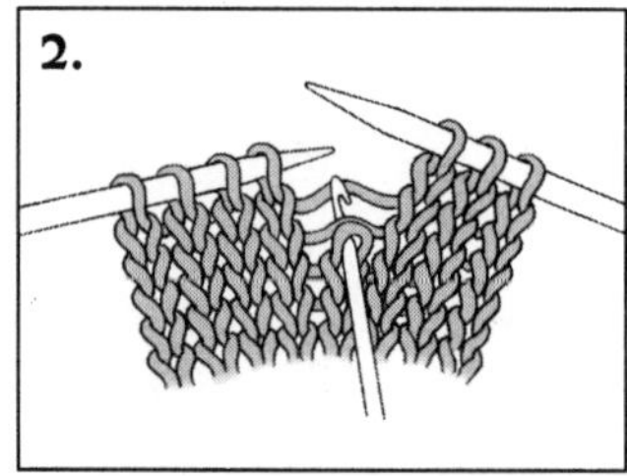

2. Knit to the place where you've dropped the stitch. Insert a crochet hook into the loop of the dropped stitch (you can also use the tip of your knitting needle, but the crochet hook will make it easier). Grab the bar of the stitch right above it in the crook of the crochet hook. Pull the bar through the stitch. If your stitch has dropped down several rows, repeat the same process until your stitch is on the same row as the rest of your knitting.

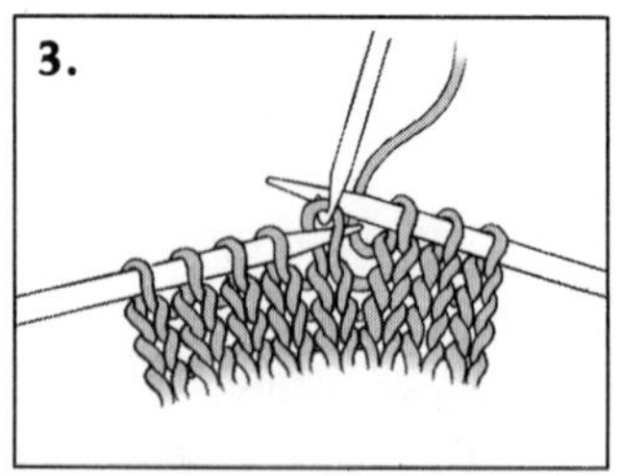

3. Slip the newly formed stitch onto your knitting needle. Be careful not to twist it when placing it back on the needle. Take a look at the stitch. It's not twisted if the yarn that makes up the stitch is coming from the front of the stitch. If it is twisted on the needle, it will appear to come from the back of the stitch.

Unraveling Stitches

Sometimes a mistake is too far down in the work to fix with a crochet hook as you would with a dropped stitch. In such cases you should unravel the work in order to fix the error. Ripping is not tragic and offers you a new chance to practice your knitting or make changes you might not have otherwise had an opportunity to incorporate into your piece.

You can unravel your knitting by taking stitches off the needle and ripping out the desired number of rows or working stitch by stitch. Working stitch by stitch is good for smaller "rip outs," and although it is slightly slower, it's a very safe method to fix your knitting.

You can also work a combination of both techniques by ripping out the majority of the rows and then, when you come to the row before the final "mistake" row, slipping your stitches back onto the needle one by one (taking care not to twist them) as shown on page 47. To complete the ripping out and get to the mistake, work stitch by stitch, following the directions here.

1. On a knit stitch, holding the yarn in the back, insert the left needle into the stitch one row below the first stitch on the right needle. On a purl stitch (not shown), hold the yarn in front and insert the needle from the back of the work.

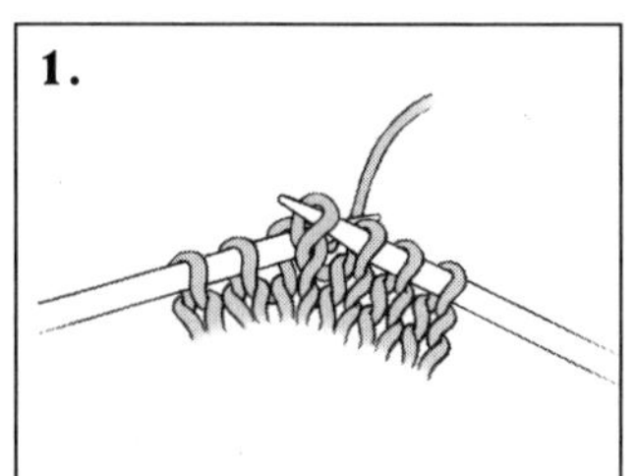

Slip the stitch onto your left needle, gently pulling the yarn out of the stitch above it. Continue in this way until you have reached your mistake.

UNRAVELING TIPS

When the section to be ripped is too large to make the individual-stitch method practical for getting to the last row to rip, it is helpful to lay the piece on a table so that you can clearly see the work. You'll have more control of the stitches, and this allows you to thread the stitches back onto the needle properly. You can use a finger to "pin" the stitch below the one being threaded to ensure it doesn't drop.

Rip to the "mistake" row and then put all the stitches of that row back onto the needle one by one as shown above. It much easier than trying to "thread" the needle into open loops of stitches—invariably this will make it easier to twist, split, or drop stitches.

Edge Stitches

Beginning knitters often feel that their edge stitches are too loose. As you practice, you'll notice this happens less and less. If it seems to persist, you can draw up a loop from the row below on the last stitch and knit or purl both the loop and last stitch.

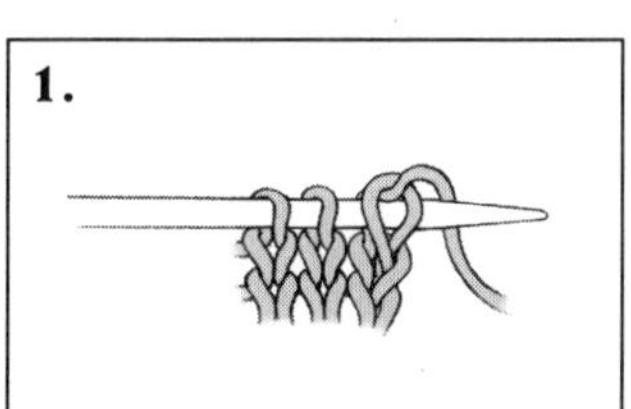

1–2. Sometimes an extra stitch appears to form at the beginning of your needle. This happens when you begin to work a row and you take the yarn *over the top* of the needle. To prevent this, bring the yarn *underneath* the knitting when moving it from front to back for a knit stitch.

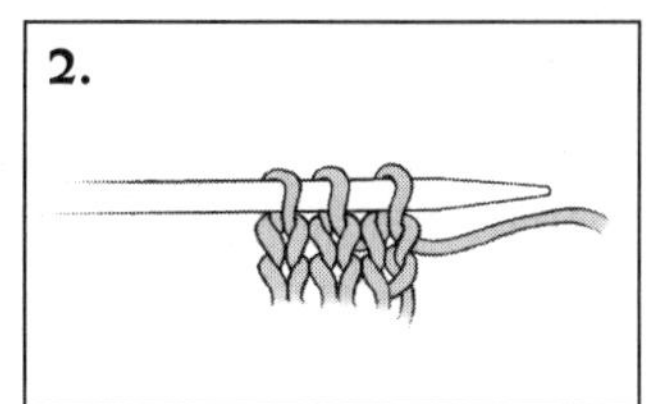

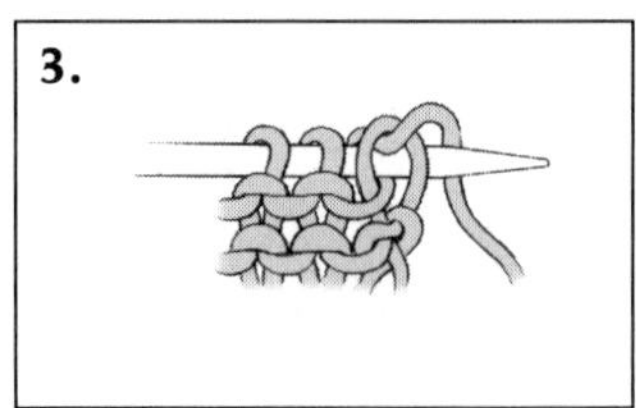
3.

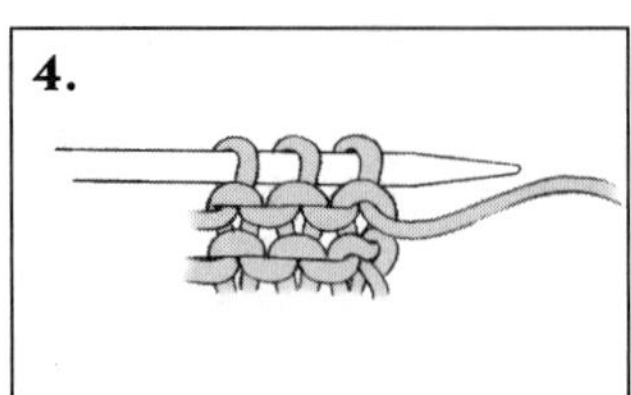
4.

3–4. You can have the same problem at the beginning of a purl row. To prevent extra stitches from forming, bring the yarn *underneath* the knitting from back to front for a purl stitch.

It Helps to Know . . .

- To avoid losing stitches, place point protectors over the needle tips. Complete a row whenever possible so you won't get confused about where to begin the next row.
- If you get confused about where you are in a row, just remember that the stitches that are attached to the yarn belong in your right hand and have already been worked. Stitches on the needle without yarn attached to them are waiting to be knitted.
- Can't remember where you left off when you put down your work? It's always a good idea to find a simple tracking system that lets you know what you have just completed, especially as you begin to work more complex patterns. You can use simple check marks on paper or a row counter to help manage your project.

  Of course, this advice doesn't help if you haven't noted your place. If your pattern is stockinette stitch, it's a matter of figuring out if you are on a knit or purl row. For other patterns, go back to the last row worked and see if you can identify the stitches worked. Compare those stitches to the pattern. Sometimes the first stitch or two will give you enough clues to figure out which pattern row you are on.
- Measuring pieces accurately can be easily achieved if you lay the piece onto a flat surface such as a table. Measure straight up and down inside the piece and don't angle the tape measure along a curve.
- Be proactive in avoiding problems with your knitting. Count the number of stitches on the needle before beginning a new row. This allows you to discover any dropped or added stitches before you go further with your work.

6

Scarves

Bias Bicolor Scarf

FINISHED MEASUREMENTS

7" x 52"

MATERIALS

• 1 skein each Lion Brand *Chenille Thick & Quick®* #149 Gray and #141 Dusty Mauve (100 yds; 91% acrylic, 9% rayon)

• Size 11 (8 mm) knitting needles, or size to get gauge

GAUGE

8 stitches and 14 rows = 4" (10 cm) with size 11 needles in stockinette stitch (knit on right side; purl on wrong side). *Be sure to check your gauge.*

NOTE

Use first increase on page 58.

SCARF

First Half of Scarf

With gray, cast on 16 stitches. **Row 1** Knit 1, increase 1 stitch in next stitch, knit to end. **Row 2** Knit 1, purl 2 together, purl to last stitch, knit 1. Repeat last 2 rows until short side of scarf measures 26", ending with row 2.

Second Half of Scarf

Attach dusty mauve and resume working rows 1 and 2 until second half measures the same as first half. Bind off all stitches.

FINISHING

Weave in ends. Lightly block.

Lengthwise Scarf

FINISHED MEASUREMENTS

6" x 62"

MATERIALS

• 1 skein each Classic Elite *Waterspun:* #5097 Moss (A) #5026 Dark Purple (B) #5065 Grape (C) #5050 Olive (D) #5027 Maroon (E); (1 ¾ oz, 138 yds; 100% felted Merino wool)
• Size 7 (4.5 mm) knitting needles, or size to get gauge
• Size H-8 (5 mm) crochet hook for fringe

GAUGE

16 stitches and 30 rows = 4" (10 cm) with size 7 needles in seed stitch.
Be sure to check your gauge.

NOTE

The scarf is worked lengthwise in stripes.

Seed Stitch

Row 1 *Knit 1, purl 1; rep from *, end knit 1. Repeat row 1 for seed stitch.

Stripe Sequence

Note Work 2-row stripes after cast-on and before bind-off and 3 rows of all other stripes. When tying on a new color, leave about an 8" tail, which will become part of the fringe.

Color C
Color D
Color E
Color A
Color B

Repeat sequence three times, ending last stripe with color C.

SCARF

With color C, cast on 247 stitches. Work in seed stitch and stripe sequence until scarf measures 6". Bind off all stitches.

FRINGE

Cut 16" lengths in assorted colors. Working with 6 strands each of two colors, work fringe following diagrams. Trim ends. See page 55 for more information about making fringe.

Tassel Scarf

FINISHED MEASUREMENTS

8" x 52"

MATERIALS

- 1 skein Lion Brand *Homespun®* #343 Romanesque (6 oz, 185 yds; 98% acrylic, 2% polyester)
- Size 10.5 (6.5 mm) knitting needles, or size to get gauge

GAUGE

10 stitches and 24 rows = 4" (10 cm) with size 10.5 needles in garter stitch (knit every row).

Be sure to check your gauge.

NOTE

Cut yarn for tassels before you begin to knit.

SCARF

Cast on 20 stitches.

Knit every row until yarn is almost gone, leaving about 2 feet with which to bind off. Bind off all stitches.

FINISHING

On one short end, take center 2½" and fold approximately 2½" from each side edge into a pleat meeting at center of scarf as shown in illustrations 1 and 2. Stitch in place. Repeat on second short end.

TASSEL

Cut 30 pieces of yarn 18" for each tassel. Follow tassel instructions on page 56. Attach one tassel in center of pleat on each end.

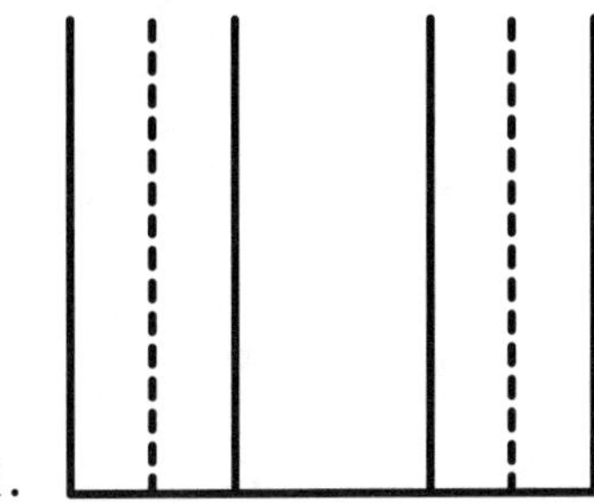

1.

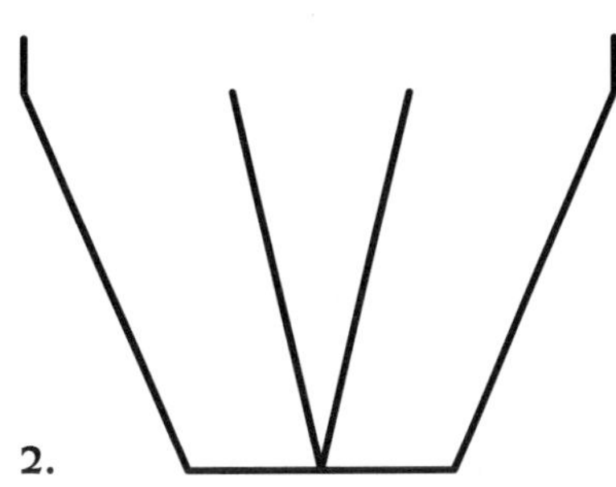

2.

Lace Rib Scarf

FINISHED MEASUREMENTS

8" x 62"

MATERIALS

• 1 skein Lion Brand *Monet* #405 Peacock (4 oz, 230 yds; 100% wool)
• Size 8 (5 mm) knitting needles, or size to get gauge

GAUGE

14 sts = 4" (10cm) with size 8 needles in pattern stitch.
Be sure to check your gauge.

NOTES

1. See abbreviations list page 71.
2. Always slip the first stitch of each row purlwise without knitting it.
3. See Chapter 7 pages 58 and 61 for techniques on slipping stitches and yarn overs.

SCARF

Cast on 29 stitches and knit 4 rows. **Row 1** Slip 1 st, knit 2, *yarn over (yo), k2tog, purl 1, knit 1; repeat from * to the last 2 sts, knit 2. **Row 2** Slip 1 st, knit 1, purl 1, *yo, p2tog, knit 1, purl 1; repeat from * to the last 2 sts, knit 2. Repeat rows 1 and 2 until desired length or most of the yarn is used up. End by knitting 4 rows. Bind off stitches loosely.

FINISHING

Weave in ends. Stretch to open up lace pattern and block.

A color photo of this item can be found in the color insert, photo number 6

Double-Strand Scarf

FINISHED MEASUREMENTS

8" x 42"

MATERIALS

• 1 skein Lion Brand *Homespun®* #34 Mediterranean (6 oz, 185 yds; 98% acrylic, 2% polyester)
• Size 19 (15 mm) knitting needles, or size to get gauge

GAUGE

11 stitches and 14 rows = 4" (10 cm) with size 19 needles in garter stitch.
Be sure to check your gauge.

NOTE

The scarf is worked with 2 strands of yarn held together. For ease in working, use one strand from outside of skein and one from inside of skein.

SCARF

With 2 strands of yarn, cast on 14 stitches. Knit every row until yarn is almost gone, leaving about 2 feet with which to bind off. Loosely bind off all stitches.

FINISHING

Weave in ends.

A color photo of these items can be found in the color insert, photo number 5

Cabled Scarf

FINISHED MEASUREMENTS

7" x 40"

MATERIALS

• 1 skein Lion Brand *Wool-Ease Thick & Quick®* #099 Fisherman (6 oz, 108 yds; 80% acrylic, 20% wool)
• Size 13 (9 mm) knitting needles, or size to get gauge
• Cable needle

GAUGE

8 stitches and 12 rows = 4" (10 cm) with size 13 needles in stockinette stitch (knit on right side; purl on wrong side).
Be sure to check your gauge.

2/2 Left Cable (over 4 stitches)

Slip 2 stitches to cable needle and hold to front, knit 2, knit 2 from cable needle

SCARF

Cast on 16 stitches. Knit 3 rows. **Rows 1, 5, 7 (right side)** Knit 5, purl 1, knit 4, purl 1, knit 5. **Row 2 (and all wrong side rows)** Knit 2, purl 3, knit 1, purl 4, knit 1, purl 3, knit 2. **Row 3 (cable row)** Knit 2, purl 4, 2/2 left cable over 4 stitches, purl 4, knit 2. **Row 8** Repeat row 2. Repeat rows 1–8 for cable pattern until yarn is almost finished (leaving enough to work several rows), ending with row 2. Knit 3 rows. Bind off. Weave in ends. Block lightly.

A color photo of this item can be found in the color insert, photo number 7

Fringe

One of the easiest ways to embellish a scarf, shawl, or afghan is to add fringe. You can vary fringe by length of the strands, by the number of strands used for each fringe and by the spacing across the piece. Use a crochet hook to manipulate the strands through the knitted piece. The hook size is not very important, but it should be large enough to hold the strands.

Cutting fringe strands can be done easily by wrapping yarn around a book, magazine, video, cardboard, or other firm but not-too-thick object. The key is to find something that will give you the desired fringe length. Cut the lower edge of the fringe and set aside. If you are fringing a large piece, you may want to do this several times to get the number of yarn strands needed. To ensure that you don't run out of yarn, prepare the fringe yarn before knitting your project.

It's best not to use a yarn that frays or unravels for fringe.

1. Once the fringe strands are cut, gather the desired number and fold in half. Insert the crochet hook into the fabric from the wrong side. Draw through a loop of all strands. Be sure to make a fairly large loop and not to miss any loop of yarn when drawing through.

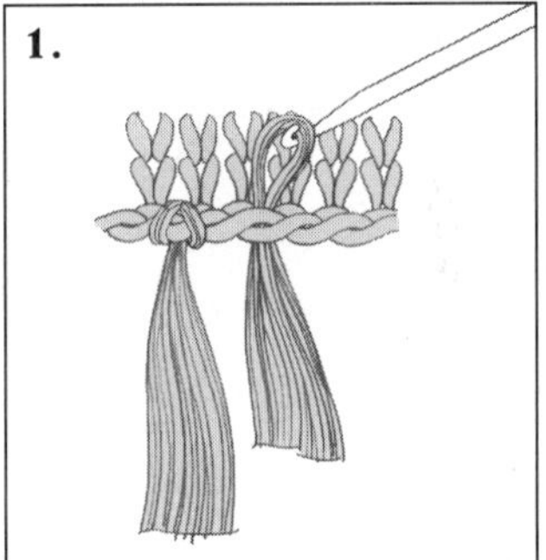

2. Using your hands, pull the loose strands through the loop and tighten as shown. Once the entire area is fringed, lay the piece on a flat surface and trim all strands with scissors.

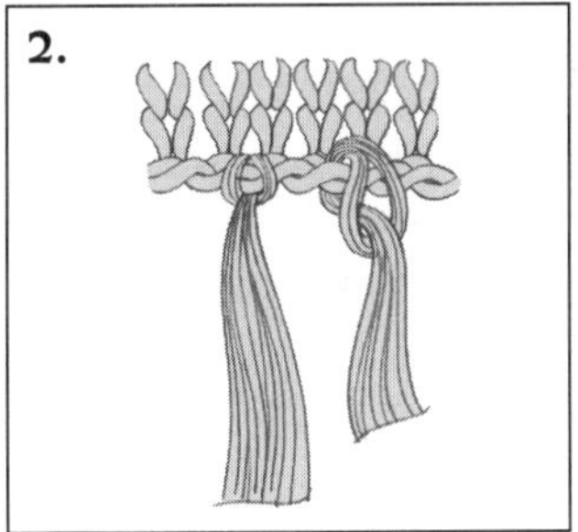

1.

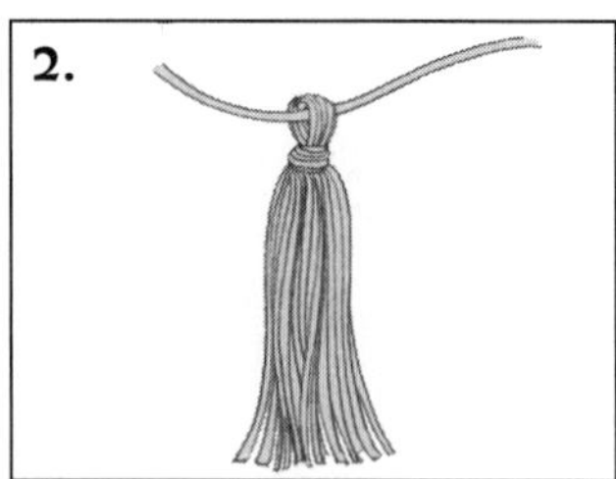
2.

Tassel

Like fringe, tassels are another easy embellishment, not only for knits but also for other decorating purposes.

1. Wrap the strands around a piece of cardboard the desired length of the tassel. Draw a piece of yarn under the top of the tassel and tie into a circle to keep in place. Cut the strands along the lower edge and remove from the cardboard.

2. Take a slightly longer strand of yarn and wrap a few times around the top of the tassel about an inch down from the top. Tie in place and allow ends to become part of the tassel. Untie the upper knot and use it to attach the tassel to the desired item. One way to do this is to thread both strands of the upper tie onto a yarn needle and sew the tassel on.

7

Increasing Your Knowledge

Once you know the basic steps to creating a flat piece of knitting, the logical next step is to make items that require some kind of shaping. This is easy! You only need to know how to increase or decrease your stitches. In your early attempts to knit, you may already have inadvertently added or lost stitches. Now let's learn how to do this on purpose.

Increases

Increasing widens your piece and adds to the number of stitches on the needle. There are many ways to increase, but most of the time, a simple method will suffice. When you learn more about knitting, you may want to learn other specific ways to increase. The most important things you'll need to know are where to make the increase and where to place the increases you make.

TIPS

- Your pattern usually won't tell you how to increase; you can use either method shown here. In many cases, it doesn't matter which you choose.
- When increasing multiple stitches across a row, making the increases between stitches is easier. When increasing at the edges (such as sleeve shaping), increasing within a stitch is just fine.
- If possible, work all increases at least one stitch in from the edge. This applies to both the beginning and end of row increases. This facilitates both seaming and picking up stitches for borders after the garment pieces are complete. Although many patterns will not spell this out, working all shaping at least one stitch from the edge is a habit that you should always practice.

INCREASING ONE

Using a stitch (not invisible)

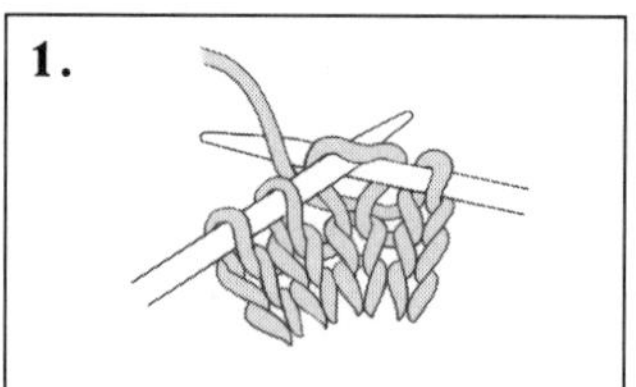

1. Insert the needle as if you were knitting the stitch, wrap the yarn and pull through the loop.

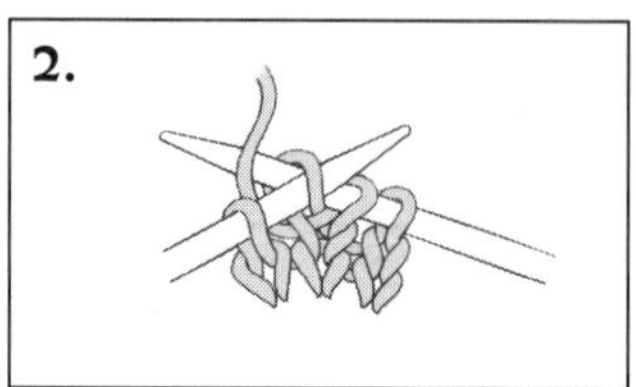

2. Leaving the loop just pulled up on your right needle, knit the stitch once again through the back of the loop. You now have created a new stitch.

BETWEEN A STITCH

This increase is called a make 1, or M1 (invisible)

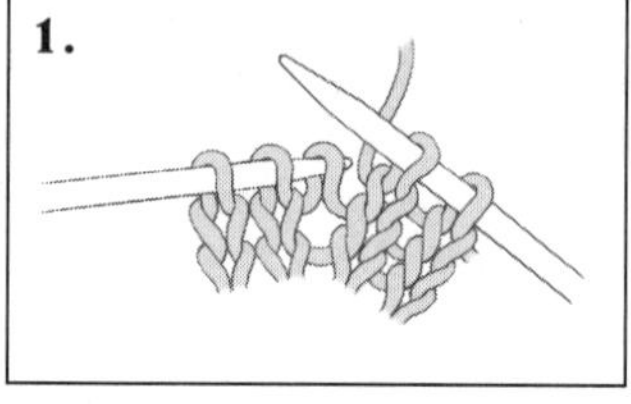

1. Insert the left-hand needle under the strand from front to back between two stitches as shown.

2. Knit the loop off the left needle, inserting right needle into the back of the stitch and knitting into the back loop of the stitch.

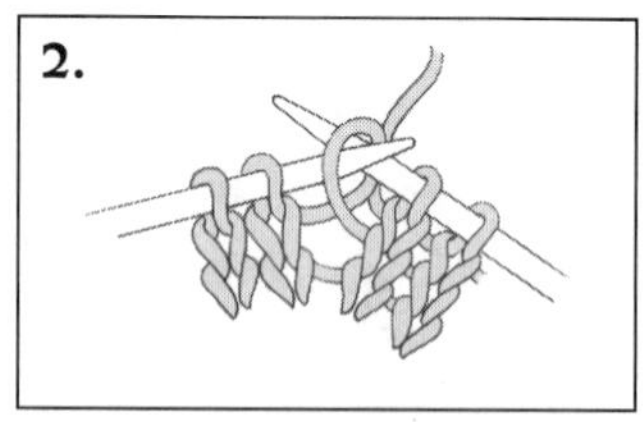

3. To purl between a stitch, insert the left needle under the strand from front to back and purl through the back loop of the stitch.

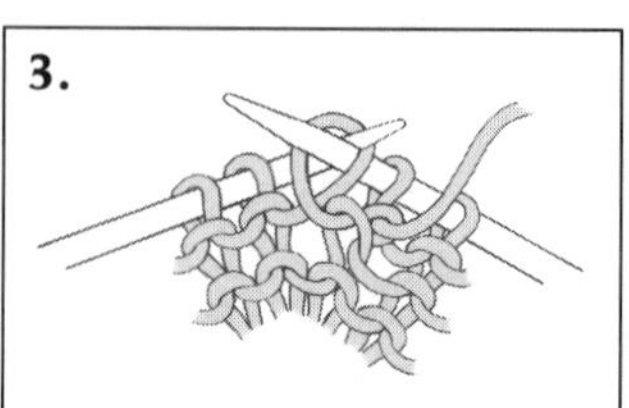

YARN-OVER INCREASE

This increase is used not only to add stitches, but also for many decorative purposes. In fact, the yarn-over is the primary building block of lace stitches, since it is designed to make a visible hole in the fabric. (See the Lace Rib Scarf in Chapter 6 on page 52.)

The yarn-over formation shown here is the simplest to do. There are other variations, such as when a yarn-over occurs either before or after a purl stitch or at the beginning of a row. These variations differ only in how you move the yarn from front to back and are easily accomplished if you remember that once completed, the purpose of a yarn-over is to leave a strand of yarn on the needle.

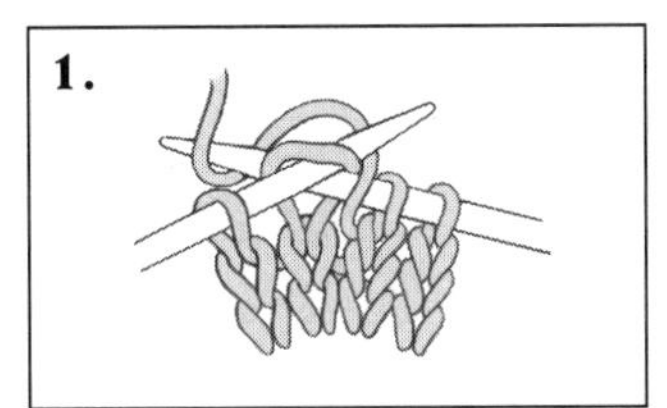

1. Bring the yarn from the back of the work to the front, and bring it back over the needle. Knit the next stitch as shown.

2. On the wrong side of the piece, purl the loop created by the yarn-over.

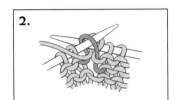

Decreases

Decreasing makes your piece narrower. There are many ways to decrease a stitch. As with increasing, one or two simple decrease methods are all you'll need. The most important thing you'll need to know is where to make the decrease and how to place the decreases you make.

Front and Back Loops

When you knit or purl, you normally work into the front of the stitch as in 1 and 2. If you are required to work into the back loop of a knit or purl stitch, do so as shown in 3 and 4. In patterns, this will be noted as "knit or purl through the back loop" and is sometimes abbreviated as k1b or k1 tb1 or p1b or p1 tb1. Note that purling through the back loop requires more effort, but is less frequently used.

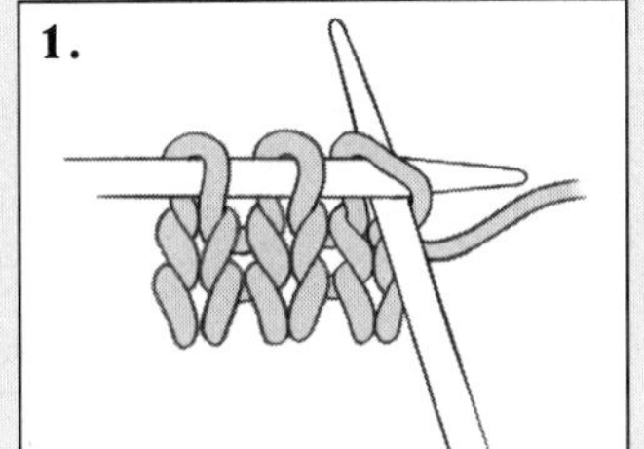

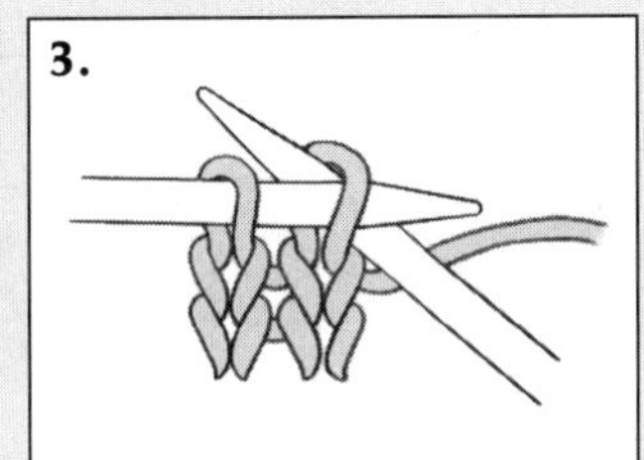

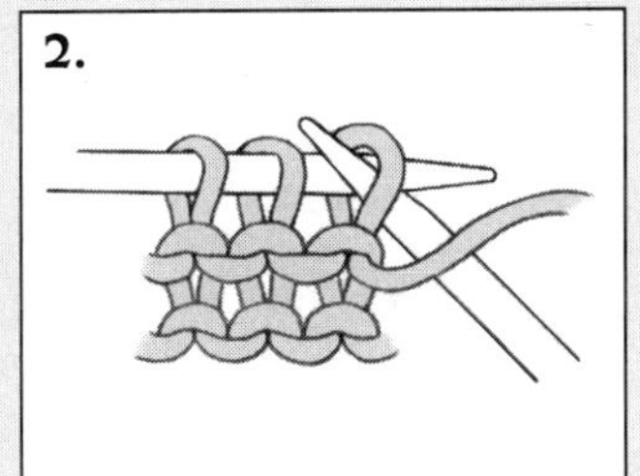

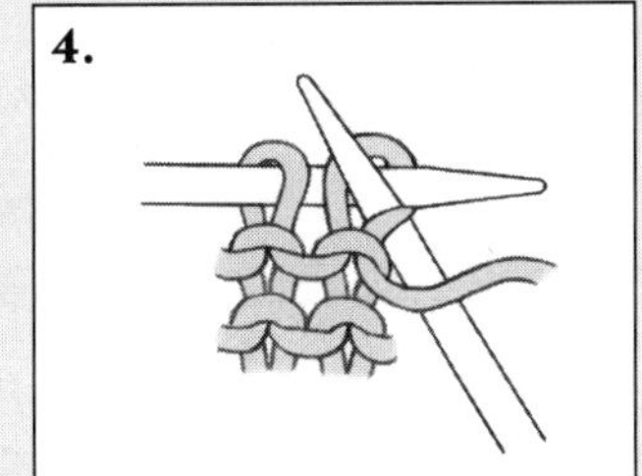

TIPS

- Patterns are more specific about decreasing than increasing. Decreases done in certain ways slant the stitches to the left or right. For many patterns this is an important element; for others it doesn't matter all that much.
- Knitting or purling two stitches together slants the stitches to the right. Working either a slip, slip, knit or slip, slip purl slants the stitches to the left.
- Although many patterns will not say so specifically, it's generally preferable to work decreases at least one stitch in from the edge, whether at the beginning or end of a row. This facilitates both seaming and picking up stitches from the edge later on in the finishing process.

DECREASING ONE

Knitting or purling two stitches together (right-leaning decreases)

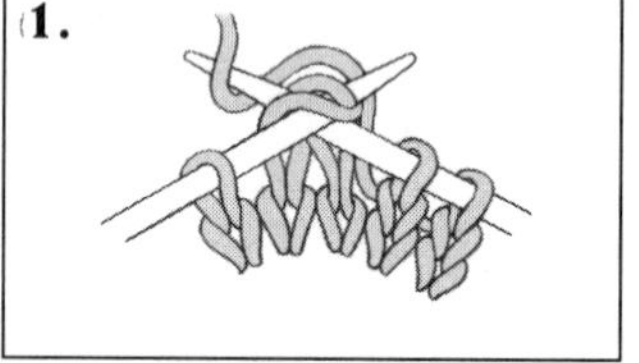

1. Insert your needle to knit, but go through two stitches. Knit as normal.

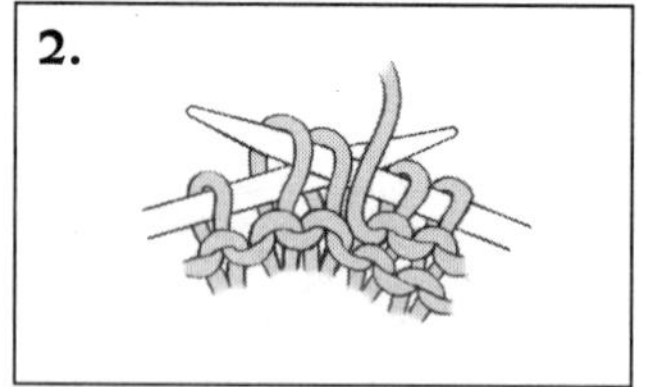

2. Insert your needle to purl, but go through two stitches. Purl as normal.

Slip, slip, knit or slip, slip, purl decrease (left-leaning decreases)

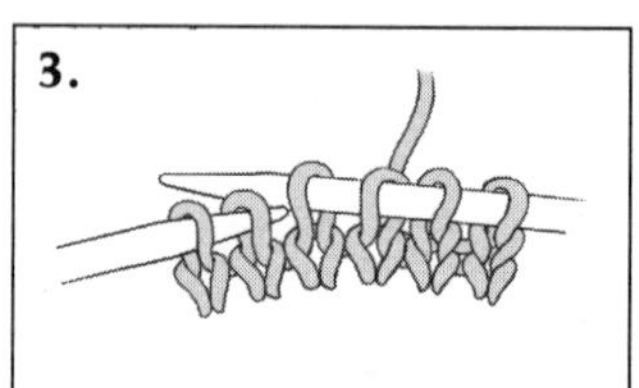

3. Slip two stitches from the left needle to the right, one at a time, as if to knit. Insert the left needle into the front of the two slipped stitches.

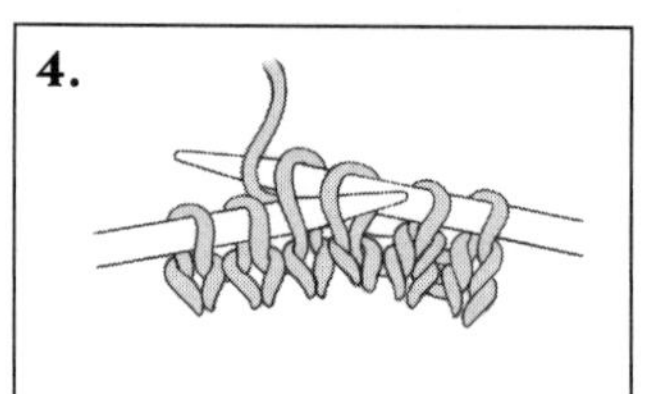

4. Knit the two stitches together as shown.

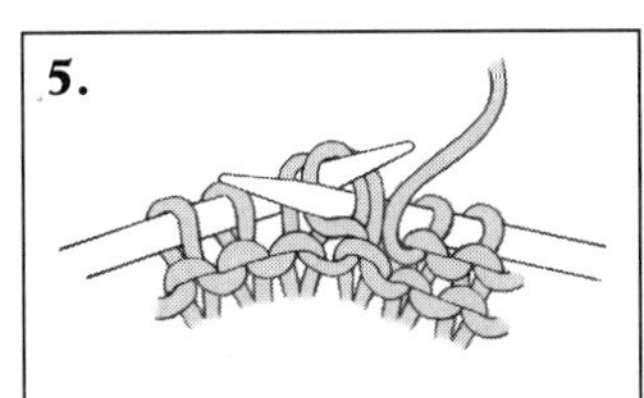

5. On the purl side, slip the stitches from the left needle to the right, one at a time, as if to knit. Pass them back to the left hand needle. Purl them together through the back loop of the stitch.

Slipping Stitches

When you slip a stitch, you neither increase nor decrease it. As a matter of fact, you don't even knit or purl it. Essentially you are merely transferring the stitch from one needle to the next without working it at all. The yarn is kept in place, ready to work the next stitch. There are a variety of uses for this technique, and knowing how to slip a stitch will prove to be very helpful. In a pattern the term used to indicate a slip stitch is "slip 1" or "sl 1."

Often stitches at the beginning of a row are slipped in one row and then worked on the next row. This is done to create a neat chain edge along the side of your piece. For example, slip stitches are used along the sides of the heel in a sock to give a neat edge to pick up stitches. This technique makes it easy to see where you need to pick up stitches.

Slip stitches are also used for decreases. For example, a double decrease that eliminates two stitches at the same time is sometimes written as follows: slip 1 as if to knit, knit 2 together, psso (pass the slipped stitch over the knit-two-together stitches). This decrease is abbreviated as sl 1 k2tog psso or SK2P. Slip stitches can be used within a specific pattern to create a unique look when making mosaic stitches or tuck stitches.

SLIP ONE PURLWISE

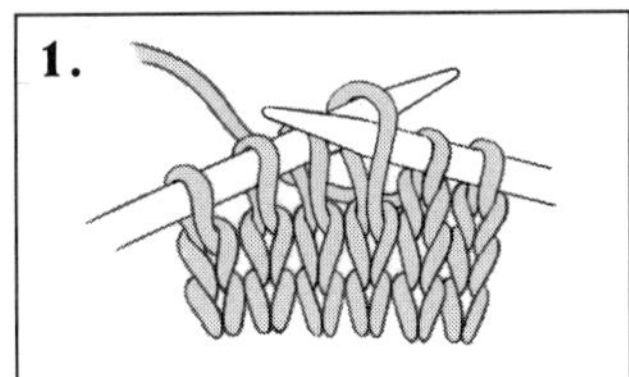

1. If your pattern does not give you an indication of how the stitch should be slipped, assume that it is purlwise. Slip 1 stitch from the left needle to the right by going into the front of the stitch as if to purl. This puts the stitch onto the right needle in the correct position without twisting it.

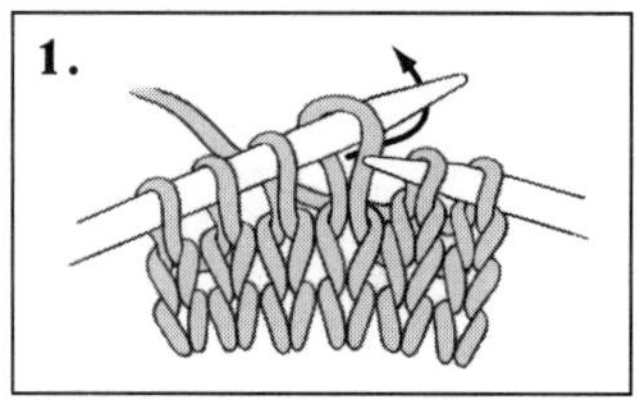

SLIP ONE KNITWISE

1. Slip 1 stitch from the left needle to the right as if to knit. This twists the stitch as it goes from the left needle to the right needle. Stitches are most often slipped knitwise when working decreases.

Increased/Decreased Baby Blanket

FINISHED MEASUREMENTS
36" square

MATERIALS
• 3 balls Lion Brand *Homespun®* #348 Gazebo; (6 oz, 185 yds; 98% acrylic, 2% polyester)
• Size 11 (8 mm) knitting needles or size to get gauge

GAUGE
9 stitches and 18 rows = 4" (10 cm) with size 11 needles in garter stitch (knit every row).
Be sure to check your gauge.

NOTE
1. Blanket is worked on a diagonal from corner to corner by increasing until half the blanket is complete (the diagonal of the square) and then decreasing back to the original number of stitches.
2. K2tog-knit 2 together.

BLANKET
Cast on 5 stitches. Knit 1 row. **Next row** Knit 3, yarn over (yo), knit 2. **Next row** Knit 3, yo, knit 3. **Next row** Knit 3, yo, knit to end. Repeat last row until there are 126 stitches on needle. **Decrease row** Knit 2, k2tog, yo, k2tog, knit to end. Repeat last row until there are 7 stitches on needle. **Last decrease** row Knit 2, k2tog, k2tog, knit 1. Bind off remaining 5 stitches. Work in ends.

A color photo of this item can be found in the color insert, photo number 8

8

Glossary of Knitting Terms

As for back To keep a pattern concise, specifics for identical operations are not spelled out more than once. You are often referred to the first time the action takes place, e.g., on the back of a sweater.

AT SAME TIME Occasionally you must complete two actions at once. For clarity, these two commands will be separated by the phrase AT SAME TIME. Make sure that you read your pattern all the way through before beginning to knit so that you don't miss any AT SAME TIME instructions.

Bind off in pattern (ribbing) Most simple bind-offs are done by knitting the stitches and working a bind-off. When binding off in pattern or ribbing, you create a flexible edge. For example, in knit 1, purl 1 ribbing you would knit 1 stitch, purl 1 stitch and then take the knit stitch over the purl stitch. Continue in this way to bind off all stitches.

Bind off from each neck edge When working a neck shaping where both sides are bound off at the same time, you bind off from the right neck edge on right-side rows and the left neck edge on wrong-side rows.

Change to larger (or smaller) needles To change needles, simply start to work your next row with the new-sized needle. Don't forget to set the smaller needle aside after that row so that you work the next row with two needles of the same size.

Cont as established (also cont in the way or cont in this manner) This follows text that sets up a pattern. You are being asked to continue the set-up pattern until the next step is outlined.

End(ing) with a wrong-side (or right-side) row Abbreviated as WS and RS, this means that the last row worked is the one stated. Ending with a WS row means that you complete a wrong-side row and are ready to work a right-side row when the next action takes place.

From beg (beginning) The phrase usually reads "work until piece measures XX" from beg." This indicates a measurement taken straight up from the cast-on row of your piece. Lay the piece flat on a hard surface to take this measurement.

Knitwise Used for a slip stitch (or sometimes in grafting instructions) and means that you insert the needle into the stitch as if to knit it.

M1 (make 1) An increase that is invisible. Insert the left-hand needle from front to back under the strand (running thread) between two stitches. Knit the loop off the left needle by inserting the right needle into the back of the stitch and knitting into the back loop of the stitch.

Next row (WS) or (RS) This indicates that the next row is either a wrong-side (WS) or right-side (RS) row. This is given to help you be sure that you are in the correct place in the pattern.

Pick up and k (knit) This term is used when you are requested to pick up stitches for a neckband or front band. Instead of picking up loops of the knitted fabric, you use a strand of yarn and knit the picked-up stitches.

Place a marker Markers can be placed in two ways. They can be put into the fabric to mark a specific spot or they can go directly onto a needle to designate a particular spot in the knitting. Markers on needles are slipped from one needle to the next as you knit.

Purlwise Used for a slip stitch (or sometimes in grafting instructions) and means that you insert the needle into the stitch as if to purl it.

Rep from * to end Stitch instructions preceded by an asterisk (*) are to be worked across the row to the end. This might appear as "k1, p1; rep from * to end." You may also see "rep from * around" for circular pieces [or "rep from *, end—" when there is an indication of stitches outside the repeated stitches such as "rep from *, end k1, p1, k1."]

Reverse shaping (or work to correspond) Usually this appears when you have worked one front (either left or right) of a cardigan and have to mirror the shaping on the second piece. On such a piece, you would work bind-offs and decreases on the fabric edge opposite to that of the first piece. Some patterns spell out how the reversal should take place; other patterns assume that it will be understood.

Ssk (slip, slip, knit) A left-leaning decrease worked by slipping the next 2 stitches knitwise, one at a time, from the left to the right needle. Insert the tip of the left needle into the front of the stitches and knit them together.

Ssp (slip, slip, purl) A left-leaning decrease that is worked with purl stitches as follows: slip the next 2 stitches knitwise, one at a time, from the left to the right needle; pass them back to left needle, then purl them together through the back loops.

With RS or WS facing The action is to take place with either the right or wrong side of the work facing you. This is often indicated when picking up stitches for a neckline, working a band, or when sewing seams together.

Work both sides at once Usually used for a neck shaping when the left and right sides are worked at the same time after center neck stitches are bound off. This is done with separate balls of yarn.

Work even Continue to the required length in the pattern stitch without shaping or other actions.

Work to end Continue in the pattern across to the end of the row.

Reading Instructions

Reading a knitting instruction is one of the most intimidating parts of the whole knitting process. When you think about it, reading a pattern is just like reading a recipe. First you are given a list of "ingredients" and then you are told the steps you must perform to complete your project. Think of the pattern as building blocks that need to be taken in small steps. Even though you should review the entire pattern before you begin to see what's ahead, once you begin to work on the project, you accomplish the project in small, easy-to-digest segments. Let's review each part of a knitting recipe and you'll begin to see how easy it is once you are familiar with the format.

SIZE AND FINISHED MEASUREMENTS

No matter what you make, you should know how big your finished piece is going to be. If you get the gauge given in the pattern, your finished item should match that of the finished measurements listed. When making a garment, compare the given sizes with the finished measurements to decide on the size to make. You may consider yourself a "small," but a small size in a specific knitting pattern may be smaller or larger than you desire. Altering the chest or bust measurement for a specific size is not done easily; however, length measurements can be readily changed.

MATERIALS

As with any good recipe, the list of materials includes ingredients and tools that you'll need to make your project. The yarn given is the one used to make the sample shown. You may decide to change that yarn, but do so carefully. The yardage of the ball is the best key to how much you'll need of another type of yarn. Multiply the number of balls of the suggested yarn by the number of yards in each ball. That is the number of yards required to finish the garment. Then divide that total by the number of yards per ball of the yarn that you would like to substitute to find out how many balls of that yarn you should buy. Turn to page 15 in Chapter 1 to read about the various weights of yarn and their approximate gauges. This is another bit of information that you'll find extremely helpful in making a substitution.

You'll notice that the needle size given always states "or size to get gauge." The needle size given is a good place to start, but getting the gauge is more important. You should use whatever needle size is necessary to accomplish this task.

GAUGE

Carefully reading the gauge information is a step that will save you countless hours in the long run. Matching your knitting to that of the given gauge is the only way to assure that you will get the correct dimensions in all of your knitted pieces. The gauge is normally given in stitches and rows over 4" (10 cm) and it's a good practice to make a swatch that is at least that large to measure your gauge. Read more about taking the gauge in Chapter 1 on page 25.

Some patterns include more than one gauge. If so, you should try them all out to make sure that your tension doesn't change from one stitch to another.

NOTES

Notes are included at the beginning of the pattern to bring your attention either to "helpful hints" for working the pattern or to special maneuvers required for the successful completion of the garment. Always read the notes before you start your project and again when you reach that point in the pattern to which a given note refers.

PATTERN STITCHES

To make the instructions more concise, sometimes the stitch pattern or a pattern sequence (such as stripes) will precede the pattern text. Read through these instructions to make sure you understand them, and then move on to the section where the pattern begins. It will probably start with a directive such as "Cast on [so many] stitches." Read along and you will come to the portion where the stitch pattern or other sequence is used.

Note that a pattern may be given in a particular multiple of stitches. This means that the instruction should be given in stitch numbers divisible by the stitch multiple. To even out a pattern, there are sometimes extra stitches included. For example, the multiple may be "9 stitches plus 2 extra." This means that you would repeat the pattern a number divisible by 9, such as 90, and have 2 extra stitches (92 stitches total). It isn't terribly important to understand this when working from a pattern that has these numbers already figured out, but it does become important if you are designing or altering pattern instructions. It can also be used if you want to use the stitch pattern in some other way than in the specific pattern where it is found.

PROJECT

When working a project that consists of pieces (such as a sweater), you will find that instructions for the different pieces are given in a specific order. Normally the back is done first. The idea behind this thinking is that if you are uneven in your knitting or don't make something exactly perfect, it will show less on the back. Also, the back has less shaping and sometimes less patterning. You then knit the front(s), followed by the sleeves. After you have completed all the pieces, the pattern will give instructions for finishing.

Many patterns offer guidance at the beginning of the instructions by stating a skill level. The way the pattern is written is often a reflection of the skill needed to complete the project. There are fewer abbreviations in beginner patterns. Ribbing and patterning rows are written out in greater detail. It is not assumed that the beginning knitter has the knowledge that comes with more experience. It should be noted that in this book we have not added skill levels because all the designs are intended to be in the beginner/easy range.

ARMHOLE SHAPING AND NECK SHAPING

Generally, shaping is worked (or at the very least begun) on a right-side row. The action that immediately precedes the beginning of shaping may indicate that you should "end with a wrong-side row." This means that the last row you work is on the wrong side.

Armholes are usually bound off at the beginning of consecutive rows, because you can't bind off at the end of a row, only at the beginning. Then both the left and right armhole decreases are performed on the same row (usually with the right side facing you), since you can decrease stitches at both the beginning and the end of a row. Neck shaping is worked in somewhat the same manner with separate balls of yarn on either side of the neck.

FINISHING

More specific information is given in Chapter 10 about how to finish and seam a garment. Generally the patterns give you instructions for blocking, followed by the order in which you should seam your pieces. You'll also be provided with details about adding button(hole) bands, neckbands, and collars, as well as how and where to make the buttonholes and sew on buttons, if required.

IT'S GOOD TO KNOW

- Many questions come up about working a piece when the instructions tell you to "reverse the shaping" of the previous piece. For example, a cardigan has a left and a right front. The pattern may detail one front and then tell you to "reverse the shaping" for the second front. Sometimes stitch pattern set-ups and shaping instructions are spelled out in detail, and sometimes there is very little information. Just remember that if you bind off stitches on the left-front armhole at the beginning of right-side rows, you'll bind off stitches on the right-front armhole piece at the beginning of wrong-side rows.

- Your instruction may include "selvage stitches" or "edge stitches." These are extra stitches that are sewn into the seam or selvage. These stitches aren't included in the finished measurements. To create a smooth seaming edge, you should work all increases and decreases inside the selvage stitches.

KNITTING PATTERN ABBREVIATIONS

approx	approximately
beg	begin(ning)
BO	bind off (rarely used)
CC	contrasting color
cn	cable needle
CO	cast on (rarely used)
cont	continue
dec	decreas(e) (ing)
dpn	double pointed needles
foll	follow(s) (ing)
inc	increas(e) (ing)
k	knit
k1 b or k1 tbl	knit into the back loop of a stitch
k2tog	knit 2 together (a decrease)
LH	left hand
MC	main color
M1	make 1 (an increase)
p	purl
pat(s)	pattern(s)
pm	place marker
psso	pass slip stitch over
p1b or p tbl	purling into the back loop of a stitch
rem	remaining
rep	repeat(s) (ing)
rev St st	reverse stockinette stitch

KNITTING PATTERN ABBREVIATIONS *(continued)*

rnd(s)	rounds
RH	right hand
RS	right side
SKP	slip 1, knit 1, pass slip stitch over knit stitch
sl	slip
sl st	slip stitch
ssk	slip, slip, knit (a decrease)
ssp	slip, slip, purl (a decrease)
S2KP2	slip 2 together, knit next st, pass the two slipped sts over knit stitch (centered double decrease)
st	stitch
St st	stockinette stitch
tog	together
WS	wrong side
wyib	with yarn in back
wyif	with yarn in front
yo	yarn over needle

MEASURES AND WEIGHTS

cm	centimeter(s)
g	gram
m	meter(s)
mm	millimeters
oz	ounce(s)
yd(s)	yard(s)

SYMBOLS

*	Repeat from * as noted
( )	Parentheses have several uses. One is to give order to sizing. For example a sweater with four sizes may be written as S (M, L, XL). The same sequence is followed throughout a pattern: Cast on 44 (46, 48, 50) stitches.

[ ] or ( )	Brackets or parentheses are used to rope off a string of commands and tell you how many times to complete this command: Knit 3, [k2tog, purl 3] twice, knit 3. In this instance, you would work the k2tog, purl 3 once and then k2tog, purl 3 again.

INTERNET LINGO

If you subscribe to a chat list that talks about knitting, be aware that you will encounter acronyms and terms you've never seen before:

FO	Finished Object (usually accompanied by many !'s)
HALFPINT	Have A Lovely Fantasy Project, I've No Time
KIP	Knitting In Public
LYS	Local Yarn Store
LYSO	Local Yarn Store Owner
NAYY	No Affiliation, Yada, Yada. Used when writing about a yarn store, knitting magazine, yarn company, or other commercial source.
SEX	Stash Enrichment eXpedition
TINK or FROG	undoing your knitting (TINK = KNIT backward. When you FROG your knitting, you rip-it, rip-it [ribbit]. Get it?)
TOAD	Trashed Object, Abandoned in Disgust
UFO	Unfinished Object
USO	Unstarted Object
WIP	Work In Progress
Y or WCZ	Yarn or Wool Containment Zone (where you keep your yarn)

Reading a Chart

One might compare knitting from a chart to driving to a destination using a map instead of written-out directions. A knitting chart is a visual representation of a knitting stitch pattern as it appears from the right side of the fabric. A "stitch key" accompanies each chart to decode the symbols. Many symbols are standardized, but some vary from publication to publication.

If you are inexperienced in working from charts, look for patterns that include both the written words and a chart. You can cross-reference between the two until you feel comfortable using just the chart.

When reading charts, you should visualize the direction of the knitting process. Since the chart mimics the right side of your knitting, you will read the right-side rows from right to left, which is the same direction that you are knitting them. Likewise, you will read the wrong-side rows from left to right on the chart, in the same way that you turn your fabric to work the wrong side. To guide you in the direction you are to work, the row numbers most often appear on the side of the row where you are to begin. And just as a knit stitch worked on the right side looks like a purl stitch worked on the wrong side, the symbol for "knit" on right-side rows is the same as for "purl" on wrong-side rows. It may be easier to think of the symbol as being for stockinette stitch rather than as knit or purl. The stitch key will spell out exactly what the symbol represents on each side of the fabric.

Charts are worked from the lower-right edge (row 1) upward. If the stitch pattern repeats vertically, knit the rows in the pattern sequence, and then return to row 1 to begin again.

Each square on a chart represents one stitch. A horizontal line of squares equals one row. Many symbols used in charts are purposely used to simulate the approximate look of the actual stitch. Stockinette stitch (knit on right side) is a vertical line or a blank square, and reverse stockinette (purl on right side) is a horizontal line.

There are two types of charts. One represents a panel of stitches that may be placed somewhere within your knitted piece. An example of this type of chart is a cable panel. You may work this chart more than once vertically, but it is not usually repeated across a row.

The second type of chart conveys an overall stitch pattern that is repeated many times across the row. This chart may include a pattern repeat ("stitch multiple") as well as stitches that fall on either side of the multiple ("edge stitches"). The actual repeat is denoted by heavy black lines and, in the written pattern, is usually set off by * (asterisks). Working from right to left, work the stitches outside the actual stitch pattern once, then work the actual stitch pattern as many times as is indicated in your pattern, and finish with the edge stitches on the left side of the chart. Reverse the direction when working wrong-side rows.

When you are required to work a decrease or increase over two stitches, this will be shown on the chart as a symbol in one square as it appears once the decreasing or increasing process is complete.

Occasionally you'll see a symbol given for a chart called "no stitch." This symbol is often given as a filled-in square. This simply means, "Ignore this square because nothing actual appears on your knitting needle. Move to the next stitch on chart and your knitting needle."

Cable symbols are given over the number of stitches involved in the cable operation. They often include lines within the square to show the direction of the cable crossing.

READING A COLOR CHART

We have been discussing stitch charts. Another type of chart is a color chart. As in a stitch chart, each square equals one stitch, and a horizontal row of stitches equals a row. Various symbols are used to denote the color to be knitted, and the key tells you what colors the symbols represent. Some publications use color rather than symbols. You may also find color charts that combine stitch patterns and color patterning. Use the chart's key to give you guidance.

CHARTING TIPS

- Make a carry-along copy of your chart. Blow it up so that you can read it more easily. Find a way of keeping track of your rows. Highlighting markers are perhaps the simplest solution for indicating the row you are working; it is helpful to alternate highlight colors so that you can more easily distinguish the row you just worked from the row you are currently working. Other solutions include movable strips, which are available in office-supply stores and magnetic boards equipped with "underlining" magnets, which are carried by many craft stores.
- Move the strip or magnet up from above the row you are working, keeping unworked rows hidden. That way you can compare your knitting with the charts of the rows you have already worked.
- If you are working several charts in a row, copy and tape your charts in sequence. This helps you to knit quickly across the row without having to refer back to the individual charts.
- Not all charts within a design necessarily have the same number of rows in a repeat. You may be working from five different charts—one with a 10-row repeat, two with 8-row repeats, two with 6-row repeats. Remember to begin at row 1 once you have worked the row repeat indicated by the chart.

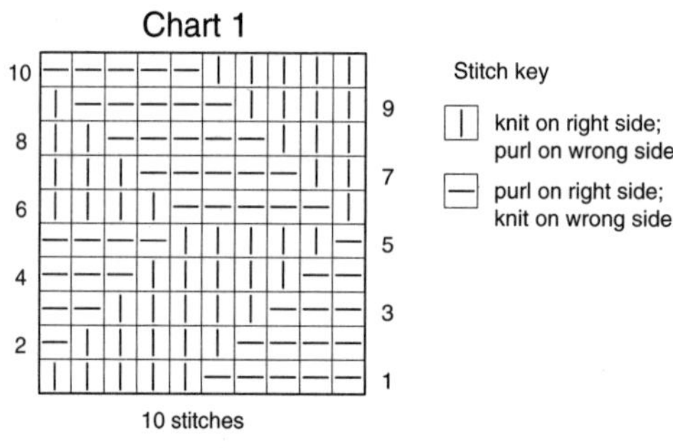

Chart 1 A Simple Knit and Purl Chart

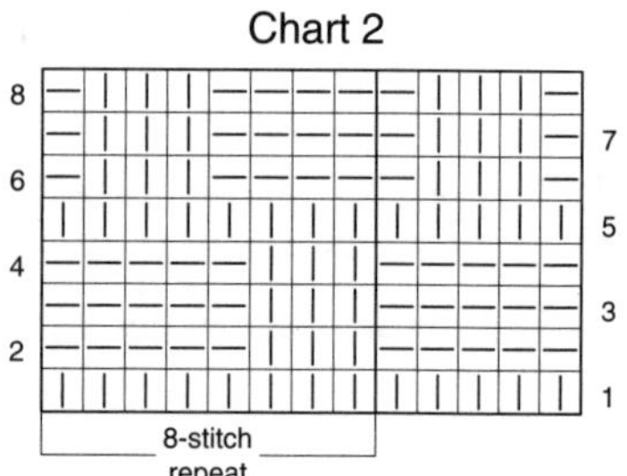

Chart 2 A Chart with Multiples and Edge Stitches

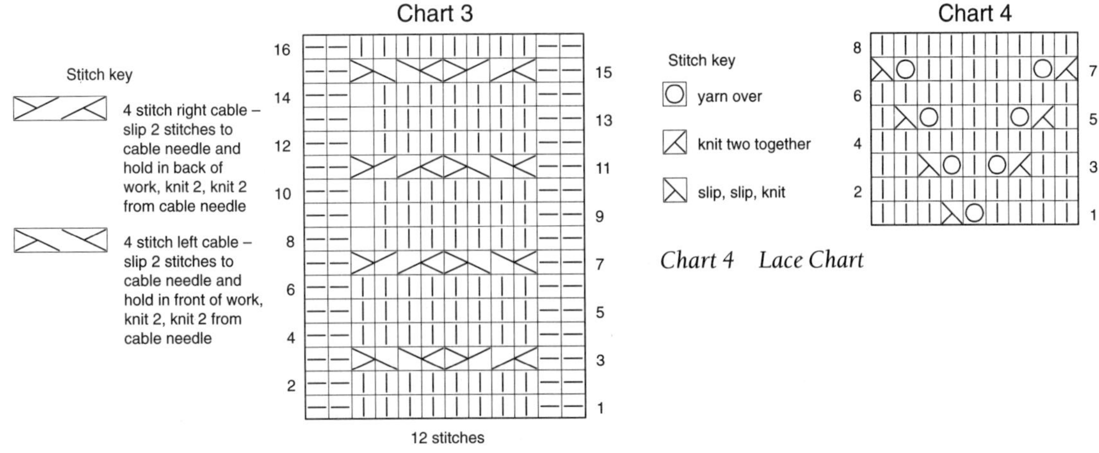

Chart 4 Lace Chart

Chart 3 A Cable Panel

Reading a Schematic Drawing

Most well-written knitting patterns include schematics of the pieces you'll be knitting. These drawings offer a great deal of information, and once you understand how to use them, you'll find them to be an invaluable aid to your knitting.

Schematics are a set of scale drawings of the pieces of a garment. They represent the actual fabric that you are knitting, including selvages; they do not, however, include edgings that you may attach later, such as collars and button bands. You may find them in a number of formats, but the information included is approximately the same for all schematics. For example, some pattern writers superimpose the front piece onto the back if the only difference between the two is the neck shaping; others draw two separate pieces. Some include measurements in both metrics and inches. Some include all the measurements, while others give only key measurements.

Normally, schematics are oriented in the direction that you are knitting the fabric. Not all sweaters are knitted from the bottom up. Schematics of garments knitted from the top down are displayed upside down, while those of sweaters that are knitted side to side are shown with the cuff at the bottom. When all pieces are shown joined (such as happens with yoked sweaters), that means that the sweater is knitted in one piece, i.e., the sleeves are joined to the body in the knitting process rather than sewn together after the pieces are knitted.

Make a copy of your schematics; then you can use them to remind yourself to alter certain measurements to your taste (like length). Just cross out the measurement given in the pattern and write in your changes.

Where multiple sizes are shown, you may want to circle those numbers that directly refer to the size that you are making.

Schematics are very important when you are blocking the garment pieces prior to seaming. Pin the pieces of fabric to the dimensions on the schematic and you are sure to have the sweater that is the size that you intended to knit.

FRONT AND BACK

Begin reading your piece just below the lower edge, and continue counterclockwise. The measurement line shown at the bottom gives the chest measurement at the widest point. If the piece is shaped, you may find two sets of numbers denoting the widest and the narrowest points.

Assuming a piece knitted from the bottom up, the right-side vertical measurement begins with the length of the ribbing, follows with the measurement to the underarm without the ribbing, and ends with the armhole depth. If there is shoulder shaping, it will also be included at the top of this line of measurements.

The measurement line across the top has one or both shoulder measurements (almost always the same set of numbers) and the width of the neck (both back and front necks).

The line shown vertically along the left edge most often includes the neck depth (two measurements if the back neck is shaped) and the remaining length to the lower edge.

FRONT PIECES

Usually only one front is shown when the left and right pieces are mirror images. The measurements are set up in a similar format to those of the back. In some drawings, a front can be shown superimposed on the back piece.

SLEEVES

Since both sleeves are normally identical, only one schematic is shown. When the sleeve is knitted from the top down, it may appear upside down.

Once again reading counterclockwise from the lower left, the set of numbers that appear just below the lower edge indicate the width of the fabric just above the ribbing. Note that the ribbed cuff is not usually as wide as this measurement.

Going vertically up the right side, you'll find first the ribbing depth and then the sleeve length. When a set-in or raglan garment is made, the sleeve cap appears at the top of the sleeve. The example shown here has a cut-in armhole where no cap is needed.

The horizontal measurement along the top of the sleeve is the measurement of the sleeve at its widest point. In the cases of sweaters with drop shoulders, cut-in or angled armholes, this top sleeve measurement is double the width of the armhole depth on the schematic for the back.

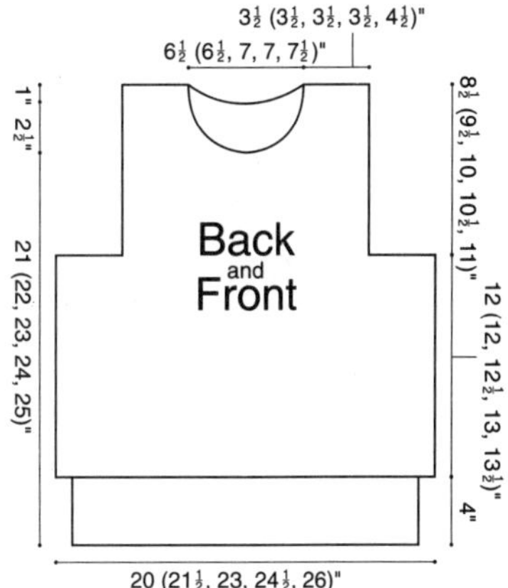

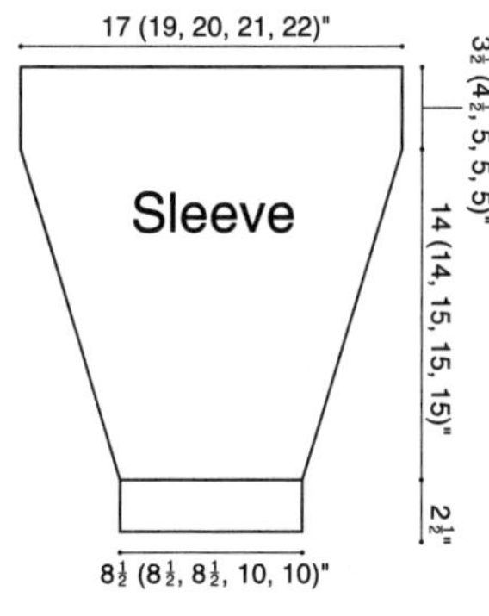

9

Making Your First Sweater

Garter-Stitch Vest

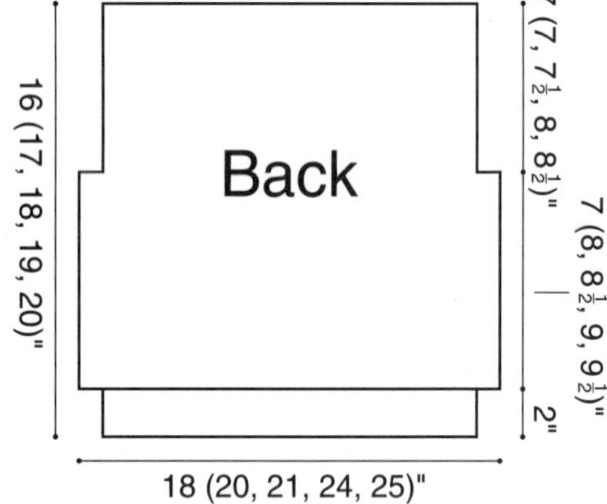

SIZES

XS (S, M, L, XL)

FINISHED MEASUREMENTS

Chest at underarm 36 (40, 43, 48, 50)"
Length from shoulder 16 (17, 18, 19, 20)"

MATERIALS

- 3 (3, 3, 4, 4) balls Lion Brand *Homespun®* #312 Edwardian (6 oz, 185 yds; 98% acrylic, 2% polyester)
- Sizes 15 and 17 (10 and 12.75 mm) knitting needles, or size to get gauge
- Four 1" buttons

GAUGE

9 stitches and 12 rows = 4" (10 cm) in garter stitch (knit every row) with 2 strands of yarn.
Be sure to check your gauge.

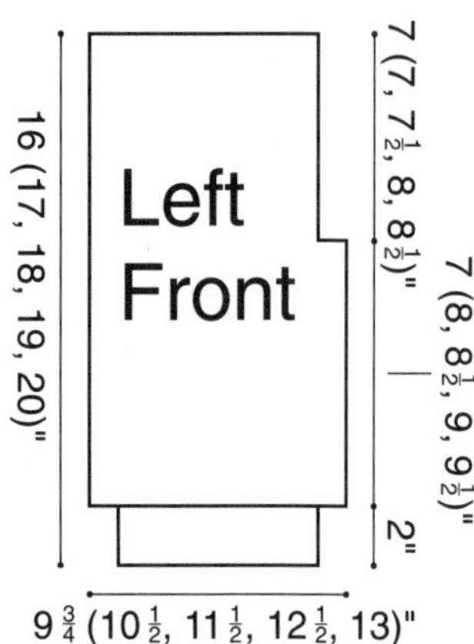

Garter-Stitch Vest *(continued)*

NOTES

1. See abbreviations page 71.
2. Vest is worked with 2 strands of yarn held together.
3. Slip first stitch of every row as if to purl for a neater edge.

BACK

With 2 strands of yarn and smaller needles, cast on 40 (46, 48, 54, 56) sts. **Row 1 (wrong side)** K1, pl; repeat from * to end. Repeat last row 4 times more. Change to larger needles. Mark right side with pin and knit every row until piece measures 9 (10, 10½, 11, 11½)" from beginning.

Shape Armholes

Bind off 3 (4, 5, 7, 8) sts at the beg of next two rows. Work even until piece measures 16 (17, 18, 19, 20)" from beginning. Bind off.

LEFT FRONT

With 2 strands of yarn and smaller needles, cast on 22 (24, 26, 28, 30) sts. Work in k1, p1 rib for 5 rows. Change to larger needles. Knit every row until piece measures same length as back to armhole.

Shape Armhole

Next row (right side) Bind off 3 (4, 5, 7, 8) sts, knit to end. Work even until piece measures 16 (17, 18, 19, 20)" from beginning. Bind off.

RIGHT FRONT

Work as for left front, binding off armhole stitches at the beginning of a wrong-side row.

FINISHING

Sew side seams. Sew shoulder seams, leaving center 9 (9, 9½, 9½, 10)" open for neck. Sew 4 buttons to left front with the first 1" down from top of neck and last ¾" from lower edge with 2 others evenly spaced between. There are no buttonholes, simply put buttons through loose openings on right front. Weave in ends.

A color photo of this item can be found in the color insert, photo number 9

Sleeveless T-neck

SIZES
XS (S, M, L, 1X, 2X)

FINISHED MEASUREMENTS
Chest at underarm, 36 (38, 40, 42, 44, 46)"
Length from shoulder 23½ (24, 24, 24¼, 24½, 25)"

MATERIALS
• 2 (2, 3, 3, 4, 4) balls Lion Brand *Lion Cotton* #142 Boysenberry (5 oz, 236 yds; 100% cotton)
• Sizes 6 and 7 (4 and 4.5 mm) knitting needles, or size to get gauge
• Size 6 (4 mm) circular needle, 16" long
• Stitch holders and large-eyed yarn needle

GAUGE
18 sts and 24 rows = 4" (10 cm) in stockinette stitch (knit on right side; purl on wrong side).
Be sure to check your gauge.

NOTES
See abbreviations page 71.

BACK
With smaller needles, cast on 80 (86, 90, 96, 100, 104) sts. **Row 1 (WS)** *K1, pl; repeat from * across. Repeat last row until piece measures 2" from beginning. Change to larger needles. Begin stockinette stitch and work even until piece measures 14" from beginning, ending with a wrong-side row.

Shape Armholes
Bind off 4 (4, 5, 5, 6, 6) sts at beg of next 2 rows—72 (78, 80, 86, 88, 92) sts. **Decrease row 1 (RS)** Slip 1 stitch, k1, p1, k2tog, knit to last 5 sts, ssk, p1, k2. **Row 2 (WS)** Slip 1 stitch, p1, k1, purl to last 3 sts, k1, p2. Repeat last 2 rows 7 (8, 8, 8, 8, 10) times more—56 (60, 62, 68, 70, 70) sts. Continue as follows: **Next row (RS)** Slip 1 stitch, k1, p1, knit to last 3 sts, p1, k2. **Next row (WS)** Slip 1 stitch, p1, k1, purl to last 3 sts, k1, p2. Repeat last 2 rows until armhole measures 7½ (8, 8, 8¼, 8½, 9)". Bind off 13 (14, 15, 17, 18, 18) sts at

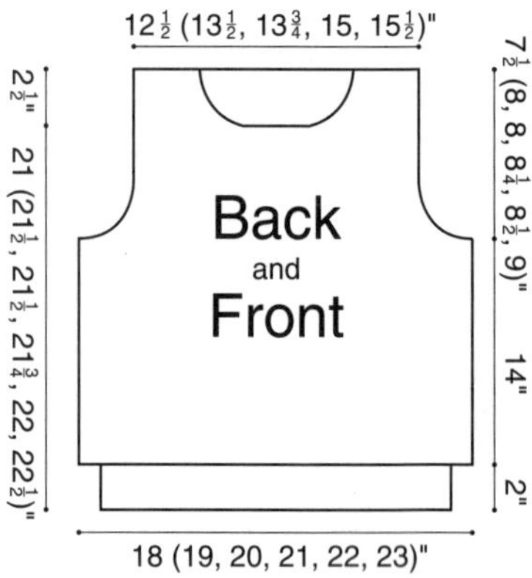

beg of next 2 rows. Place remaining 30 (32, 32, 34, 34, 34) sts onto a stitch holder for back neck.

FRONT
Cast on and work ribbing as for back. Change to larger needles and stockinette stitch and work even until same length as back to beginning of armhole shaping.

Shape Armholes
Bind off 4 (4, 5, 5, 6, 6) sts at beg of next 2 rows—72 (78, 80, 86, 88, 92) sts. **Decrease row 1 (RS)** Slip 1 stitch, k1, p1, k2tog, knit to last 5 sts, ssk, p1, k2. **Row 2 (WS)** Slip 1 stitch, p1, k1, purl to last 3 sts,

Sleeveless T-neck *(continued)*

k1, p2. Repeat last 2 rows 7 (8, 8, 8, 8, 10) times more—56 (60, 62, 68, 70, 70) sts. Continue as follows: **Next row (RS)** Slip 1 stitch, k1, p1, knit to last 3 sts, p1, k2. **Next row (WS)** Slip 1 stitch, p1, k1, purl to last 3 sts, k1, p2. Repeat last 2 rows until armhole measures 5 (5½, 5½, 5¾, 6, 6½)," ending with a WS row.

Shape Neck

Next row (RS) Slip 1 stitch, k1, p1, k13 (14, 15, 17, 18, 18), ssk, k2, place next 16 (18, 18, 20, 20, 20) sts onto a stitch holder. Attach a separate ball of yarn and continue on other side of neck as follows: k2, k2tog, k13 (14, 15, 17, 18, 18), p1, k2. Working both sides at the same time, work next row even and then decrease 1 st from each neck edge on right side rows 6 times more. When front measures same as back to shoulder, bind off 13 (14, 15, 17, 18, 18) sts for shoulders.

FINISHING

Block pieces. Sew shoulder seams.

Neckband

With right side facing and circular needle, and beginning at back neck, knit 30 (32, 32, 34, 34, 34) sts from back neck holder, pick up and k8 sts along front neck, work across 16 (18, 18, 20, 20, 22) sts from front neck holder, pick up and k8 sts along second neck—62 (66, 66, 70, 70, 70) sts. Join and work in rounds as follows: **Round 1** *K1, p1; repeat from * around. Repeat last round until neckband measures 3" Loosely bind off all sts. Sew side seams.

A color photo of this item can be found in the color insert, photo number 10

Roll-Neck Raglan Pullover with Hat

SIZES

S (M, L, 1X, 2X, 3X)

FINISHED MEASUREMENTS

Chest at underarm 37 (41, 45, 49, 53, 57)"

Length from shoulder 25½ (26, 26½, 26½, 27, 27)"

MATERIALS

Sweater

• 5 (5, 6, 6, 7, 7) balls Lion Brand *Wool-Ease®* *Chunky* #145 Concord (5 oz, 153 yds; 80% acrylic, 20% wool)

• Size 10.5 (6.5 mm) knitting needles, or size to get gauge

• Size 10.5 (6.5 mm) circular needle, 16" long

• Stitch holders and large-eyed yarn needle

Hat

• 1 ball Lion Brand *Wool-Ease®* *Chunky* #145 Concord

• Size 10.5 (6.5 mm) knitting needles

• Large-eyed yarn needle

GAUGE

13 sts and 20 rows = 4" (10 cm) in stockinette stitch (knit on right side; purl on wrong side).

Be sure to check your gauge.

NOTES

1. See abbreviations on page 71.
2. For ease in working, circle all numbers that pertain to your size.
3. Body diagram chest measurements include 1 stitch each side to sew into seam (selvage stitches), so measurements vary from finished chest measurements given.

BACK

Cast on 63 (69, 75, 82, 88, 94) sts. Work in St st for 15½ (16, 16, 17, 17, 17)" (or desired length to underarm), ending on a WS row.

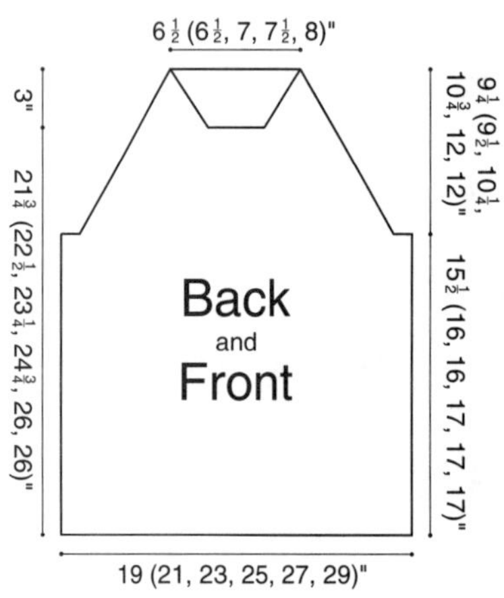

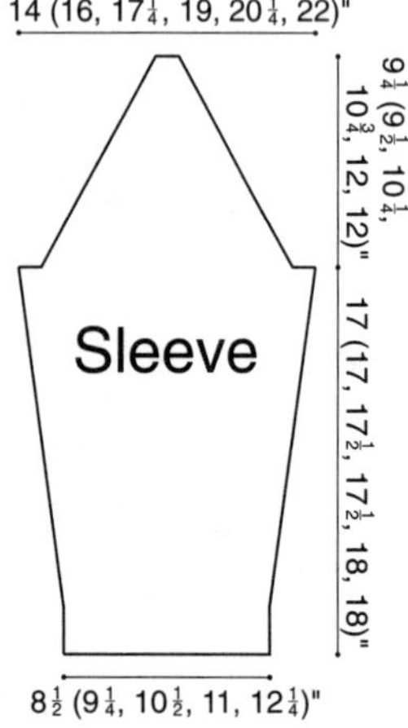

Roll-Neck Raglan Pullover with Hat (continued)

Shape Raglan Armholes

Bind off 3 (3, 4, 5, 6, 7) sts at the beg of next 2 rows—57 (63, 67, 72, 76, 80) sts. Work 2 rows even. **Next decrease row** K1, ssk, k to last 3 sts, k2tog, k1. Rep decrease row every 4th row 4 (2, 3, 2, 4, 2) times, then every other row 12 (17, 17, 20, 19, 23) times, ending with a WS row. **Last row** Ssk, k to last 2 sts, k2tog. Put remaining 21 (21, 23, 24, 26, 26) sts onto holder for back neck.

FRONT

Work as for back, including all raglan shaping, AT SAME TIME, when piece measures 3" less than back, ending with WS row.

Shape Neck

Mark center 9 (9, 11, 12, 14, 14) sts. **Next row (RS)** K1, ssk, k to marked center sts and place holder for front neck. Join a separate ball of yarn and knit to last 3 sts, k2tog, k1. Working both sides at once and continuing armhole shaping, dec 1 st at each neck edge every other row 3 times as follows: Work to last 3 sts before neck edge, k2tog, k1; on second side of neck edge, k1, ssk, work to end. Purl WS row. Then repeat these last two rows 3 times more. **Last row** Slip 2 as if to knit, k1, pass the slip stitch over the knit stitch (center), slip 2 sts as if to knit, k1, pass 2 slip stitches over the knit stitch. Place last st on each side on holder.

SLEEVES

Cast on 28 (30, 34, 36, 38, 42) sts. Work 2" even in St st. **Next increase row** K2, k in front and back of next st, k to last 3 sts, k in front and back of next st, k2. Rep inc row every 4 rows 0 (0, 0, 0, 0, 5) times, every 6 rows 0 (6, 6, 12, 13, 9) times, and every 8 rows 8 (4, 4, 0, 0, 0) times—46 (52, 56, 62, 66, 72) sts.

Shape Raglan Sleeve

When sleeve measures 17 (17, 17½, 17½, 18, 18)" (or desired length) bind off 3 (3, 4, 5, 6, 7) sts at beg of next 2 rows—40 (46, 48, 52, 54, 58) sts. Work raglan decreases as for back. **Last row** Ssk, k2, k2tog. Place last 4 sts on holder.

FINISHING

Block pieces. Sew raglan armholes. Sew sleeve and side seams.

Roll Neck

With right side facing and 16" circular needle, and beginning at front neck edge, pick up and knit 14 sts along side of neck edge, knit up 9 (9, 11, 12, 14, 14) sts from front neck holder, pick up and knit 14 sts along 2nd side of neck edge, knit up 1 st from front neck holder, 4 sts from sleeve holder, 21 (21, 23, 24, 26, 26) sts from back neck holder, 4 sts from sleeve holder, and 1 from front holder—68 (68, 72, 74, 78, 78) sts. Knit even for 2 inches (or desired length). Bind off loosely. Let roll. Weave in ends.

Roll-Neck Raglan Pullover with Hat (continued)

ROLL-BRIM HAT

Cast on 72 sts. Work even for 7", ending on WS row.

Decreasing Crown

Next row K1 *k 8, k2tog; rep from * to last st, k1—65 sts. Purl next row. **Next row** K1 *k7, k2tog; rep from * to last st, k1—58 sts. Purl next row. **Next row** K1 *k6, k2tog; rep from * to last st, k1—51 sts. Purl next row. **Next row** K1 *k5, k2tog; rep from * to last st, k1—44 sts. Purl next row. **Next row** K1 *k4, k2tog; rep from * to last st, k1—37 sts. **Next WS row** P1, *p2tog, p3; rep from * to last st, p1—30 sts. **Next row** K1, *k2, k2tog; rep from * to last st, k1—23 sts. **Next row** P1, *p2tog, p1; rep from * to last st, p1—16 sts. **Last row** K1, *k2tog; rep from * to last st, k1—9 sts. Using the yarn needle, bring yarn through remaining stitches several times and pull tight.

Finishing

Block hat. Sew side seam with wrong side facing for 2½", then finish seaming with right side facing. Weave in ends.

A color photo of this item can be found in the color insert, photo number 11

Easy Cardigan

SIZES
S (M, L, XL, XXL)

FINISHED MEASUREMENTS
Chest at underarm (buttoned) 48 (50, 52, 54, 58)"
Length from shoulder 26 (27, 27, 28, 29)"

MATERIALS

- 8 (9, 10, 10, 11) balls Reynolds *Lopi* #241 Putty (3½ oz. 109 yds; 100% wool)
- Sizes 9 and 10.5 (5.5 and 6.5 mm) knitting needles, or size to get gauge
- Size 9 (5.5 mm) circular needle, 29" long
- Four 1" (25 mm) wooden buttons

GAUGE
13 sts and 17 rows = 4" (10cm) with larger needles in stockinette stitch (knit on right side; purl on wrong side).
Be sure to check your gauge.

NOTES
1. See abbreviations on page 71.
2. For ease in working, circle all numbers that pertain to your size.

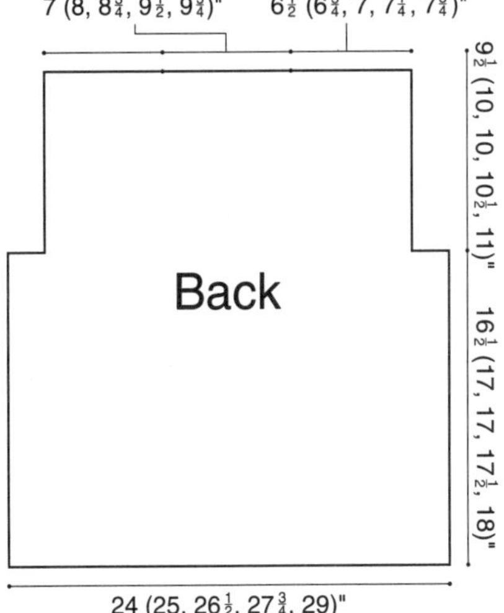

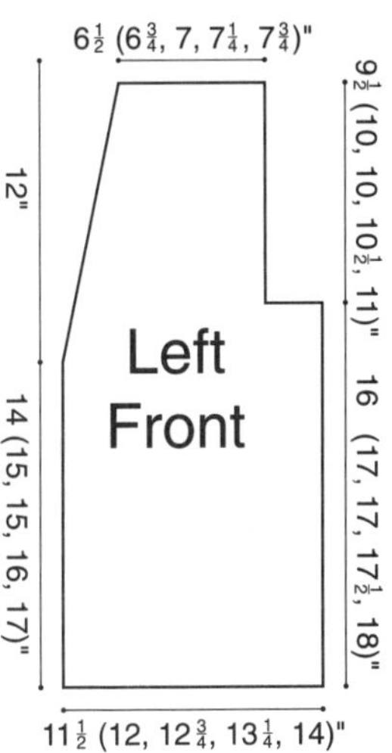

BACK
With smaller needles, cast on 78 (82, 86, 90, 94) sts. **Row 1 (RS)** K2, p2 across to last 2 sts, k2. **Row 2 (WS)** P2, k2 across to last 2 sts, p2. Rep rows 1 and 2 once. Change to larger needles and St st. Work even until piece measures 16½ (17, 17, 17½, 18)" from beginning.

Shape Armholes
Bind off 6 sts at beginning of next 2 rows—66 (70, 74, 78, 82) sts. Work even until armhole measures 9½ (10, 10, 10½, 11)". Bind off all sts.

LEFT FRONT
With smaller needles, cast on 37 (39, 41, 43, 45) sts. **Row 1 (RS)** K2, p2 across to last st, k1. **Row 2 (WS)** P1, then k2, p2 across row. Repeat rows 1 and 2 once. Change to larger needles and St st. Work even until piece measures 14 (15, 15, 16, 17)" from beginning, ending with a WS row.

Easy Cardigan *(continued)*

Shape V-neck

Decrease row (RS) Knit to last 3 sts, ssk, k1. Repeat decrease row every 4th row 4 (5, 10, 11, 13) times, then every 6th row 5 (5, 1, 1, 0) times; AT SAME TIME, when piece measures 16½ (17, 17, 17½, 18)" from beginning, bind off 6 sts at beginning of next RS row. When all armhole and V-neck decreases have been worked, work even on 21 (22, 23, 24, 25) sts until armhole measures 9½ (10, 10, 10½, 11)". Bind off all sts.

RIGHT FRONT

With smaller needles, cast on 37 (39, 41, 43, 45) sts. **Row 1 (RS)** K1, *k2, p2; repeat from * to end of row. **Row 2 (WS)** K2, p2 across row to last st, p1. Rep rows 1 and 2 once. Change to larger needles and St st. Work even until piece measures 14 (15, 15, 16, 17)" from beginning, ending with a WS row.

Shape V-neck

Decrease row (RS) K1, k2tog, knit to end. Repeat decrease row every 4th row 4 (5, 10, 11, 13) times, then every 6th row 5 (5, 1, 1, 0) times; AT SAME TIME, when piece measures 16½ (17, 17, 17½, 18)" from beginning, bind off 6 sts at beginning of next WS row. When all armhole and V-neck decreases have been worked, work even on 21 (22, 23, 24, 25) sts until armhole measures 9½ (10, 10, 10½, 11)". Bind off all sts.

SLEEVES

With smaller needles, cast on 38 (42, 42, 46, 46) sts. **Row 1 (RS)** K2, p2 across row. **Row 2 (WS)** K2, p2 across row. Repeat rows 1 and 2 once.

Change to larger needles and St st. Work even until piece measures 3" from beg, ending with a WS row. **Inc row (RS)** K2, inc 1 st in next st, knit to last 3 stitches, inc 1 st in next st, k2. Repeat inc row every 4th row 7 (3, 5, 2, 7) times more and every 6th row 4 (7, 6, 8, 5) times—62 (64, 66, 68, 72) sts. Work even until piece measures 17½ (18, 18½, 18½, 19)". Bind off all sts.

FINISHING

Block pieces. Sew shoulder seams. Place markers for buttons and buttonholes on both fronts with the first 1" from lower edge and the last at beg of neck shaping and with 2 more evenly spaced between the two.

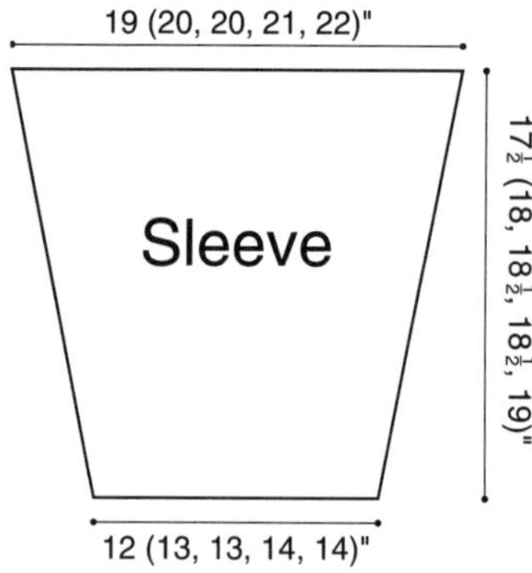

Easy Cardigan *(continued)*

Left Front Band

With circular needle, beg at lower left front edge, pick up 113 (117, 117, 125, 129) sts along front and up to half of center back neck. **Row 1 (WS)** P1, *k2, p2; repeat from * to end. **Row 2** *K2, p2; repeat from *, end k1. Bind off loosely. Repeat last 2 rows once more. Place markers on band with the first at beginning of V-neck and the last 1" from lower edge with two others evenly spaced between.

Right Front Band

With circular needle, beg at lower right front edge, pick up 113 (117, 117, 125, 129) sts along front and up to half of center back neck. **Row 1 (WS)** P1, *k2, p2; repeat from * to end. **Buttonhole row** *K2, p2; repeat from *, end k1, AT SAME TIME, working buttonholes across from markers by working a yarn over and then working the next 2 sts together.

Work 2 more rows in ribbing. Bind off loosely. Sew sleeves into armhole of body. Sew sleeve and underarm seams. Sew on buttons.

A color photo of this item can be found in the color insert, photo number 12

10

Finishing and Sizing

Sizing Garments

Once you gain some confidence as a knitter, you'll soon be considering moving beyond simple hats, scarves, and other one-size-fits-most accessories. As a matter of fact, many knitters choose to make a sweater or other garment shortly after they learn to knit. Having the skill to understand how to pick out the correct garment size and how to make alterations will take you to new heights. You will unlock a very important door, enabling you to make garments that perfectly fit you or those for whom you knit.

A good starting point is to try on sweaters that fit you well. Look at why you like them and how they fit. Look at how they fall on your shoulders and how the sweater fits at the bustline. Examine the sleeve length. Look at where the lower edge falls. All of these places are important in terms of proper fit.

Ease

Simply put, ease is the difference between the measurement of an actual body part and that of the finished garment. Usually ease is discussed in relationship to the chest/bust measurements of a knitted garment.

The amount of ease can vary from very close-fitting to extremely oversized and everything in between. How much ease is desired is both a matter of personal taste and the type of style being made. For instance, a casual outdoor sweater would have more ease than an evening-wear camisole. The chart on pages 93 and 94 will help you to evaluate the differences in measurements for a wide range of bust/chest sizes.

Remember that one of the wonderful points about knitted garments is their forgiving nature. Unlike stiff woven fabric garments, knits have a certain amount of ease and give of their own. Depending on the fiber used, the flexibility of your chosen stitch pattern, and the looseness of your gauge, the garment will have more or less drape.

The yarn weight also affects the amount of ease. If you are working with an extra-bulky yarn, you'll want to make a sweater with considerably more ease than if you are working the same sweater in a lighter-weight yarn.

Taking Measurements

As you take your measurements, write them down in a journal or notebook for future reference. Periodically update your measurements, as invariably some measurements will change over time. When you measure yourself, wear a leotard or bathing suit so that you can take accurate measurements. It's easier if you have a friend help you.

There are some measurements that don't change. Your body structure and height change very little. Your shoulder width and arm length will be fairly constant even when you lose or gain weight. Measurements that do change are your bust and hip area. If these change radically, you may have to consider making a longer or shorter garment to accommodate more or less weight in these areas.

Even though you won't need every measurement for each garment you make, you should include bust/chest, waist, hips, length from back neck to waist, shoulders, and sleeve length from center back neck.

- **Bust** Naturally, the most important is the bust/chest. This should be measured loosely at the widest point.
- **Waist** This measurement is not essential, but may help you determine the width needed on a tight-fitting sweater. Also, estab-

lishing your waistline will help you measure from the back neck to waist.

- **Hips** Again, this is not always a necessary measurement. It becomes important when making longer sweaters or tunics. If your hip area is a great deal larger than your bust, this can help you decide where you want your sweater to fall. A more flattering line would be to have the sweater end below or above the widest point of your hip.
- **Length from back neck to waist** Essentially, this measurement gives you guidance when determining sweater length. If you are long- or short-waisted, you may want to alter the length of a pattern that may be sized for someone who falls between those two lengths. Look at the finished length and use your tape measure to see where that length falls on your body.
- **Shoulders** Measure shoulder bone to shoulder bone straight across your back. This is where your friend will come in handy, as it's not so easy to do by yourself. While this measurement is rarely given specifically in a sweater pattern, you can often find it on a schematic. You may have to add each shoulder plus the neck width to determine the total measurement. Depending on the garment's style, you may want to choose a size that best fits you in this area.
- **Sleeve length from center back neck** Take this measurement from the center-back neck bone to the wrist bone with the arm slightly bent (for ease). With a simple drop-shouldered garment, you can easily determine how long your sleeve should be by adding one half the body width to the total sleeve length. Of course, with set-in sleeves and raglan armholes, you may need to take a measurement from the point where the underarm falls on your body to the wrist. You can use actual sweater pieces to help you with this mission.

Adjusting to Fit

Now that you have your measurements in hand, the next step is to go directly to your sweater and review the given sizes. Begin with the bust/chest measurement. Look at the other measurements for that size to determine if they fit your needs.

It's easier to alter the length of a garment than to change its width. However, if you are making a simple drop-sleeve sweater with no specific pattern or shaping, you can add or subtract from the width as needed. The ease with which you can alter the length depends on two variables—patterning and shaping, usually you can alter the measurements between the lower edge and the underarm without difficulty. If you change the length above the underarm, you will also have to change the measurement of the finished sleeve cap.

To change a sleeve length, you must consider the increases made between the wrist and upper arm. These increases are generally designed to be worked from just above the ribbing to a couple inches short of the desired length to the underarm. If you shorten

WOMEN'S SIZING GUIDELINES

Women's sizes	**X-Small**	**Small**	**Medium**	**Large**	**1X**	**2X**	**3X**
Actual bust	**28–30"**	**32–34"**	**36–38"**	**40–42"**	**44–46"**	**48–50"**	**52–54"**
Metric equivalent	71–76	81–86	91–96	101–106	112–117	123–128	132–137
Very close-fitting	**28"**	**32"**	**36"**	**40"**	**44"**	**48"**	**52"**
	71	81	91	101	112	123	132
Close-fitting	**30"**	**34"**	**38"**	**42"**	**46"**	**50"**	**54"**
	76	86	96	106	117	128	137
Standard-fitting	**32"**	**36"**	**40"**	**44"**	**48"**	**52"**	**56"**
	81	91	101	112	123	132	142
Loose-fitting	**34"**	**38"**	**42"**	**46"**	**50"**	**54"**	**58"**
	86	96	106	117	128	137	147
Oversized	**35"**	**39"**	**43"**	**47"**	**51"**	**55"**	**59"**
	89	99	109	119	129	139	150

INFANTS' SIZING GUIDELINES

Sizes	**3–6 month**	**9 month**	**12 month**	**18 month**	**2 years**
Finished chest	**20"**	**22"**	**24–25"**	**26"**	**27–30"**
Metric equivalent	51	56	61–63	66	68–76
Length	**9½–11"**	**12"**	**13"**	**14"**	**15"**
	24–28	31	33	36	38
Sleeve length	**7"**	**7½"**	**8–9"**	**9½"**	**10"**
	18	19	20–23	24	26
Armhole depth	**4–5"**	**5"**	**5–5½"**	**6"**	**6¼"**
	10–13	13	13–14	15	16
***Neck opening**	**4½"**	**4½"**	**5"**	**5"**	**5½"**
	12	12	13	13	14

* Neck opening may require shoulder or back opening to accommodate head

KIDS' SIZING GUIDELINES

Sizes [in years]	**4**	**6**	**8**	**10**	**12**
Finished chest	**29–32"**	**32–34"**	**34–36"**	**36–38"**	**38–44"**
Metric equivalent	74–81	81–86	86–91	91–96	96–112
Length	**16–17½"**	**17½–19"**	**18–20"**	**22–23"**	**23"**
	41–45	45–48	46–51	56–59	59
Sleeve length	**10–11"**	**11–12½"**	**12–13"**	**14½–16"**	**15–16"**
	26–28	28–32	31–33	37–41	38–41
Armhole depth	**6½"**	**7"**	**7"**	**8"**	**8"**
	17	18	18	20	20
Neck opening	**5½–6"**	**6"**	**6–6½"**	**6½–7"**	**7½"**
	14–15	15	15–17	17–18	18

MEN'S SIZING GUIDELINES

Men's Sizes	**X-Small**	**Small**	**Medium**	**Large**	**1X**	**2X**
Actual chest	**30–32"**	**34–36"**	**38–40"**	**42–44"**	**46–48"**	**50–52"**
Metric equivalent	76–81	86–91	96–101	106–112	117–123	128–132
Length	**24"**	**25"**	**25½"**	**26"**	**26½"**	**27"**
	61	63	65	66	67	68
***Sleeve length**	**31–32"**	**32–33"**	**33–34"**	**34–35"**	**35–36"**	**36–37"**
	79–81	81–84	84–86	86–89	89–91	91–94

* from center back neck to wrist with elbow slightly bent

* for tall men, add approximately 2" to length and 1" to sleeve length

or lengthen this distance, you must consider how this alteration affects the rate at which you make the sleeve increases. If you add or subtract a small amount such as an inch or so, you can probably work your pattern as written. More drastic changes will require a bit of refiguring.

For example, suppose that you want to shorten a 17-inch sleeve by 2 inches and your pattern calls for an increase from 40 stitches at the cuff to 80 at the underarm. Your pattern directs you to increase 1 stitch each side every 6 rows 20 times, because, assuming a row gauge of 8 stitches to the inch, you have a total of 120 (17 x 8 = 136 [sleeve length] minus 2 x 8 = 16 [2" worked even just below underarm]) rows in which to work your increases. If you shorten the 17" to 15", you'll have exactly 120 rows for the total sleeve length, so you may want to change your rate of increase to every 4th row 10 times and every 6th row 10 times (for a total of 100 rows) plus 20 rows to be worked even.

Once you have the general idea about how to calculate this formula, you can experiment until you get the desired result.

Finishing Touches

A whole book could be (and quite a few have been!) written on how to finish knitted projects, especially sweaters. How you complete your sweater is as important as the techniques you use to make it. It's not difficult, but it is a part of the craft worthy of learning how to do well.

If you have a deadline, allow plenty of time to finish your knitted project. Once the knitting is complete, you are most likely anxious to be at the end of the process, but a little extra time will make a garment that you'll love for a lifetime. You may want to do it in stages, leaving time for your pieces to dry after blocking, or "seam preparation," before you put them together.

When you finish knitting your pieces, you may notice that the edges don't lie flat and the stitching may appear to be a bit uneven. This has nothing to do with your knitting ability, but rather, is inherent to the nature of knitted fabric. The first step in the finishing process is to prepare the pieces for seaming by an all-encompassing technique that is sometimes referred to as blocking. Since the word "blocking" sounds a bit harsh, it might be better to call this process "seam preparation."

Seam preparation can be done in a number of ways, such as steaming with a steamer or iron and wet blocking. The type of fiber used for the project determines how you prepare the fabric for seaming. Natural fibers such as wool can be steamed or pressed, while synthetic fibers require a no-heat process such as dampening and pinning, because heat can actually melt or take the life out of the knitted fabric.

Begin by finding a convenient spot to pin your pieces in place. It can be as simple as putting a large bath towel on a clean, carpeted floor and pinning (use rustproof T-pins) your pieces there. Small pieces can be pinned to an ironing board or on a blocking board covered with a towel or sheet. Use enough pins so that the pieces lie flat without stretching or gapping, and check the measurements as you pin, comparing them to the pattern schematic. Do not stretch out your ribbings.

You can wet the pieces before pinning or simply use a spray bottle to mist them once they are pinned. Leave them in place until completely dry. If the weather is damp, you may want to turn the piece over and/or replace the towels during the drying process.

Another way to prepare your pieces is to steam or lightly press them. Be very careful with this method. If you have any doubts about how the yarn reacts to heat, first practice with a knitted swatch. Any pressing should be done lightly after placing a damp cloth or towel over the knitted piece. Once you have steamed or pressed the pieces, allow them to dry before seaming. Pin them out to help keep their shape or just lay them flat until they are dry.

If you plan to add embellishments such as embroidery, this might be a good time to do it, rather than working on a full garment.

Next you are ready for seaming. You'll need a large-eyed yarn needle, large pins such as T-pins (metal or plastic), and a good pair of scissors or snips. After you have sewn all your seams, weave in any loose ends; you can bury ends in the seams rather than in the actual knitted fabric. When weaving in ends, it is a good idea to weave them in one direction and then in another to keep them in place.

Now try your sweater on to make sure that it fits properly. If it does, you are ready to add bands or edges and sew on buttons.

Seaming

The way you sew pieces together is a very important element in making a nicely finished knit. The type of seam you use depends on several factors—the type of stitch to be seamed and the location of the stitching (vertical or horizontal seaming). There are many ways to accomplish this process. Here we'll cover the most basic ones that can be used for most of your knitting.

Most often, seams are worked with the same yarn used for your project. If you are using a yarn that can't easily be used for sewing (such as highly textured or fragile yarns), find a similar-color plain yarn for seaming.

Your knitting instructions will usually give the order for seaming. For sweaters, the shoulder seams are joined first; then the sleeves are sewn into the armholes, and the side and sleeve seams are sewn last. This order can vary depending on the style of garment being made.

Vertical Seams

Vertical seams are used for side and sleeve seams on sweaters, for any straight pieces being joined in panels, and for seams on hats and other accessories. Both of the techniques described are worked from the right side of your pieces.

INVISIBLE SEAMING ON STOCKINETTE STITCH

This seam is smooth, flat and nearly invisible. Place the pieces of fabric to be joined side by side, with right sides up. Beginning at the lower edge of one of the pieces, attach the yarn without making a knot by running it in and out of the edge stitches closest to the spot where the seaming will begin. Start seaming by inserting the needle under the running thread between the edge stitch and second stitch on the first piece and pulling it back up through to the front. Pull the yarn through. Now insert the needle under the corresponding running thread on the second piece, pull it up and through. Alternate stitching on both sides along the entire seam length. Do not pull the yarn taut; the seam should have the same elasticity as the rest of the knitted fabric. As you continue to work, the seam will fall to the wrong side and appear almost invisible.

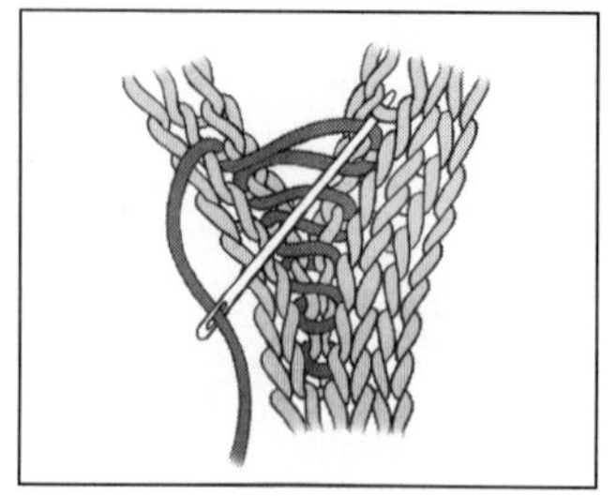

INVISIBLE SEAMING ON GARTER STITCH

Work in the same manner as on stockinette stitch, but inserting the needle into the edge "bump" on either side of the pieces to be joined. On garter stitch, the edges will be flush, with no discernable seam falling to the wrong side.

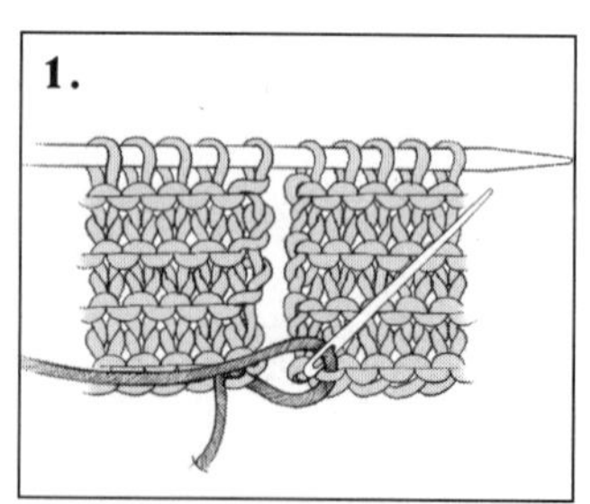

1. With the seams side by side and beginning at the lower edge, join the two pieces with a large-eyed yarn needle and a strand of yarn.

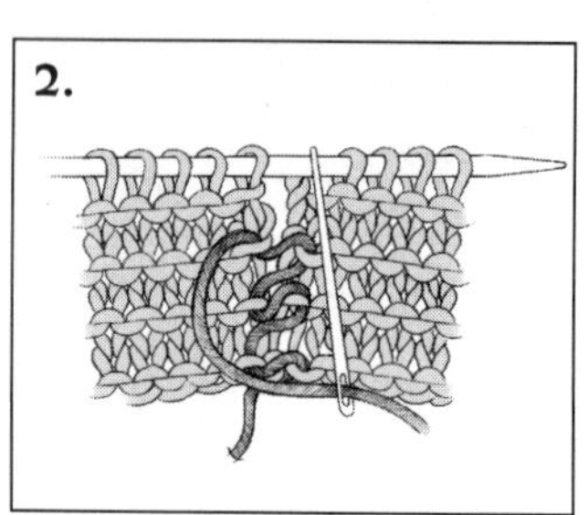

2. Stitch up the seam, going from side to side into the loops as shown.

Horizontal Seaming

Horizontal seams are generally used to join shoulders of garments. They can either be worked invisibly to hide the seam or joined in a decorative manner to accent the seam. Shoulder seams are very important, because they are the key points for holding a sweater on the body. The shoulder be worked firmly without pulling in the stitching. With more fragile or stretchy yarns, you may want to reinforce the inside seam. For heavy garments such as coats, reinforcing the shoulder seams is also a good idea. To reinforce, you can stitch over the seam with an overcasting stitch or sew on a piece of twill ribbon.

INVISIBLE SEAMING ON STOCKINETTE STITCH

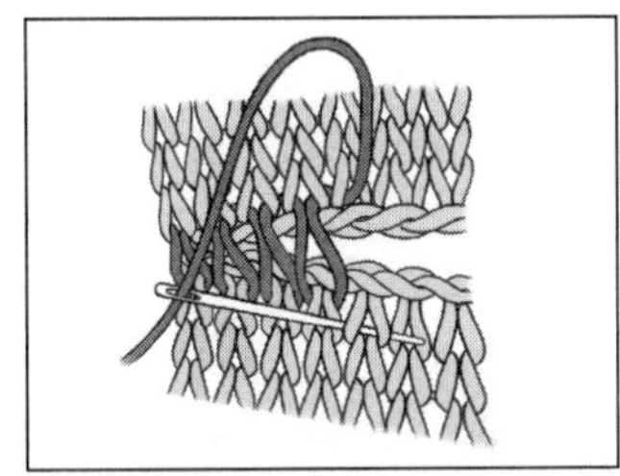

Line up the two seams to be sewn and begin as for the vertical invisible stockinette seam by running the yarn in and out of edge or bound-off stitches. Insert the needle over each bound-off edge stitch into the center of the first stitch just below the bind-off and bring it out through the center of the next stitch. Pull the yarn through. Now insert the needle into the center of the first stitch below the bind-off on the opposite side, bring it out through the center of the next stitch, and pull the yarn through. Continue alternating between the pieces of fabric. (Hint: Look for the V's and connect them up.) Once again, do not pull the seaming yarn too tightly; the seam should be strong but flexible.

THREE-NEEDLE BIND-OFF

This wonderful technique is very useful. It creates a neat, firm seam, as it is worked directly from live stitches and it's easy to do. You can work it with the right sides together so that the seam is on the inside, as shown, or decoratively with the wrong sides together so that the seam is on the outside of your sweater.

Set up the seaming process by moving your stitches from holders to knitting needles. You will need two knitting needles to hold stitches and a third knitting needle to work the bind-off. Make sure that both needles with the shoulder stitches are facing in the same direction.

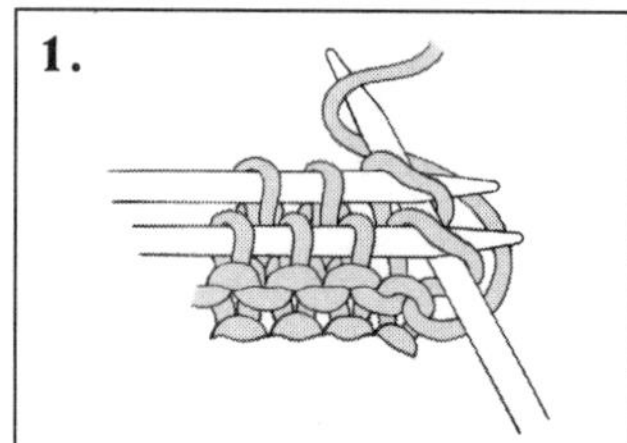

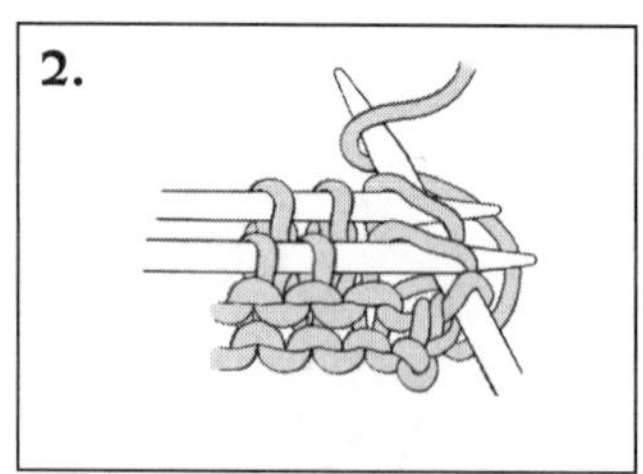

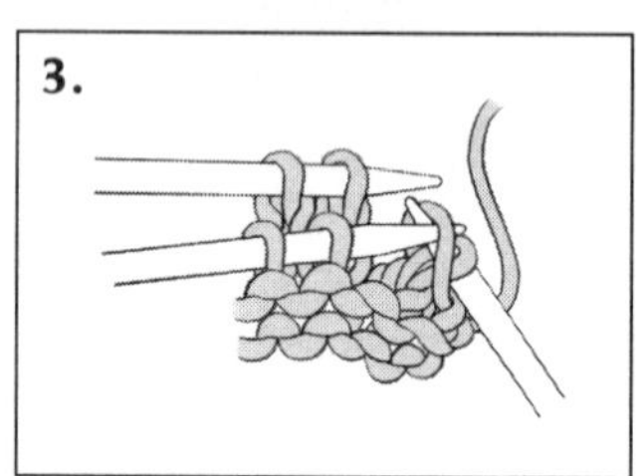

1. With the right side of the pieces together, insert the right needle into the first stitch on the front and back needle and knit them together.

2. Insert the right needle into the next stitch on the front and back needle and knit them together—two stitches remain on right needle.

3. Bring the first stitch on the right needle over the second stitch to bind it off. Repeat steps 2 and 3 until you have worked all the stitches off both needles. Fasten off last stitch as you would for a regular bind-off.

Seaming with Crochet

Crocheting a seam is fast and easy, but it can be a little bulky. This technique is very handy for joining larger items such as blankets or throws. If you are making a reversible piece such as a throw, however, take care to work the seam neatly so that both sides look good. For more on making crochet stitches, see page 110.

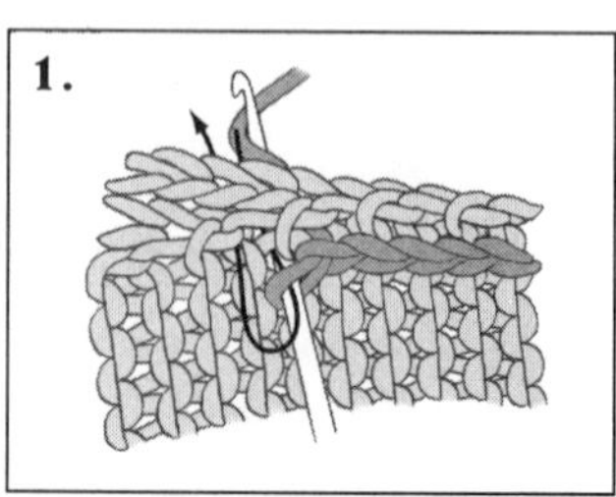

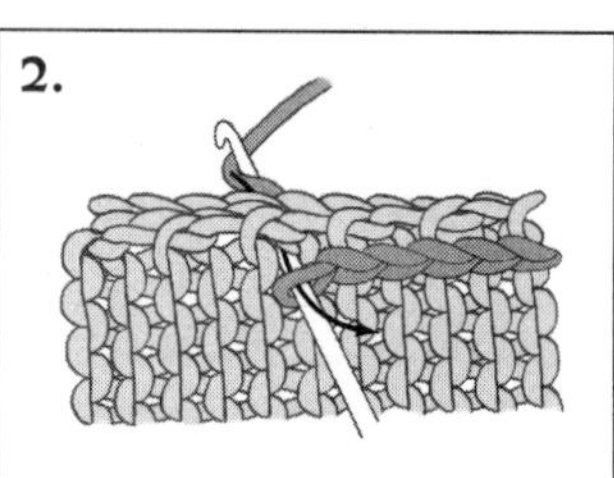

CROCHET SLIP-STITCH SEAM

1. Working from the wrong side with the right sides together begin by inserting the hook through both thicknesses.

2. Place the yarn over the hook and draw through the seam and the loop on the hook. This makes a slip-stitch seam. Continue in this way until the seam is completely joined. Fasten off the yarn and weave in the remaining tail.

Weaving In Ends

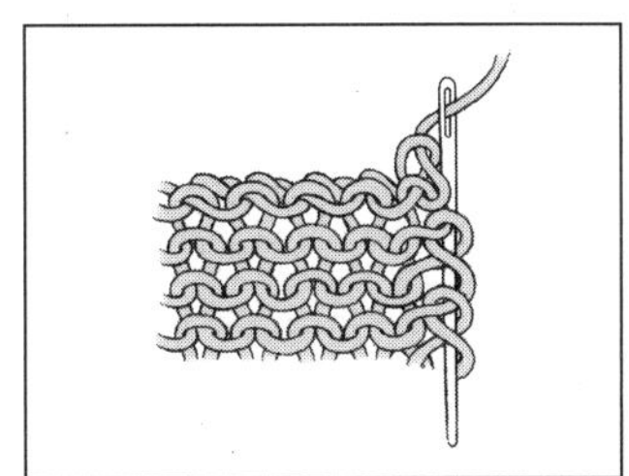

Ends where you've added new yarns or strands from the cast-on and bind-off areas are worked directly into the knitted fabric. This is best done once the seaming is complete, as you can sometimes work the ends into or near the seam.

Thread a large-eyed yarn needle with the end of yarn and run it in and out of the fabric in the most inconspicuous place. Go in one direction for an inch or so and then reverse direction. Snip off any remaining yarn.

Working Edges and Bands

The foundation of most edgings, neckbands, and front bands is the knitted piece itself. Instead of having to stitch these finishing touches to the piece, they are knitted from the right side directly onto the knitted fabric.

The number of stitches to be picked up is normally given in the pattern instructions. Sometimes there is a total figure and sometimes it is divided into segments. The instructions may say pick up 50 stitches evenly around neck edge or 20 stitches from back neck and 30 from front neck. If you are told to "pick up evenly around the neck edge," you may find it easier to do if you mark off 2" sections and pick up the same number of stitches in each section.

This process of picking up stitches, as outlined in the illustrations on page 102, is also sometimes referred to in patterns as "pick up and knit." This simply means that you are knitting the loop onto your fabric, not picking up a loop from the fabric itself.

Even within a simple neckline, you'll be required to pick up stitches in several directions—horizontally, vertically, and along a curved edge. The information that follows gives details on picking up in any of these directions.

Hint: Even if you plan to work your bands in contrasting colors, work the pickup row in the same color as the body—you'll get a neater edge.

Round necklines can be joined and worked with double-pointed or circular needles. A circular needle is also particularly useful if you are working back and forth on a band with a large number of stitches, such as a V-neck cardigan button band.

Although our illustrations are given on stockinette stitch, the process is the same when working into other stitch patterns.

Horizontal Stitch Pickups

This technique is most often used along a back neck or along the bound-off section of the front neck. Generally, you pick up one stitch for each stitch along the neck area.

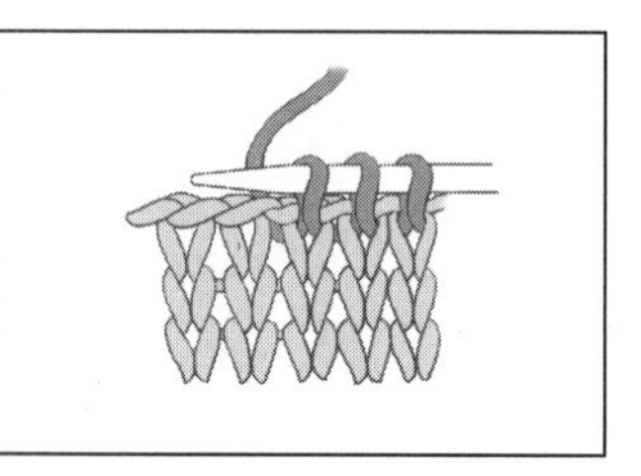

PICKING UP STITCHES ON STOCKINETTE STITCH

With the right side facing, insert the knitting needle from the front to back into the center of the stitch under the bound-off stitch above. Wrap the yarn around the needle as if to knit and pull through a loop. Repeat this step until you have picked up the desired number of stitches.

Vertical Stitch Pickups

Vertical pickups are most often worked on front bands or other such side edges. Rarely will you pick up a stitch for every row; the number of stitches that you pick up along a side edge depends on the stitch/row ratio of your gauge. In stockinette stitch, a default pickup is three stitches for every four rows. This means that you'll pick up loops in three stitches and then skip one stitch. Repeat this sequence along the entire edge.

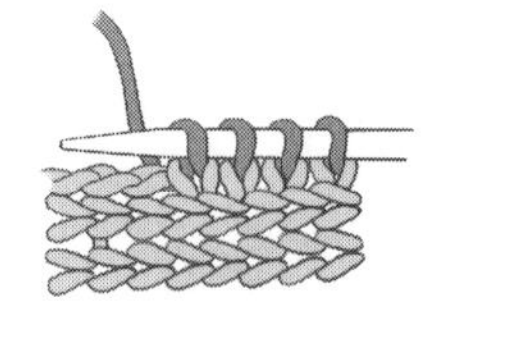

PICKING UP STITCHES ON STOCKINETTE STITCH

With the right side facing, insert the needle between the first and second stitches. Wrap the yarn around the needle as if to knit and pull through a loop. Continue in this manner along the entire edge, skipping stitches as necessary.

Curved Stitch Pickups

Necklines have curved portions where stitches are decreased and/or bound off. This actually creates a not-so-neat line. The key point to remember when picking up stitches in this area is that you want to eliminate any holes, hide any imperfections, and create a smooth line. This may take a bit of practice.

PICKING UP STITCHES ON STOCKINETTE STITCH

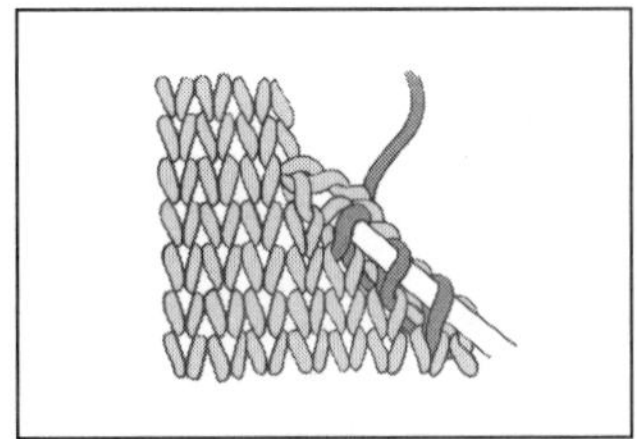

As with straight edge, insert the needle into the stitch, working inside the bound-off or edge stitches. Wrap the yarn as if to knit and draw through a loop. Continue in this way until you get to the next vertical or horizontal area.

Care of Knits

Once you have completed a sweater or other knitted item, proper care is necessary to keep it in heirloom condition. Knits are designed for easy wear, and the laundering process is now easier than ever.

BEFORE YOU LAUNDER

The good thing about yarn labels is that they usually contain directions for washing; always save a yarn label from each project to help you clean your sweaters and other knits.

Before washing, you should remove any nonwashable pieces, such as trims and wooden buttons. You should also test the colorfastness of the yarn, especially when a garment includes several colors. Always test-wash a swatch before washing the finished garment—a ruined swatch is much less traumatic than a ruined hand-knitted sweater!

Another pre-washing step is to measure the width, length, and sleeve length of your sweater so that you can reshape it to its original size after laundering it. If you don't have a tape measure handy, draw a line around the garment on brown paper or interfacing and cut out the shape to create a template upon which to dry your sweater.

READY, GET SET, WASH!

Contrary to conventional wisdom, you can wash your knits using a washing machine. In fact, it's a good tool for laundering hand knits because a machine can spin out far more water than you could possibly get out by hand.

Wool has a reputation for shrinking and becoming matted, and indeed, this can happen with animal fibers that are not washed carefully. There are three main factors that cause felting, matting, and shrinking—a shocking change in temperature from hot to cold, agitation, and harsh (highly alkaline) detergents. If you are working with a synthetic or mostly synthetic yarn or wool that is treated with a superwash treatment, you have no concern about these factors.

Avoid agitation by washing garments separately so they can't create friction as they rub against each other. Fill the tub with lukewarm water and mild detergent, put in the garments, soak them for 20–30 minutes, spin out the water, refill to rinse, let soak, and spin once again.

Choose a mild washing solution without detergents for your knits—Dawn dishwashing liquid is highly recommended. Other options include gentle washes sold at supermarkets or special wool washes often advertised in knitting publications, some of which require no rinsing. Fill your machine with lukewarm water, add your knits, soak, and then allow the machine to spin gently. Never, ever use bleach on wool or other protein fibers—the bleach will dissolve them. It's a good idea to avoid bleach or soaps that contain bleach when washing plant fibers and synthetics as well, unless your yarn label specifically states that you can use bleach (see Chapter 1, page 12 for bleaching symbol).

Let your knits soak for anywhere from 15 to 30 minutes before spinning out the water. It's better to rewash a piece than to leave it soaking for a long period of time.

Get as much water out of the garment as possible. Even if you hand-wash your garment, you may want to pop it into a machine just for the spinning. If this is not possible, roll it in a clean towel and stand on it to absorb excess moisture.

DRYING

Before you choose a drying method, look again at the yarn label so see if care is indicated. Garments made from hair fibers such as wool should be dried flat, away from heat and direct sunlight. If the yarn can be machine-dried, use a low setting and remove immediately after drying to avoid wrinkling.

The main aim in the drying process is to dry the piece quickly to prevent mildew. This is especially important with yarns such as cotton. If placing the garment on towels, replace damp towels as necessary. Air circulation speeds the drying process. Directing air flow from a portable fan at a drying sweater will cut the drying time by hours. You also can dry your knit on a handy screen device, placing it over a bathtub or across two chairs. (These are sold in catalogs and available at chain stores in the departments where ironing boards and other such items are sold.)

HOW TO STORE KNITS

Everyone has favorite storage areas and devices. While in season, keep your sweaters in a place that isn't near a heat source, where they'll remain clean and dry. When you get ready to pack away your knits, make sure they are clean. Pack them loosely in tissue paper rather than plastic bags. It may be easier to care for them if they are grouped by fiber. For example, place all wool sweaters in one box and cotton and acrylic sweaters in another.

If you are concerned about moths (attracted to wool and animal-hair fibers), add moth preventive. There are a number of herbal alternatives to mothballs, such as lavender; you can also use cedar chips or blocks.

IT'S GOOD TO KNOW

- Along with a label, save a butterfly of yarn for repairs. You may want to keep this information in a notebook that's handy for times when you'll be laundering or repairing your sweaters. If making a gift, send the recipient the label and a yarn reeling.
- Launder your sweaters before they become too soiled. Not only is it easier to get rid of spots that aren't embedded into the piece, but you will also discourage moths, which are attracted to soiled garments.
- When washing a large item such as a throw, you may have to fold it in half to dry. Keep turning it to circulate air. Throws made from yarns that can be machine-washed are indeed a blessing when it comes to their care.
- You can fluff up a sweater by placing it in a dryer on a cool-air setting. This is especially good for garments made from mohair and other fuzzy yarns.
- If you make a project that includes more than one yarn type, check the washability of all the yarns in the item. Choose your laundering method by the one that needs the most care.
- You can dry-clean sweaters, but most yarn (with the notable exception of some rayon yarns) is washable. In fact, water is much better for the fibers than harsh dry-cleaning chemicals; manufacturers often label a yarn "dry clean only" merely to protect themselves from legal action. Again, clean a small swatch to be sure.
- Repair your sweaters before washing. Check the seams and buttons to make sure that there is no damage before you proceed. Little holes become big holes when wet!

11

Bells and Whistles

Now that you've been introduced to the basics, we want to explore easy techniques that will bring you even greater enjoyment of the craft. These are the building blocks that will make you a skillful knitter. While you can find complete books on each of the following techniques, just knowing a few simple steps is all you'll need to try something new and exciting.

Each technique is followed by one or more projects. We've included several children's sweaters (quick and easy to make), home-décor items, and socks.

Keep in mind that every new technique is performed using the same two stitches that you have been making—knit and purl. If you can knit and purl, you can make cables. If you know how to make ribbing, you can make socks. If you can work stockinette stitch, you can work with more than one color in the same design.

What do you do if you get stuck? Try to figure out where you are having trouble. If you are having difficulty reading a stitch pattern, break it down into small, easily manageable segments. If you don't find your answer in this book, go to one or more of the good basic knitting books that is likely to have a solution. Sometimes you may want to read more than one book about the same subject to be sure you understand. If you can find a friend, teacher, or yarn-shop owner who will give you some personal assistance, all the better.

Cabling

When a non-knitter or beginning knitter looks at a garment with cables, she or he is truly amazed at what looks like a complex pattern. In truth, cables are extremely easy to knit. Once you can knit and purl, you can make cables. Begin with easy cables such as the ones illustrated. Making a project with one or two areas using the same cable is an easy way to begin your cabling career. Here are a few hints to make cabling even more simple.

Cables pull in knitted fabric more than stockinette stitch. The number of cables, the size of each cable, the rate at which the cable crosses are made, and the type and thickness of the yarn all determine how much the fabric will pull in. Usually smaller cables pull in less than larger ones. If you work 10 or 12 cables across the front of your sweater, the fabric will pull in more than if you knit just one center cable. The size of a cable is dictated by the number of stitches in that cable—a 4-stitch cable is considered small, compared to a 10-stitch cable. Large cables in thick yarn and smaller cables in fine yarn create very different fabrics in textural depth, width, and drape.

Cables can be used in interesting and creative ways. Small cables paired with purl stitches can be used as overall ribbing for a sweater body or on bands. Cables are most often set off on either side by purl stitches to emphasize their "sculptural" dimension. The number of stitches between cables will vary from pattern to pattern. Cable motifs are versatile—they can be worked as panels or as one or two repeats scattered on a section of a sweater.

Cables show up better worked in light-colored, plain yarns, but they can also be used successfully with variegated, tweedy, or other textured yarns. Dark variegated, deep navy, and black tones subdue cable patterns. An intricate sweater done in dark shades is basically a lot of knitting without much payoff for the time and effort involved. When in doubt about the pattern, work a large swatch and look at it from a distance before you embark on your whole project.

Cables are formed by switching the positions of two or more stitches on your needle. This "stitch turning" is achieved by placing a number of stitches (outlined in the pattern) onto a cable needle and holding those stitches in the front or back of the piece while you knit the next few stitches. The cable is then completed by working stitches from the cable needle. As you work the stitches from the holder, take care not to twist them. Be sure that your cable needle is smaller than the stitches you are working. (For more information on cable needles, see Chapter 1, page 9.)

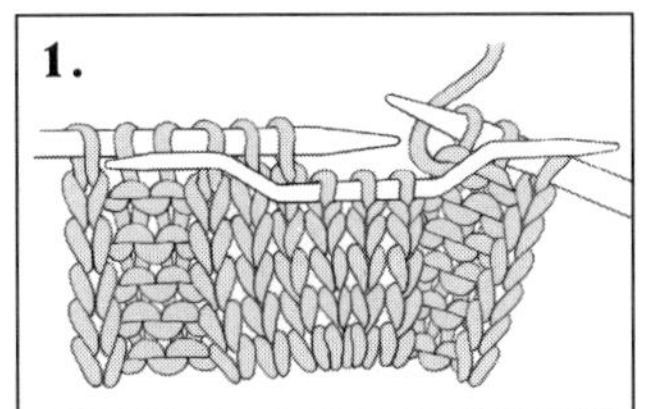

When making cables, it is critical to count the number of rows between cable crossings. Even a seasoned knitter may find that it's not easy to determine the number of rows from one cross to the next without a tracking system, especially when using fuzzy novelty yarns.

When looking at knitting instructions, you are sure to find differences in the way cables are described. "Front" cables are also known as "left-cross" cables; "back" cables are called "right-cross" cables.

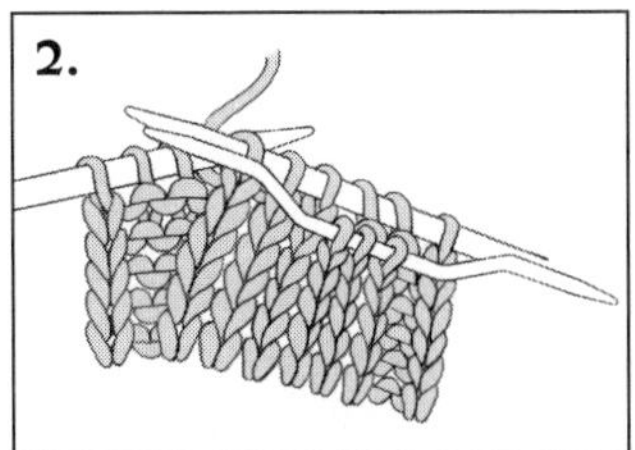

Often the number of stitches in the cable is used as part of the description. For example, "6-stitch left-cross cable" and "3/3 left-cross cable" both mean the same thing.

Note that a combination of left and right cables can be (and often are) worked in the same sweater.

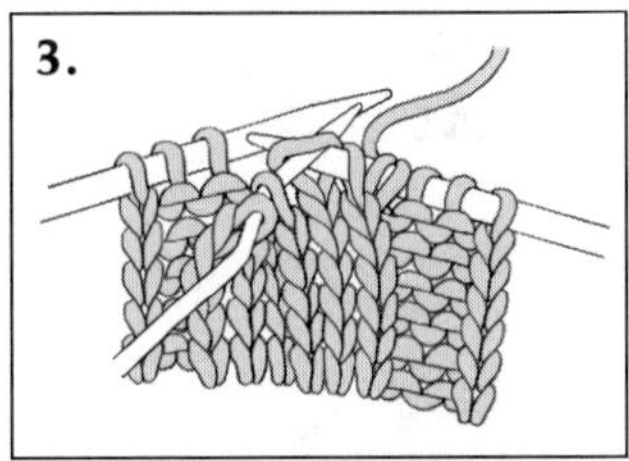

6-STITCH LEFT (FRONT) CABLE

Cables are usually crossed on right-side rows. Work to the spot where the cable crossing occurs.

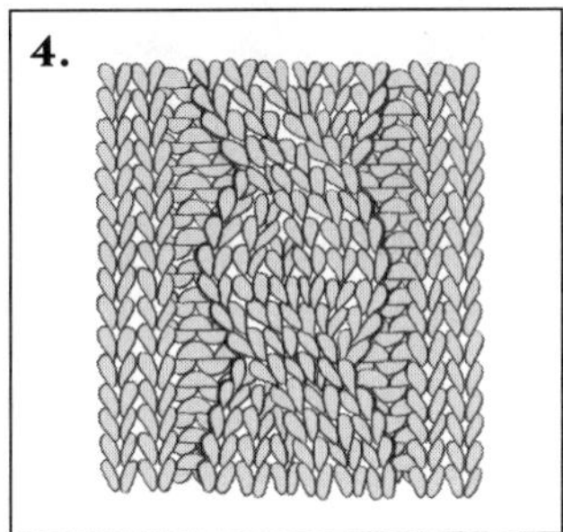

1. Slip 3 stitches onto a cable needle and allow the stitches to remain in the front of the work.

2. Knit the next 3 stitches on the needle.

3. Without twisting, knit 3 stitches from the cable needle.

4. Completed cable, showing two crossings.

6-STITCH RIGHT (BACK) CABLE

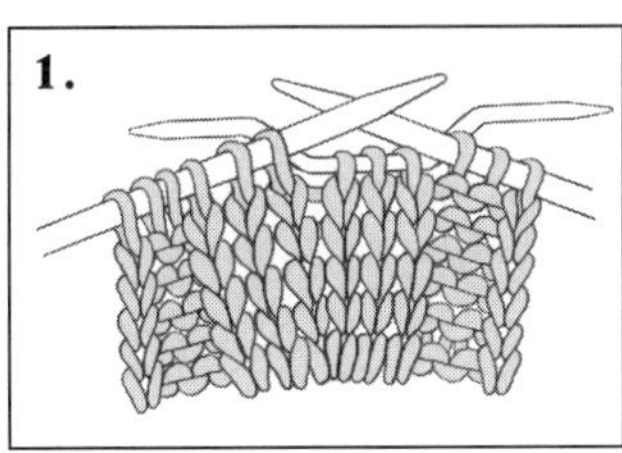

Work to the spot where the cable crossing occurs.

1. Slip 3 stitches onto a cable needle and allow the stitches to remain in the back of the work.

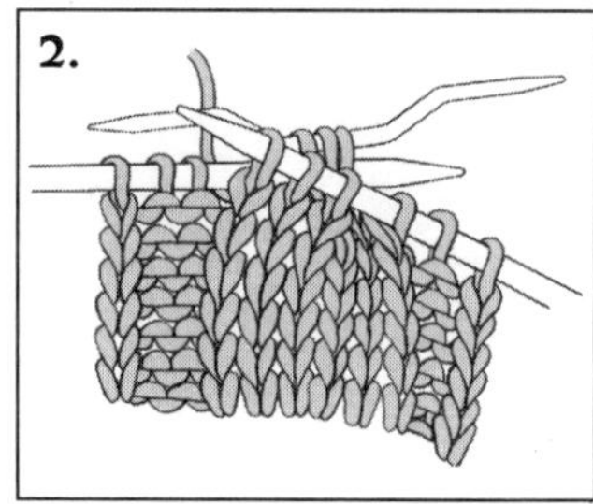
2.

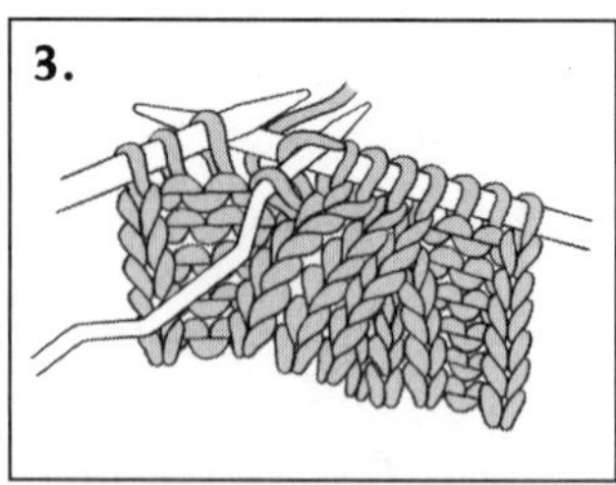
3.

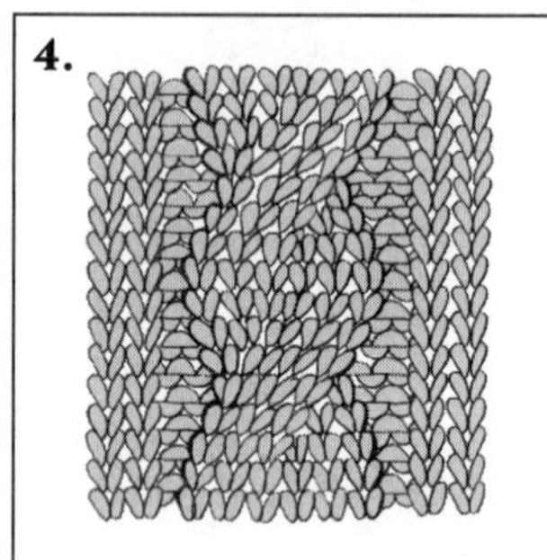
4.

2. Knit the next 3 stitches on the needle.

3. Without twisting, knit 3 stitches from the cable needle.

4. Completed cable, showing two crossings.

Crocheted Edges

Learning a couple of easy crochet stitches will greatly enhance your knitting career, even if you don't plan to become a crocheter. You can use these basic stitches in numerous ways. Once you learn them, you'll find that crocheting an edge is fast and uncomplicated. A bonus with crochet is that it's very easy to rip out and work again if you aren't completely satisfied with your first results.

As with knitting, practice is the best way to become skilled. If you decide to go further with crochet, there are many books that go beyond these preliminary steps.

The main difference in basic crochet stitches (such as slip stitch, single crochet, half double crochet, double crochet, and treble crochet) is the height of the stitches created. The list here goes from shortest to tallest, with the shortest three being the most useful crochet stitches for the average knitter.

Crochet and knitting differ in that crochet is worked one loop at a time, while knitting is performed over an entire row of open stitches. Therefore, when you finish crocheting, there is no need to bind it off as you do when knitting. To end your crocheted piece, simply cut the yarn, leave a 3" or 4" strand and pull it through the last loop to fasten it off. Weave in the remaining strand.

Please note that the illustrations given here assume that they are done holding the crochet hook in the right hand. Left-handed crocheters should transpose these instructions.

GETTING STARTED

A chain is the first step in making a free-standing crocheted piece. If you are making an edging, you won't have to make a chain—you already have your knitted fabric to crochet into. However, crocheted chains have many other uses for the knitter, such as cording, ties, straps, and trim.

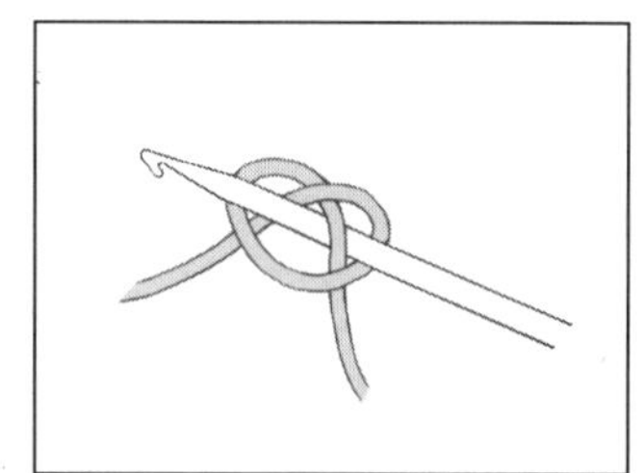

MAKING A SLIPKNOT

A slipknot is the foundation stitch of a crocheted chain. Make it around the crochet hook as shown. To complete, pull on one end of the yarn and tighten around the hook.

MAKING A CHAIN (ABBREVIATED AS CH)

1. With the hook in your right hand (between the thumb and the index finger) and the yarn in your left hand wrapped as shown over your index finger, insert the hook under and over the strand of yarn. Catch a loop on the hook (called a yarn over).

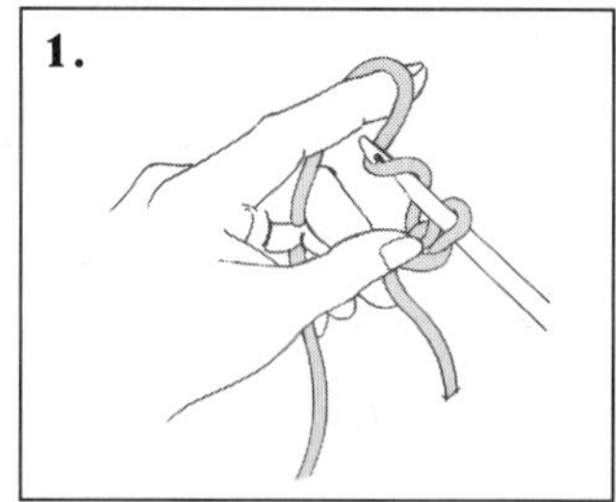

2. Pull the loop on the hook through the slipknot that's already on the hook. When this is complete, you have made one chain. Repeat this step until you have as many chains as necessary.

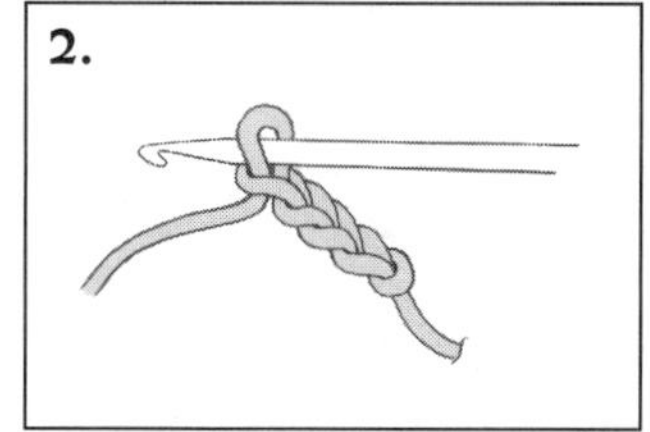

SLIP STITCH (ABBREVIATED AS SLIP ST)

A slip stitch is the shortest of all crochet stitches. It is ideal if you want to create a "no edge" edging on a knitted piece. This stitch has many uses. For example, it can be used to outline a band or neckline, it can be used to reinforce a seam, or it can be used to make a less visible seam.

1. Working with the initial chain or directly into the fabric, insert the hook as shown.

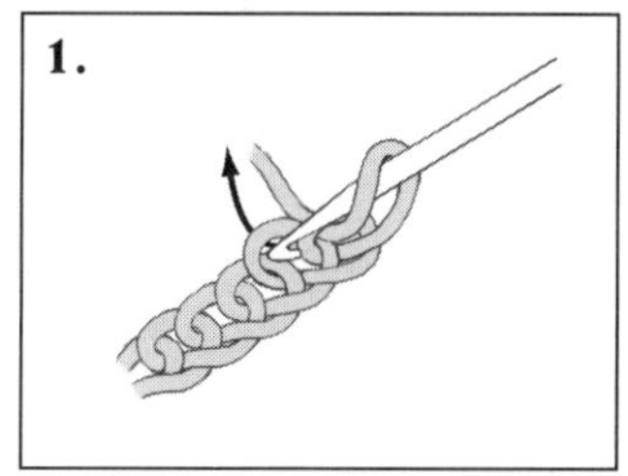

2. Place the yarn over the hook and pull through the loop that results from the yarn over. The stitch is complete.

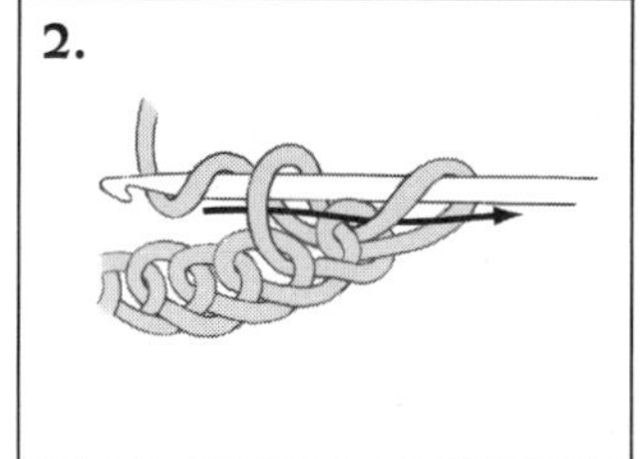

SINGLE CROCHET (ABBREVIATED AS SC)

Single crochet is very often used to edge pieces. It helps knit fabric to lie flat. It can also be used for seaming. Sometimes it is

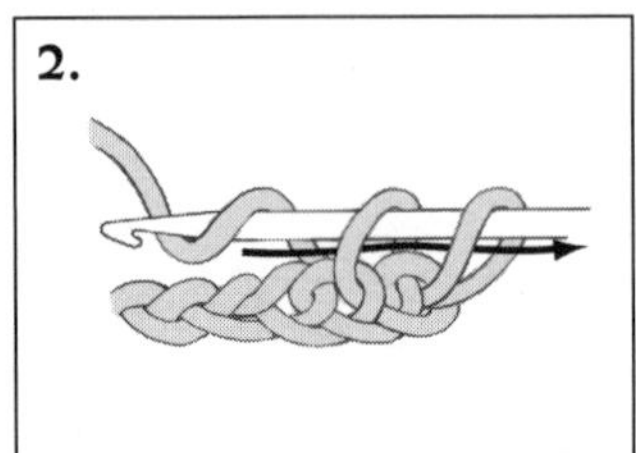

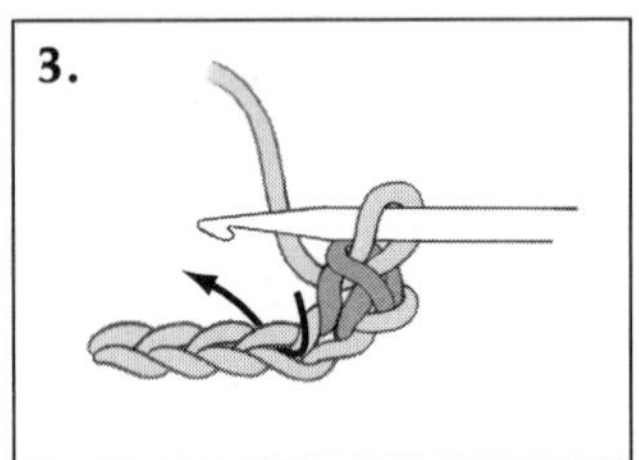

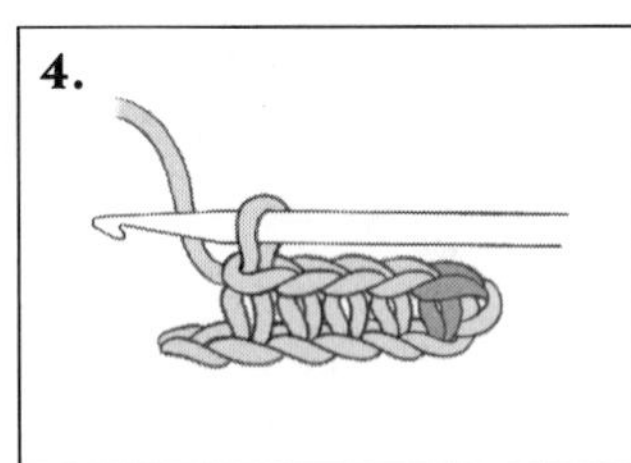

used to neaten an edge before additional crochet stitches are worked on the next row or round.

1. Insert the crochet hook into the chain or fabric as you are directed. Place the yarn over the hook and draw through a loop and leave this loop on the hook—2 loops remain on hook.

2. Yarn over the hook once again and draw the new loop through the two loops already on the crochet hook.

3. One single crochet has been completed.

4. Insert the hook into the next stitch and repeat steps 1 and 2.

Making Socks

If you are a beginning knitter, making socks is a great exercise in learning a number of uncomplicated knitting techniques. If you think of sock-making merely as a series of simple steps, you will find that it easy to complete the whole sock. The eight steps are 1. cuff/leg; 2. heel flap; 3. turning (shaping) the heel; 4. instep (picking up stitches); 5. instep gusset (decreasing stitches); 6. foot; 7. shaping the toe; 8. closing the toe.

Once you understand each of these steps, you can make almost any type of sock. The formula is basically the same.

GETTING STARTED

Socks are most often worked in the round using double-pointed needles to avoid uncomfortable seams. Some sock knitters use 12" circular needles for this purpose. The cast-on of the cuff should be loose and elastic so that you can easily put your foot into the sock. If you find it hard to cast on loosely, cast on over two needles to make a more flexible cast-on edge.

In the example given here, we shall work with 24 stitches. This number of stitches will make a toddler or small child's sock in a worsted-weight yarn using approximately size 7 or 8 (4.5 or 5 mm) needles. Note that rows worked in a circular manner are referred to as "rounds."

DOUBLE-POINTED NEEDLES

Begin with four double-pointed needles. If your set includes five needles, set aside the fifth needle. Hint: Many people find wooden or bamboo double points easier to knit with than metal needles because they don't slip out of the stitches as readily. Cast all 24 stitches onto one needle and then separate them onto 3 needles, 8 stitches on each.

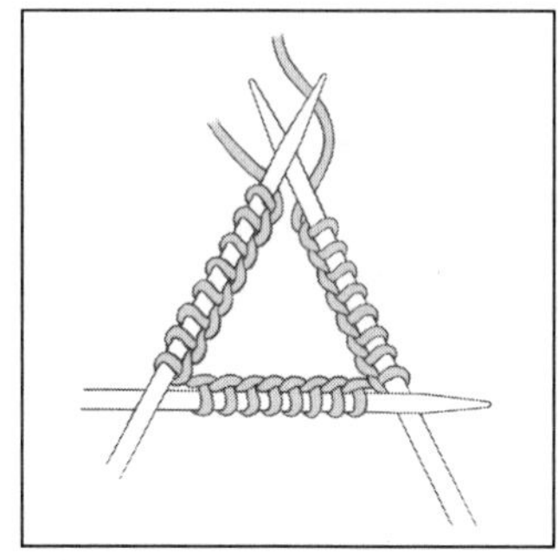

Slip a marker onto the needle with the last cast-on stitch or place a safety pin into the edge. This marker indicates the beginning of your round, which will be at the back of the sock. Lay the three needles down and make sure that all the stitches are going in the same direction and that the cast-on edge is below each of the needles before joining the work. If the stitches are twisted on this crucial joining row, they will remain twisted as you work, and you won't end up with a tube.

Before you begin to knit the first stitch, you can reverse the placement of the last cast-on stitch with the first cast-on stitch. You can also cast on one extra stitch and knit this last stitch with the first stitch on the needle. Either method locks the three needles in place and makes it easier to work the first few rounds.

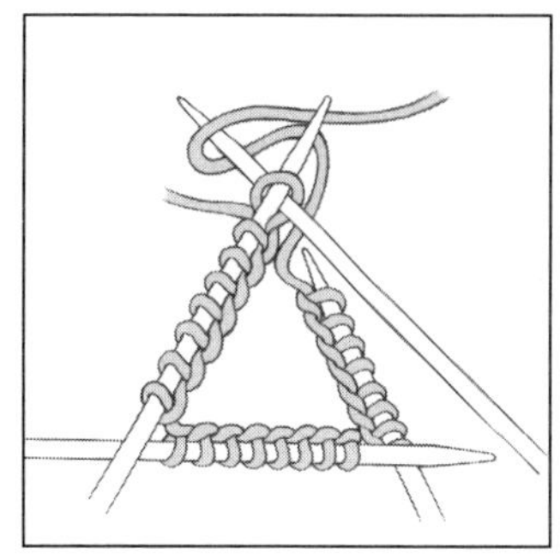

The first stitch knitted is the first stitch cast on as shown in this illustration. Work across all the stitches on the first needle with the needle in your right hand; then, with the next empty needle, work across the next needle. Always work the first stitch on a needle a bit more tightly than the rest so that you avoid "ladders" of loose stitches at the needle joins. Continue in this way around the piece. When you get back to the marker, be sure to carefully tighten the yarn as you begin the second round. Remember that even though there are three needles plus your working needle, you are always working with just two needles at any one time.

CUFF/LEG

Ribbing is ideal for an elastic cuff. Work in rounds of knit 1, purl 1 until the cuff measures 2–2½" from the beginning. You can then knit a few rounds of plain knitting before making the heel. On an adult sock, there would most likely be a few inches or more of plain knitting, depending on the desired length. End so that you are ready to begin a new round.

HEEL FLAP

The heel flap is a rectangular straight piece that comes directly from the cuff/leg portion of the sock. The heel flap is worked back and forth on half the stitches (in this case 12 stitches), with the instep stitches being placed on hold on the other two needles (6 on each). Therefore, before you begin the heel, you need to rearrange your stitches. Follow these steps exactly and you'll have your heel flap set up.

Using the empty needle (needle 1), knit the first 6 stitches at the beginning of the round (2 stitches remain unworked). Take the needle holding these two unworked stitches (needle 2) and slip the first 4 stitches from the next needle (needle 3) onto it. You now have 6 stitches on needle 2, and 4 stitches remaining on needle 3; slip the first two stitches from the last needle (needle 4) onto needle 3, so that there are also 6 stitches on needle 3. Needles 2 and 3 hold the 12 instep stitches that will remain unworked as you make your heel flap. Slip the last 6 stitches from needle 4 to needle 1, which holds the knitted 6 stitches—you now have 12 stitches for the heel flap and are ready to begin a wrong-side row.

As the heel of a sock rubs against your shoe, it receives the most wear. There are a number of different stitch patterns that can be worked to help reinforce the heel. In our example, we are going to work a knit 1, slip 1 stitch (known as heel stitch) heel flap. You can also add a strand of nylon specially designed for sock knitting or even a strand of polyester sewing thread for additional strength.

On *the wrong-side row,* slip the first stitch as if to purl and then purl across the remaining 11 stitches. On *the right-side row,* keeping the yarn to the back, slip the first stitch as if to purl, knit the next stitch; continue to slip 1 stitch with the yarn in the back and knit 1 stitch across the row. Repeat these two rows 5 times more—12 rows in total.

TURNING (SHAPING) THE HEEL

The purpose of "turning," the heel is to curve the fabric at the bottom of the heel. It is done by making partial rows of knitting (also known as short rows).

In our sample, the next row (wrong side) is worked as follows: Slip the first stitch, purl 6, purl 2 together, purl 1. Turn the work, leaving 2 stitches unworked. **Next row** Slip the first stitch, knit 3, work the slip, slip, knit decrease (ssk), knit 1, turn the work, leaving 2 stitches unworked again. **Next row** Slip the first stitch, purl 4, purl 2 together, purl 1, turn the work—no stitch remains unworked. **Next row** Slip the first stitch, knit 5, ssk, knit 1, turn the work, leaving no stitches unworked—8 stitches remain.

It's time to rearrange your needles once more (and for the final time). Place the 12 instep stitches on one needle, and use the extra needle to divide the 8 heel stitches in half with 4 on each needle. The new round begins in the center of these 8 stitches, so place your marker accordingly.

INSTEP (PICKING UP STITCHES)

By slipping the stitch at the beginning of each row, you have created 6 neat double loops to pick up in. Take the needle with the yarn coming out and pick up and knit 6 stitches along the nearest side of the heel flap.

Next knit across the 12 instep stitches, after which you will be ready to pick up along the second side of the heel flap. You should take care to pick up the same number of stitches on both sides of the heel. You have 4 stitches on the far end of the needle and will be picking up 6 stitches to join these 4 stitches.

Note You can avoid the little hole that often appears between the gusset and the instep stitches by picking up an extra stitch at the top of the heel flap on each side and putting these two stitches onto each end of the instep needle; eliminate the hole by decreasing these 2 stitches away on the second round.

INSTEP GUSSET (DECREASING STITCHES)

You now have a total of 32 stitches: 10 stitches on each of the back two needles and 12 stitches on the front needle. The extra stitches are the gusset stitches. The next step is to form the triangular gussets by decreasing the number of stitches on the back two needles until 6 stitches apiece remain. Your total stitch count will then be back to the original 24.

Knit one round without shaping. **Next round** Knit to 3 stitches before the end of the first needle, knit 2 together, knit 1; knit across the 12 instep stitches; knit 1, work an ssk decrease, knit to the end of the round. Repeat these two rounds until you have 6 stitches on the back two needles.

FOOT

The variation in sizing takes place in two areas: the width and length of the cuff/leg and the foot length. Note that foot lengths vary from child's sizes to large men's sizes. For example, a child of 2–3 years of age would have about a 5½" foot length and a man would have an 11" foot length.

For this sock, knit even until you have worked about 2" from the last gusset decrease.

SHAPING THE TOE

The toe is shaped in the same manner as the instep gusset, except that there will be decreasing on all needles. **Next round** Knit to last 3 stitches of first needle, knit 2 together, knit 1; on next needle, knit 1, work ssk decrease, knit to the end of the round. **Next round** Knit without making any decreases. Continue to repeat last 2 rounds until 8 stitches remain.

CLOSING THE TOE

On a toddler sock such as this one, the remaining few stitches can be drawn together with the remaining strand of yarn using a tapestry needle.

Color With Stripes

Striping is an easy, creative way to add color. Easy, because you knit with only one color per row. Creative, because your striping options are limitless. You can limit yourself to one contrasting color in your project or add as many as space allows. Stripes can be wide or narrow. They can be knitted in the same kind of yarn or in a yarn with a contrasting texture. Stripes can be worked in plain stockinette stitch or in other stitch patterns. Creative striping adds a new dimension to your knitting.

ADDING A NEW COLOR OF YARN

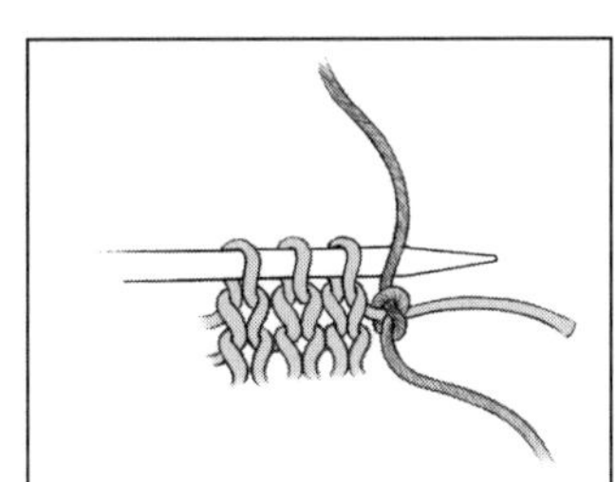

When you reach the place where you want to add a new ball of yarn, do it at the beginning of a row. Loosely tie a knot with the new yarn around the old yarn, leaving a tail of at least 4". Slide the knot up the tail of the old yarn as close as possible to your work.

STRIPING IN STOCKINETTE STITCH

Working stripes in simple stockinette stitch is an easy way to try them out. You can keep it simple by knitting stripes that are all an even number of rows wide. In this way you always begin your new color additions, on right-side rows.

Once a stripe is complete, you can leave the yarn at the edge, ready to work the next stripe in that color, or you can cut the yarn.

The choice is most often dictated by the distance that the yarn is carried before the next time it is used. If that distance is just a couple of inches, it's easier not to cut it and to carry it up the side of the fabric. You should also bear in mind how the finished piece will be used. If you are making a blanket or scarf where this edge will be visible, it might be best to cut the yarn when you begin a new stripe. When the project is done, invisibly weave the yarns into the fabric. As an alternative, you can carry the yarn and then work a crocheted or knitted edging that will cover the yarn carries.

THE PURL SIDE OF YOUR WORK

When you add a new row of color, take a look at what is usually considered the wrong side (purl side) of your knitting. You will have a bar of the old color plus a bar of the new color that you are adding. This natural occurrence can be used to your advantage and become a design choice. If you work two-row stripes of several colors and decide to use the purl side as the right side of your work, you'll make a nice tweedy effect.

GARTER-STITCH STRIPES

Knitting every row makes a soft, spongy fabric, and the addition of stripes of color enhances this fabric. Just remember that you should decide which would be your right and wrong side so that when you add new colors, the side with the bars of old and new color will all be the same. Placing a safety pin on the right side will help you remember.

UNEVEN STRIPES

Making stripes of uneven rows entails carrying the yarns up both sides of your fabric because you are not limited to changing colors on even (right-side) rows. If you are working a pattern calling for uneven stripes, working back and forth on a circular needle will make it easier to "retrieve" and work with yarns left on the "far" edge of the fabric; this would be impossible to do if you are knitting with straight, one-ended needles. With circular (or two-ended) needles, you can work from either side of the piece depending on what color you are adding or dropping and where the yarn happens to be.

MAKING COLOR STRIPES IN RIBBING

To make crisp, well-defined rows of striping when working ribbing omit the ribbing pattern and knit the entire first row of the new color. On the next row, resume your ribbing pattern. This will eliminate the color "grin-through" created by the purl blips of the ribbing. You can use this technique when working any stitch pattern that involves a combination of knit and purl stitches, such as seed stitch. However, it should be noted that you can create an interesting tweedy fabric in seed stitch by using the natural occurrence of the purl stitches as an asset.

COMBINATION OF COLOR AND STITCH PATTERNS

Textural colored striping can be worked by combining simple stitches, such as stockinette stitch, with garter stitch. Two garter-stitch rows worked in a contrasting color will create a ridge that stands away from the main-color stockinette stitch fabric. You can also make dash lines as a contrasting stripe by knitting one row in one color and then working a knit 5, purl 5 pattern in a second color.

Child's Cabled Cardigan

SIZES

Child's 2 (4, 6, 8)

FINISHED MEASUREMENTS

Chest at underarm (buttoned) 32 (34, 36, 38)"
Length from shoulder 13 (14, 15, 16)"

MATERIALS

- 2 skeins Lion Brand *Babysoft®* in #099 Cream (4 oz, 367 yds; 60% acrylic, 40% nylon)
- Size 6 (4 mm) knitting needles, or size to get gauge
- Cable needle and stitch markers
- Five ¾" buttons

GAUGE

22 sts and 30 rows = 4" (10 cm) in stockinette stitch (knit on right side; purl on wrong side) using size 6 needles.
Be sure to check your gauge.

NOTES

1. See abbreviations on page 71.
2. Place markers at beginning and end of each cable until pattern becomes familiar.
3. For ease in working, circle the numbers that apply to your size.

CABLE PATTERN (2/2 RIGHT CABLE)

Over 4 stitches **Rows 1 and 3 (right side)** Knit. **Rows 2 and 4** Purl. **Row 5** Slip 2 sts onto cable needle and hold in back, knit 2 sts, knit 2 sts from cable needle. **Rows 6 and 8** Purl. **Rows 7 and 9** Knit. **Row 10** Purl. Repeat rows 1–10 for cable pattern.

REVERSE STOCKINETTE STITCH

Purl on right side; knit on wrong side.

BUTTONHOLES

For each buttonhole, bind off 2 sts on first row and cast on 2 sts over the bound-off sts on next row.

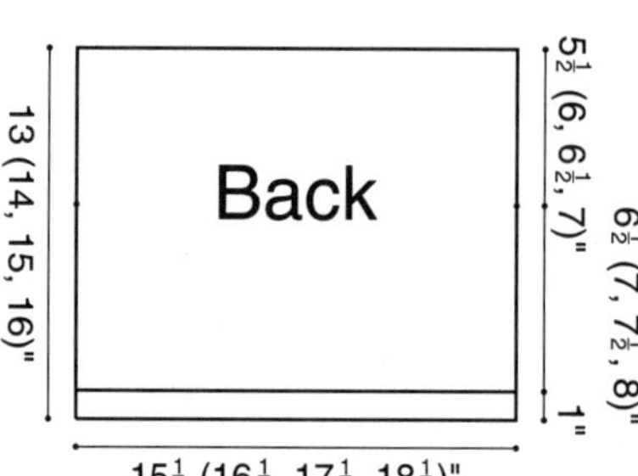

BACK

Cast on 86 (92, 98, 102) sts.
Row 1 K1, *k1, p1; repeat from * to last st, k1. **Row 2** P1, *k1, p1; repeat from * to last st, p1. Repeat last 2 rows 3 rows more. Begin for cable pattern as follows: **Row 1 (right side)** P9 (10, 11, 12), [work row 1 of cable pattern, p6 (7, 8, 8)] twice, [work row 1 of cable pattern, p8 (8, 8, 9)] twice, [work row 1 of cable pattern, p6 (7, 8, 8)] twice, work row 1 of cable pattern, p9 (10, 11, 12). **Row 2 (wrong side)** K9 (10, 11, 12), [work row 2 of cable pattern, k6 (7, 8, 8)] twice, [work row 2 of cable pattern, k8 (8, 8, 9)] twice, [work row 2 of cable pattern,

k6 (7, 8, 8)] twice, work row 2 of cable pattern, k9 (10, 11, 12). Continue in this way working rows 1 and 2 and continuing to work 10 rows of cable pattern. When piece measures 7½ (8, 8½, 9)" from beg, place marker for underarm. Continue to work even until piece measures 13 (14, 15, 16)" from beginning. Bind off all sts.

LEFT FRONT

Cast on 44 (47, 50, 52) sts. Work rib as for back for a total of 8 rows. Begin for cable pattern as follows: **Row 1 (right side)** P9 (10, 11, 12), [work row 1 of cable patterns, p6 (7, 8, 8)] twice, work row 1 of cable pattern, p11 (11, 11, 12). **Row 2 (wrong side)** K11 (11, 11, 12), [work row 2 of cable pattern, k6 (7, 8, 8)] twice, work row 2 of cable pattern, k9 (10, 11, 12). Continue in this way working rows 1 and 2 and continuing to work 10 rows of cable pattern. When piece measures 7½ (8, 8½, 9)" from beg, place marker for underarm. Work even until piece measures 10½ (11½, 12½, 13½)" from beginning, ending with a right-side row.

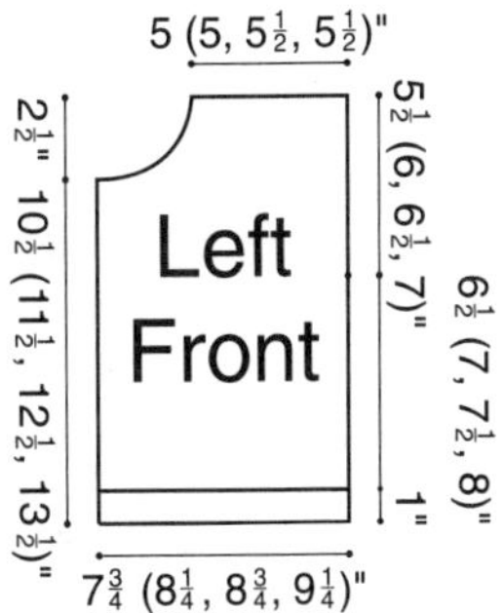

Shape Neck

Next row (wrong side) Bind off 7 (9, 9, 11), work to end. Continuing in pattern, bind off 2 sts at neck edge twice, then decrease 1 st at neck edge every other row 4 times. Work even on 29 (30, 33, 33) sts until same length as back. Bind off all sts.

RIGHT FRONT

Cast on 44 (47, 50, 52) sts. Work rib as for back for a total of 8 rows. Begin for cable pattern as follows: **Row 1 (right side)** P11 (11, 11, 12), [work row 1 of cable pattern, p6 (7, 8, 8)] twice, work row 1 of cable pattern, P9 (10, 11, 12). **Row 2 (wrong side),** K9 (10, 11, 12) [work row 2 of cable pattern, k6 (7, 8, 8)] twice, work row 2 of cable pattern, k11 (11, 11, 12). Continue in this way working rows 1 and 2 and continuing to work10 rows of cable pattern and when piece measures 7½ (8, 8½, 9)" from beg, place marker for underarm. Work even until piece measures 10½ (11½, 12½, 13½)" from beginning, ending with a wrong-side row.

Shape Neck

Next row (right side) Bind off 7 (9, 9, 11), work to end. Continuing in pattern, bind off 2 sts at neck edge twice, then decrease 1 st at neck edge every other row 4 times. Work even on 29 (30, 33, 33) sts until same length as back. Bind off all sts.

SLEEVES

Cast on 40 (44, 46, 48) sts. Work rib as for back for a total of 8 rows. Work in reverse

stockinette, increasing 1 stitch each edge every 6th row 10 (11, 14, 15) times, every 8th row 1 (1, 0, 0) times—(62, 68, 74, 78 sts). Work even until sleeve measures 11 (12, 13, 14)" from beg. Bind off loosely.

FINISHING

Sew shoulder seams, matching cables on front and back.

Neckband

With right side facing, pick up 20 sts to shoulder seam, 30 (34, 36, 40) sts to opposite shoulder seam, 20 to front edge—70 (74, 76, 80) sts. Work 1 rib as for back for 5 rows. Bind off all sts loosely in ribbing.

Left Front Band

With right side facing, pick up 65 (71, 77, 83) sts. Work in K1, p1 rib for 5 rows Bind off all sts in ribbing. Place markers ½" from top and bottom edges and 3 more evenly spaced between for buttonhole placement.

Buttonhole Band

Work as for front band, binding off for buttonholes on 3rd row and closing them on the 4th row. Complete as for left-front band. Sew sleeves to body between markers. Sew side and underarm seams. Sew on buttons. Weave in ends.

A color photo of this item can be found in the color insert, photo number 13

Cabled Pullover

SIZES

S (M, L, XL, XXL)

FINISHED MEASUREMENTS

Chest at underarm 40 (44, 46, 50, 54)"
Length from shoulder 24 (24, 25, 26, 26)"

MATERIALS

• 11 (12, 13, 14, 15) balls Classic Elite *La Gran* #1515 Seafoam (1½ oz, 90 yds; 76.5% mohair, 17.5% wool, 6% nylon)
• Sizes 8 and 9 (5 and 5.5 mm) knitting needles, or size to get gauge
• Cable needle and stitch markers

GAUGE

16 sts and 20 rows = 4" (10 cm) with larger needles in reverse stockinette stitch (purl on right side; knit on wrong side). *Be sure to check your gauge.*

NOTES

1. See abbreviations on page 71.
2. For ease in working, circle all numbers that pertain to your size.
3. When working decreases for front neck, work as follows: On wrong-side rows on first side: knit to last 3 sts, k2tog, kl; on second side, k1, k2tog. On right-side rows on first side: knit to last 3 sts, p2tog, p1; on second side, p1, p2tog.

CABLE PATTERN (OVER 10 STS)

Row 1 Knit 10. **Row 2** Purl 10. **Row 3** Slip next 5 sts onto a cable needle and leave in back of work. K5, then K5 from cable needle. **Row 4** Purl 10. **Row 5–12** Rep rows 1 and 2 a total of 4 times. Repeat rows 1–12 for cable pattern.

BACK

With smaller needles, cast on 81 (89, 93, 101, 109) sts. **Row 1 (RS)** K1, p1 across to last st, end K1. **Row 2 (WS)** P1, k1 across to last st, p1. Rep rows 1 and 2 for seed st for 1", decreasing 1 st and ending with a WS row—80 (88, 92, 100, 108) sts. Change to larger needles and rev St st, beg first row with a purl row. Work even until piece measures 24 (24, 25, 26, 26)" from beginning.

Shape Shoulders

Bind off 8 (9, 9, 10, 11) sts at beginning of next 4 rows, then 8 (10, 10, 12, 13) sts at beg of next 2 rows—32 (32, 36, 36, 38) sts. Bind off remaining sts.

FRONT

Cast on and work seed st as for back, dec 1 st on last row—80 (88, 92, 100, 108) sts. Change to larger needles. **Row 1 (RS)** Purl 35 (39, 41, 45, 49), place

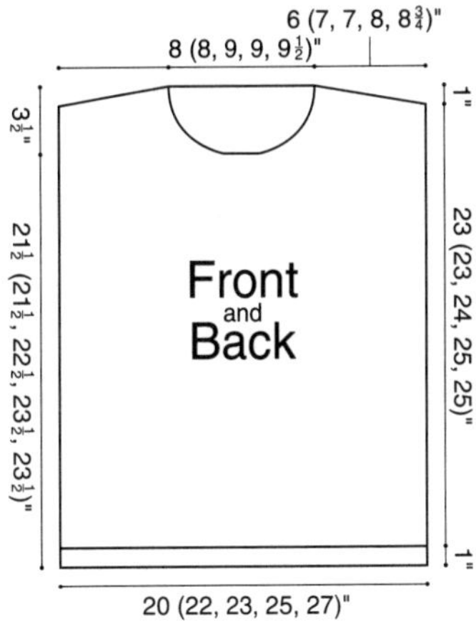

Cabled Pullover *(continued)*

marker, work cable pattern row 1 over 10 sts, place marker, purl to end. **Row 2 (WS)** Knit 35 (39, 41, 45, 49), slip marker, work cable pattern row 2 over 10 sts, slip marker, knit to end. Repeat last 2 rows, slipping markers on each row and working 12 rows of cable pattern over center 10 sts. Continue until piece measures 21½ (21½, 22½, 23½, 23½)" from beg, ending with a WS row.

Shape Neck

Next row (RS) Purl 35 (39, 39, 43, 46) sts, join another ball of yarn and bind off next 10 (10, 14, 14, 16) sts, work to the end. Working both sides of the piece at the same time, decrease 1 st from each neck edge 11 times. (See note 3.) Work even until piece measures 24 (24, 25, 26, 26)" from beginning.

Shape Shoulders

Bind off 8 (9, 9, 10, 11) sts at beginning of next 4 rows, then 8 (10, 10, 12, 13) sts at beg of next 2 rows.

SLEEVES

With smaller needles, cast on 35 (35, 37, 41, 45) sts. **Row 1 (RS)** K1, p1 across row to last st, k1. **Row 2 (WS)** P1, k1 across row to last st, p1. Repeat rows 1 and 2 for seed st for 1". Change to larger needles and rev St st. **Inc row (RS)** P1, inc 1 st in next st. purl to last 2 sts, inc 1 st in next st, p1. Repeat inc row every other row 3 times, then 4th row 15 (17, 18, 18, 18) times—73 (77, 81, 85, 89) sts. Work even until piece measures 17 (18, 18, 18, 18)" from beg. Bind off all sts.

FINISHING

Block pieces. Sew right shoulder seam.

Neckband

With right side facing and larger needles, pick up 76 (76, 86, 86, 90) sts around neck edge. Beg with a purl row on the WS. Work in St st (k on RS, p on WS) for 2½". Bind off. Sew left shoulder and neckband seam. Mark underarm down 9 (9½, 10, 10⅓, 11)" from shoulders on front and back. Sew in sleeves between markers. Sew sleeve and side seams.

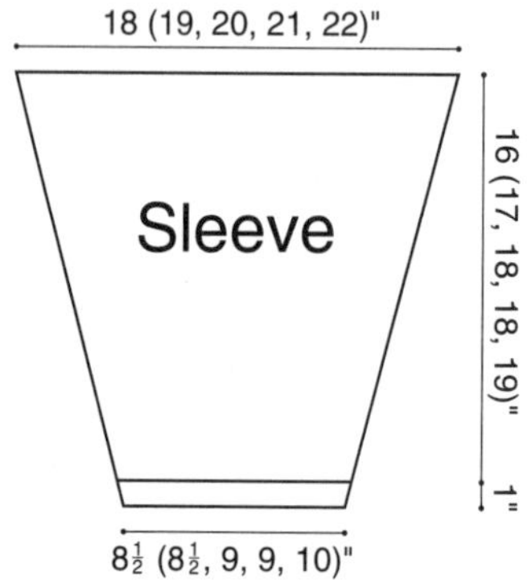

A color photo of this item can be found in the color insert, photo number 14

Striped Sailor Pullover

SIZES
Child's 18 months (2, 4, 6)

FINISHED MEASUREMENTS
Chest 26 (28, 30, 32)"
Length from shoulder 14 (15, 16, 17)"

MATERIALS
• 1 skein each Lion Brand *Babysoft*® in #111 Navy Blue (A) and #099 Cream (B) (4 oz, 367 yds; 60% acrylic, 40% nylon)
• Size 6 (4 mm) knitting needles or size to get gauge
• Four 1" (25 mm) buttons

GAUGE
22 sts and 30 rows = 4" (10 cm) in stockinette stitch (knit on right side, purl on wrong side) with size 6 needles.
Be sure to check your gauge.

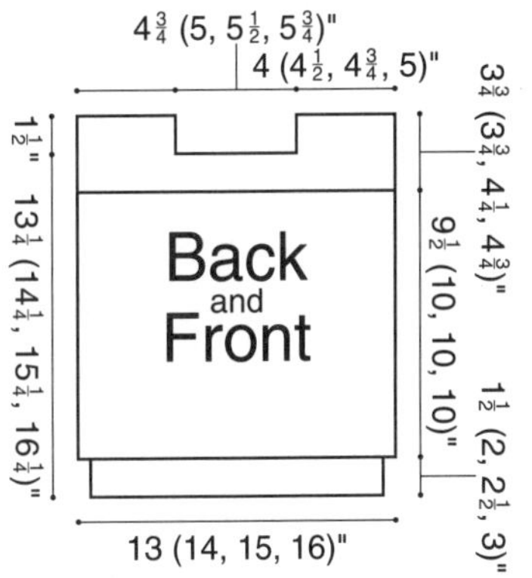

NOTE
See abbreviations on page 71.

STRIPE PATTERN
Working in stockinette stitch:
Rows 1–6 in A.
Rows 7–16 in B.

BACK
With A, cast on 74 (78, 82, 90) sts. **Row 1** K1, *k2, p2; repeat from * to last st, k1. **Row 2** P1, *k2, p2; repeat from * to last st, p1. Repeat these two rows until ribbing measures 1½ (2, 2½, 3)", ending with a right-side row. Purl 1 row. Change to B (do not cut A, but carry yarn up side of work) and work 6 (10, 10, 10) rows of stockinette stitch. Change to A and work 4 complete pattern stripes.

Yoke
Change to A and knit 1 row. Work in ribbing rows 1 and 2 as for lower edge until yoke measures 2¼ (2½, 2¾, 3¼)".

Shape Neck
Work across 24 (25, 26, 29) sts, join new yarn, bind off center 26 (28, 30, 32) sts, work to end. Working both sides at the same time work until yoke measures 3 (3, 3½, 4)". Bind off all stitches loosely in ribbing.

FRONT
Work as for back until yoke measures 3¼ (3¼, 3¾, 4¼)".

Buttonhole Placement (Left Shoulder)
Rib on 5 (5, 6, 7) sts, yarn over, k2tog, rib 10 (11, 10, 11) sts, yarn over, k2tog, rib 5 (5, 6, 7) sts. Work right shoulder reverse buttonhole placement. Work even in ribbing, complete as for back.

SLEEVES
With A, cast on 38 (42, 46, 46) sts. Work ribbing as for back 2", ending with a right-side row. Purl 1 row in A. Change to B and work 6 (4, 6, 4) rows in B in stockinette st, then work 4 (5, 5, 6) repeats of stripe pattern, AT SAME TIME, increas-

Striped Sailor Pullover (continued)

ing 1 st each side every 6th row 11 (12, 14, 15) times—60 (66, 74, 76) sts. End working 6 rows A. Bind off all sts.

FINISHING

Lap 1½" of front over back at shoulders, sew these side rib bands together. AT SAME TIME, place a marker at each edge when garment measures 8 (8½, 9, 9½)" from beg for underarm. Sew sleeve to sweater between markers. Sew side and underarm sleeves. Sew on buttons. Weave in ends.

A color photo of this item can be found in the color insert, photo number 15

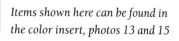

Items shown here can be found in the color insert, photos 13 and 15

Socks

SIZE

Average adult woman (size can be altered by making leg and foot longer or shorter than given measurements)

MATERIALS

- 1 ball Lion Brand *Wool-Ease® Sportweight* #152 Oxford Grey (5 oz, 435 yds; 80% acrylic, 20% wool)
- One set of four size 5 (3.75 mm) double-pointed knitting needles, or size to get gauge
- Yarn circle marker

GAUGE

21 sts and 28 rows = 4" (10 cm) with size 5 needles in stockinette stitch (knit every round).

Be sure to check your gauge.

SOCKS

Loosely cast on 48 stitches onto 1 needle. Divide so that there are 16 sts on each of 3 needles. Join first and last needles, placing a marker in the fabric between the needles to identify the beginning of the round.

Round 1 *K2, p2; repeat from * around. Repeat last round until cuff of sock measures 7" from beginning and ending at marker.

Divide Stitches to Begin Heel

Next round Knit 12, slip next 24 sts onto 2 needles (instep that remains unworked during this process), slip last 12 sts onto the needle with the 12 knitted stitches.

Heel Flap

Row 1 (wrong side) Slip first stitch, purl to end—24 sts.

Row 2 Slip first stitch, knit to end. Repeat last 2 rows until flap measures 2 ¼", ending with row 2.

Turning Heel

Next Row Slip first stitch, purl to center, p2, p2tog, p1, turn piece. Slip first stitch, k5, ssk, k1, turn piece. Slip first stitch, p6, p2tog, p1, turn. Slip first stitch, k7, ssk, k1, turn. Slip first stitch, p8, p2tog, p1, turn. Slip first stitch, k9, ssk, k1, turn. Slip first stitch, p10, p2tog, p1, turn. Slip first stitch, k11, ssk, k1, turn. Slip first stitch, p12, p2tog, turn. Slip first stitch, k13, ssk—14 sts.

Instep

With the right side facing, pick up 16 stitches along the left side of the heel flap, transfer the center 24 stitches to one needle and knit across those stitches. With another needle, pick up 16 stitches along the right heel flap as you did on the left side; using the same needle, knit across the next 7 stitches. This is the new beginning of your rounds. You will now have 23 stitches on 2 needles and 24 on the instep needle. Knit 1 round. **Next Round** Knit across first needle to last 3 stitches, k2tog, k1; k24 on 2nd needle; k1, ssk, k to end of 3rd needle. Repeat last 2 rounds until 48 sts remain.

Foot

Work even by knitting every round until foot measures 7" or 2" short of desired length, ending at the marker for beginning of round.

Socks (continued)

Shape Toe

Next round Knit to last 3 stitches of first needle, k2tog, k1; k1, ssk, knit to last 3 stitches of 2nd needle, k2tog, k1; k1, ssk, work to end of 3rd needle. Knit 1 rnd. Repeat last 2 rounds twice more, then work decrease rounds only until 12 stitches remain. Break yarn, leaving approximately an 8" tail.

Finishing

Thread a large-eyed yarn needle and run through the remaining stitches twice to close toe. Work ends into inside of sock.

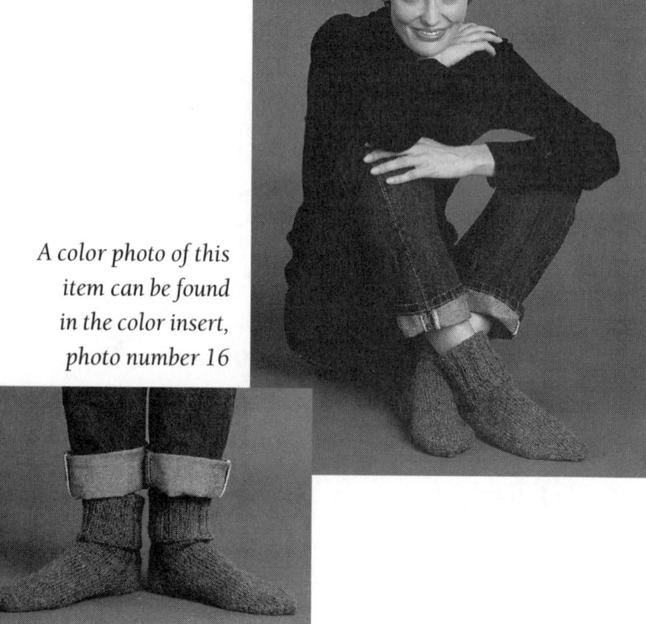

A color photo of this item can be found in the color insert, photo number 16

Easy Strip Throw

SIZE

50" x 54" including edging

MATERIALS

• 4 skeins each Lion Brand *Homespun*® #302 Colonial (A) and 4 skeins #320 Regency (B) (6 oz, 185 yds; 98% acrylic, 2% polyester)
• Size 10 (6 mm) knitting needles or size to get gauge
• Size J-10 (6 mm) crochet hook

GAUGE

12 sts and 24 rows = 4" in garter stitch (knit every row). *Be sure to check your gauge.*

NOTES

1. See abbreviations on page 71.
2. Make 4 panels using color A and 3 panels using color B.

PANEL

Cast on 22 sts. Work in garter stitch until piece measures 53" from beginning. Bind off. For easier finishing, make sure that each panel has the same number of rows by counting the ridges.

FINISHING

With right sides of 2 panels (1 color A, 1 color B) together and using color B and crochet hook, chain 1 through both layers at right corner edge. Work 1 single crochet in each garter-stitch "valley" through both layers along sides of panels to end, 1 single crochet in end stitches. Join all 7 panels together in this manner following chart, alternating panel colors.

Edging

With right side facing, join B at top right corner of afghan with chain 1. *Work 1 row single crochet evenly across, 3 single crochet in corner stitch, 1 single crochet in each garter stitch "valley" along side, 3 single crochet in corner stitch. Repeat from *, ending join with slip stitch in chain 1. Fasten off and weave in loose ends.

A color photo of this item can be found in the color insert, photo number 17

12

Branching Out

Now that you're a full-fledged knitter, you are ready for more challenges. You'll want to learn more than just the basics. For example, you probably want to experiment with new techniques, substitute different yarns in projects, and come up with ideas of your own. Where do you begin? Every time you work on a new project, you expand your horizons. You can learn a great deal by just experimenting and trying new things.

One great reason to knit is to produce one-of-a-kind items, individualized with your own touches. You pick the color and the yarn, and then make something to suit your taste and style. Even the most straightforward pattern can be personalized in countless ways. You'll find that even if you were to make the same sweater a dozen times, you could come up with a dozen completely different-looking garments. There are any number of ways to change a basic sweater or, as a matter of fact, anything that you knit. We'll explore several options for expanding your horizons in this chapter. With practice, you'll master new techniques and learn how to ascertain what will work and what won't in any given situation.

Using Your Pattern as a Jumping-Off Point

You, like even the most experienced knitters, will probably prefer to use a pattern when you knit. This doesn't mean that you are required to follow the instructions exactly as they are written. Rather, your pattern will become a framework from which you can deviate so that you create a sweater (or other knitted item) that will truly be yours.

Your experience level will be a big factor in deciding what type of changes you want to make to a pattern. Knowing whether or not your ideas make sense and will enhance the design will come with practice. You may want to get the opinion of a knitting friend or a professional before attempting a major change to a pattern.

Alterations

Garment patterns are written for a person with average proportions, and the pattern writers make certain assumptions that don't work for every body type. You may be either shorter or taller than the average person, or you may be shorter or longer just in certain parts of your body (e.g., short- or long-waisted).

The length of a given sweater may also be dictated by a certain fashion that is in vogue at the moment; it might be cropped at the midriff or descend to the hip, or even reach tunic length. However, you may not like cropped sweaters (or tunics) and may want to change the sweater length to better fit your personal style. It's always good to try on a few sweaters of your own to find ones that you like and take their measurements.

It's usually fairly simple to change the length of a sweater body or to change the sleeve length. These two adjustments greatly change the look of any sweater. However, changing the width of a garment is more challenging than altering its length. In order to make a sweater narrower or wider, you must change the number of stitches in the pattern or somehow adjust the gauge, and possibly both. These are major changes, and, while not difficult to do, the math involved is beyond the scope of this book. Should you want to alter the width of a sweater, the information is readily available in sweater design books.

Read more on sizing and adjusting patterns to fit in Chapter 10, page 93.

The Yarn Choice Is Yours

When you find a pattern in a magazine or book, the yarn listed in the pattern is the one that was used to make the sweater in the picture. You may decide not to use that yarn for the project for a whole variety of reasons.

The easiest change that you can make when buying yarn is to

get a different color of the same brand. You don't want a red sweater like the one in the picture? Buy purple yarn instead!

If you are going to use an entirely different yarn, the two key points to note in the pattern are the gauge at which the original yarn knits up and the fiber type and amount of twist in that original yarn. The gauge gives you some idea of the weight of the yarn. For example, if the pattern has a gauge of 20 stitches to 4" (10 cm), you can assume that it is approximately a standard worsted-weight yarn.

The fiber content and amount of twist of a yarn greatly affect the look and drape of your finished garment. If you love the look of a sweater shown in soft, hairy mohair, you won't get that look with a mercerized cotton or flat wool yarn. You can change yarns, but choosing one that has mohair or simulates a mohair look would be a better solution.

Before making a change, reread the information in Chapter 1 on yarns on page 14. This will give you a point of reference for understanding yarn weights and types.

Then, prior to beginning the project, knit a good-sized gauge swatch in the stitch pattern you'll be using to see how the substituted yarn reacts and drapes.

Stitch Patterns

Changing stitch patterns for a project can be very simple or it can be complex, depending on the similarities between the original stitch pattern and the new one. Making a wise choice takes a bit of experimenting.

Stitch patterns change not only the texture, but also sometimes the width and length of knit fabric. By this point you have knitted garter stitch (knit every row) and stockinette stitch (knit on right-side rows; purl on wrong-side rows) and have seen the differences between the two. Garter stitch is very textured and compact, while stockinette stitch is flat and slightly elongated.

When changing from one stitch pattern to another, always knit sizeable swatches of both stitches to see if they have the same width and length dimensions. For example, an allover cable pattern will pull the fabric in widthwise and will require additional stitches to make a piece of fabric the same width as one knitted in stockinette stitch.

Since stitch patterns are described in terms of "multiples" (i.e., a k2 p2 rib has a multiple of 4), try to substitute a stitch pattern with the same multiple as the original; mathematically, it will fit into your total garment stitches without any changes. For example, you might change from stockinette stitch to seed stitch (Row 1: Knit 1, purl 1 across. Row 2: Purl 1, knit 1 across).

Invest in a good anthology of knitting-stitch patterns, which often feature hundreds of pattern options. You are sure to find stitch patterns that suit your needs.

Edges

Knit 1, purl 1 and knit 2, purl 2 ribbings are not the only options you have for edging a garment or piece. The practical function of an edging (especially on a stockinette-stitch body) is to keep the edges from rolling up.

There are a number of stitches that are non-rolling and are ideal for edgings. On the other hand, you can opt to use the propensity of stockinette stitch to roll to your advantage.

Keep in mind that most edges are worked on needles one or two sizes smaller than the body of the piece. Tighter ribbings that cinch the waist or wrist are also worked on fewer stitches than the body. If you just want an edge that lies flat but doesn't pull in, you can work it with the same-size needles as for the body.

OTHER KNIT/PURL OPTIONS

You can work a number of combinations of knit and purl stitches to make a ribbing. You might try a knit 3, purl 3 ribbing or a knit 3, purl 2 ribbing for a more gutsy edge.

Keep in mind that any stitch pattern where the knit stitches greatly outnumber the purl stitches might cause the edge to roll. For example, a knit 5, purl 2 ribbing may not be appropriate as an edge ribbing depending on the yarn used, the depth of the ribbing, and/or the width of the piece.

ROLLED EDGE

If you begin your piece with a number of rows of stockinette stitch, the edge will naturally curl out, and you will have a rolled edging. You can work this rolled edge in the same color as the main body of the project or in a contrasting color.

GARTER-STITCH EDGE

Garter stitch is a good non-rolling stitch. It tends to be wider than stockinette, so is better worked with fewer stitches and on a smaller needle.

MOCK CABLE EDGE

This pattern is worked with a multiple of 4 stitches plus 2 extra stitches at the end.

To make the mock cable (a left twist over 2 stitches), reach behind the first stitch on the left-hand needle and knit the second stitch, leaving it on the needle; then knit the first stitch and drop both stitches from the needle.

Row 1 (RS) Purl 2, *knit 2, purl 2; repeat from * to end. **Rows 2 and 4 (WS)** Knit 2, *purl 2, knit 2; repeat from * to end. **Row 3 (RS)** Purl 2, *work left twist over 2 stitches, purl 2; repeat from * to end.

Repeat these 4 rows for mock cable pattern, ending pattern with row 4.

Color Knitting

Although color-knitting technique could fill several chapters, we chose to include it in an abbreviated fashion. It is not a beginning technique, but it is one with which you will certainly want to familiarize yourself.

There are two very different methods for working with more than one color in a row. You can carry both yarns along the row (stranding, or Fair Isle technique) or you can work each section of the fabric separately, each using its own yarn source, without carrying the colors along the back of the fabric (intarsia). Your pattern will usually tell you which method you should use—it depends largely on whether you are working small, equally spaced patterns (stranding) or large, often "picture-like" areas of color (intarsia).

STRANDING

When you carry both colors along at one time, keep the yarns not in use loose so that you don't pucker the fabric. Periodically, spread out the stitches that you have just knitted to keep the stranding yarn from being pulled too tightly.

INTARSIA

When you come to a different-colored section, drop the first yarn and bring the new color up from under the first yarn, thereby linking the two yarns. It is very important to twist the yarns on the wrong side to prevent holes from occurring in the fabric.

With a number of yarn strands at the back of the work, it is important to have some sort of organizational system to keep them from becoming tangled as you knit. Rather than working from a full ball of yarn, there are several options to more effectively handle your yarn. You can make a simple butterfly of yarn or wrap yarn around a plastic bobbin specially designed for this purpose. Some knitters swear by using shorter lengths of yarn that simply dangle free in the back of the piece and are easy to untangle.

TWISTING YARNS

When you are stranding, it is important to twist the working yarn and the yarn that is not in use around each other to avoid long, loose floats at the back of the work.

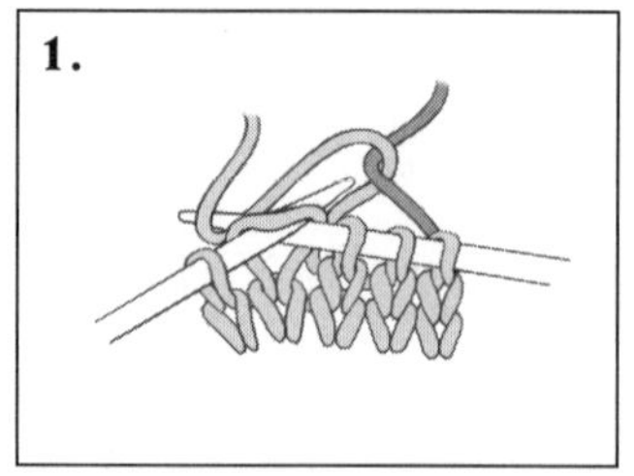

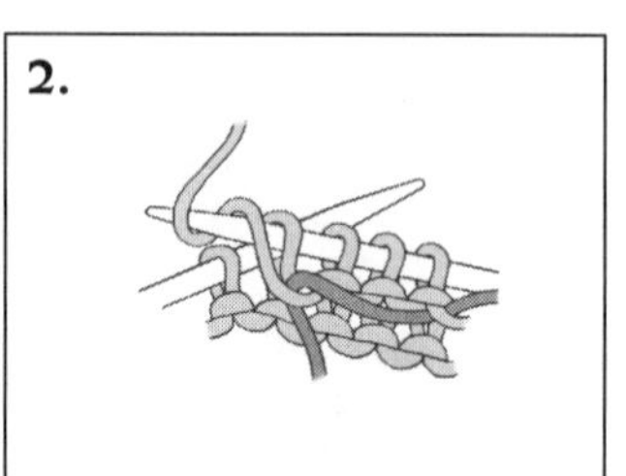

When working in intarsia, you will twist the yarns in this fashion but not carry the color not in use.

1. When working a knit row, bring the working color over the carried color to lock the strand in place on the back of the work and knit the next stitch as shown.

2. On the purl side, bring the carried color over the working color and purl the stitch.

Necklines

One of the easiest changes you can make to a neck is to alter the length and shape of the band. You can change a basic crewneck into a turtleneck by making a longer neckband that folds over. You can separate the neckband in the center and create a polo collar. To have a polo collar that folds nicely, work the last couple of inches using a larger needle. You can also use a different stitch on the neckband. For example, you could replace all plain ribbed bands (neck, bottom, and wrist bands) with a simple cable rib or a lacy rib.

Another option would be to work the neckband in a contrasting-colored yarn. For a neater edge, pick up from the neckline fabric in the same color as you used for the body and change to the contrasting color on the second round. Remember, if you are doing a ribbed band, the color change will be much cleaner if you work the first row of the contrasting color in stockinette stitch.

For a quick, yet simple neckline, work a simple crocheted edge rather than a knitted band.

You can also change the shape of the neckline, say from a crewneck to a V-neck. It isn't difficult to do, but requires mathematical calculations, which are beyond the scope of this book. Refer to one of the many excellent books on sweater design.

Buttonholes

Buttonholes are easy, and working them on a cardigan is essential. Make the band where the buttons will be sewn first; calculate the placement and identify and mark the spots where the buttons will be placed.

There are many ways to make a buttonhole. The easiest one is to work to the place where you wish to make the buttonhole, knit two stitches together, and work a yarn-over. Even though you can't alter the size of the buttonhole, it usually works out fine if the buttons you choose are in proportion to the yarn. For example, when using a very fine yarn, you will get a smaller buttonhole than when using a thicker yarn.

The second-easiest buttonhole to work is a horizontal buttonhole. Bind off a number of stitches and cast them back on, using a firm tension in the same spot on the next row. You can alter the size of your buttonhole using this method. If the number of bind-off stitches is not given, err on the side of smaller rather than larger, as knitted fabric stretches. If you find your buttonhole a bit too large, you can stitch one end slightly closed.

Pockets

Pockets in knits (especially jackets and coats) add a practical dimension to a garment. The two basic types are patch pockets (sewn onto the outside of the fabric) or set-in pockets (which have a pocket lining).

Naturally, a patch pocket is the easiest to make, as you simply knit a pocket and sew it to the piece. Take care to line up the pockets carefully. Use the lower edge and the side or front edges as a guide. This is especially helpful if you are placing two pockets on a piece. Neatly sew the pocket on with the same-color yarn as used for the body to make the stitching less noticeable.

Making set-in pockets is a four-step process:

1. Make a pocket lining and place live stitches on a holder.

2. Work to the position where you want to place the pocket and either bind off the same number of stitches as you have knitted for the pocket lining or put them on a holder. Take the pocket-lining stitches from the holder and line them up in back of the fabric and work across those stitches in pattern. Continue until you finish the piece.

3. When you have completed the piece, place the stitches left on hold or bound off and work a pocket edge such as a few rows of ribbing. Bind off the edging and sew the edge sides to the front. Alternatively, if you have bound off the top stitches, you can just crochet across the bind-off for a neat edge.

4. Neatly stitch the pocket lining to the inside of the garment, leaving the top edge open.

Six additional patterns that involve the techniques you have learned in Part I are presented in Chapter 23 of this book. But first, let's delve into the world of knitting.

PART II

The World of Knitting

13

Knitting for Charity

As you navigate the world of knitting, from the Internet to the knitting guilds, from retreats to societies of friends and neighbors who frequent yarn shops, you are likely to encounter knitting for charity. Over the years, knitters have embraced the causes of knitting for the troops (in every war from the Revolutionary War to the war in Bosnia), for hospital patients, for those experiencing a crisis (victims of floods and earthquakes), and for the underprivileged and homeless. When you make donations through an established charity, you play a part in providing a consistent flow of items to a chosen cause.

Knitting charities are usually run entirely by volunteers. From the organizers to those who knit and distribute the hand-knits, these groups tend to be composed of knitters who have been moved to address a cause and have created an organization the same way they knit—one step at a time, with the work of their own hands.

A hand-knitted donation has unique qualities. First, there is the warmth provided by knits, both practically, in keeping out the cold, and in the emotional association of comfort, closeness, and love. Unlike donations of used clothing, or even money, something that was hand-knitted for a hospital or homeless shelter expresses the idea of "giving of oneself" in a way that only volunteer work can do. Hand-knits carry with them the character and efforts of the giver. From selecting the type and color of yarn and the pattern, to spending time creating a one-of-a-kind blanket or hat, a personal touch permeates every aspect of a hand-knit gift.

As anyone who has inherited a hand-knitted or crocheted piece from a family member can attest, there is a sense that something of the knitter remains with the garment. The evenness of the stitches as well as the imperfections in the fabric speak to the human hand behind the effort. When we realize that a throw or sweater was made over a period of days, weeks, or months, we can visualize the maker spending time with it as it moved from her home to her tote bag and traveled with her on the train to a doctor's appointment or a business meeting.

The generosity of a hand-made gift is not lost on the recipients. One woman, whose baby might otherwise have gone home from the hospital in only a diaper, received a set of booties, a blanket, a sweater, and a hat. "I look at the beautiful work that someone poured her heart into and it touches me to think someone did this for me," she said.

Joan Hamer, the unofficial archivist of knitting charities, puts it this way: "Many people who are poor, alone, or suffering a loss may not feel good about themselves at the time that they receive a donation." Receiving something that was handmade by another person has a special power, according to Hamer. "They think, someone out there gave their time to make this, and it helps their self-esteem."

Joan created the special role for herself of communicating about knitting charities in April 1993, when she received a notice that the *Spring Valley Knitting Club,* a newsletter about charity knitting, was going to stop publishing. She wrote to the publisher, Lois Greene, asking if there was anything she could do to help. Lois, unable to continue because of other commitments, gave Joan the 200-name mailing list and the suggestion that she "make it her own." Joan asked her mentor, author Meg Swansen, for advice about taking on the project and Meg counseled her to do it. In 1993 Joan launched the newsletter with only 28 subscriptions. Today, with about 1000 subscriptions and a Web site, Joan puts scores of hours a month into the *Pine Meadow Knitting News,* a project she describes as continually evolving. Every issue features a story on at least one charity. Her Web site, www.fibergypsy.com/pmkn, has free patterns for charity knitting and highlights of back issues. Joan has also compiled a list of charities collected on the Internet at www.woolworks.org, a site that offers a state-by-state listing of knitting charities including contact information and a description of their missions.

Joan works for her church three days a week, as well as designing knitwear for yarn companies and magazines, when she is not

1
Cell Phone Holder
(pattern on p. 36)

2
Tie Hat
(pattern on p. 37)

3
Striped Stocking Cap
(pattern on p. 40)

4
Easy, Bright Ribbed Pullover
(pattern on p. 43)

5
Scarves
(patterns on pp. 49, 50, 51, 53, 54)

6
Lace Rib Scarf
(pattern on p. 52)

7
Cabled Scarf
(pattern on p. 54)

8
Increased Decreased Baby Blanket
(pattern on p. 63)

9
Garter-Stitch Vest
(pattern on p. 80)

10
Sleeveless T-Neck
(pattern on p. 82)

11
Rolled Neck Raglan Pullover with Hat
(pattern on p. 84)

12
Easy Cardigan
(pattern on p. 87)

13
Child's Cabled Cardigan
(pattern on p. 120)

14
Cabled Pullover
(pattern on p. 123)

15
Striped Sailor
(pattern on p. 125)

Striped Sailor, with
Child's Cable Cardigan
(shown in photo 13)
(patterns on pp. 120 and 125)

16
Socks
(pattern on p. 127)

17
Easy Strip Throw
(pattern on p. 129)

19
Baby Soft 'n' Seamless Cardigan
(pattern on p. 151)

18
Preemie Caps
(pattern on p. 149)

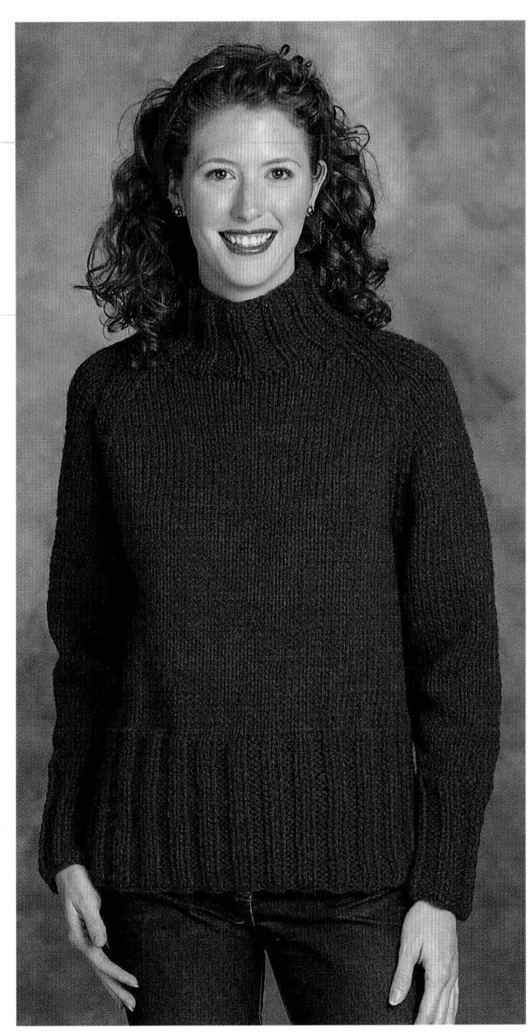

20
Deep Rib Pullover
(pattern on p. 234)

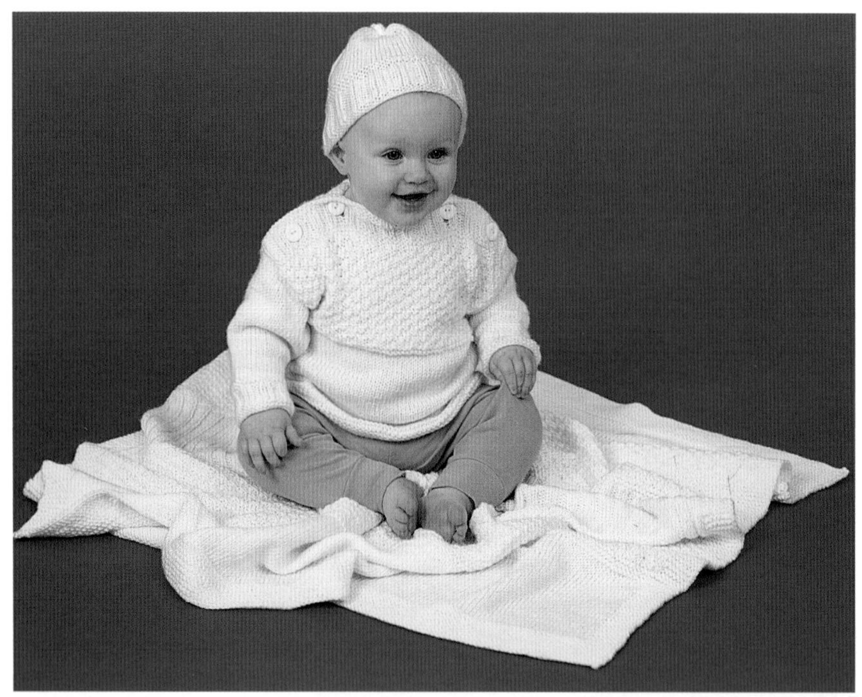

21
Baby Guernsey Set
(pattern on p. 238)

22
V-neck Bicolor Tunic
(pattern on p. 241)

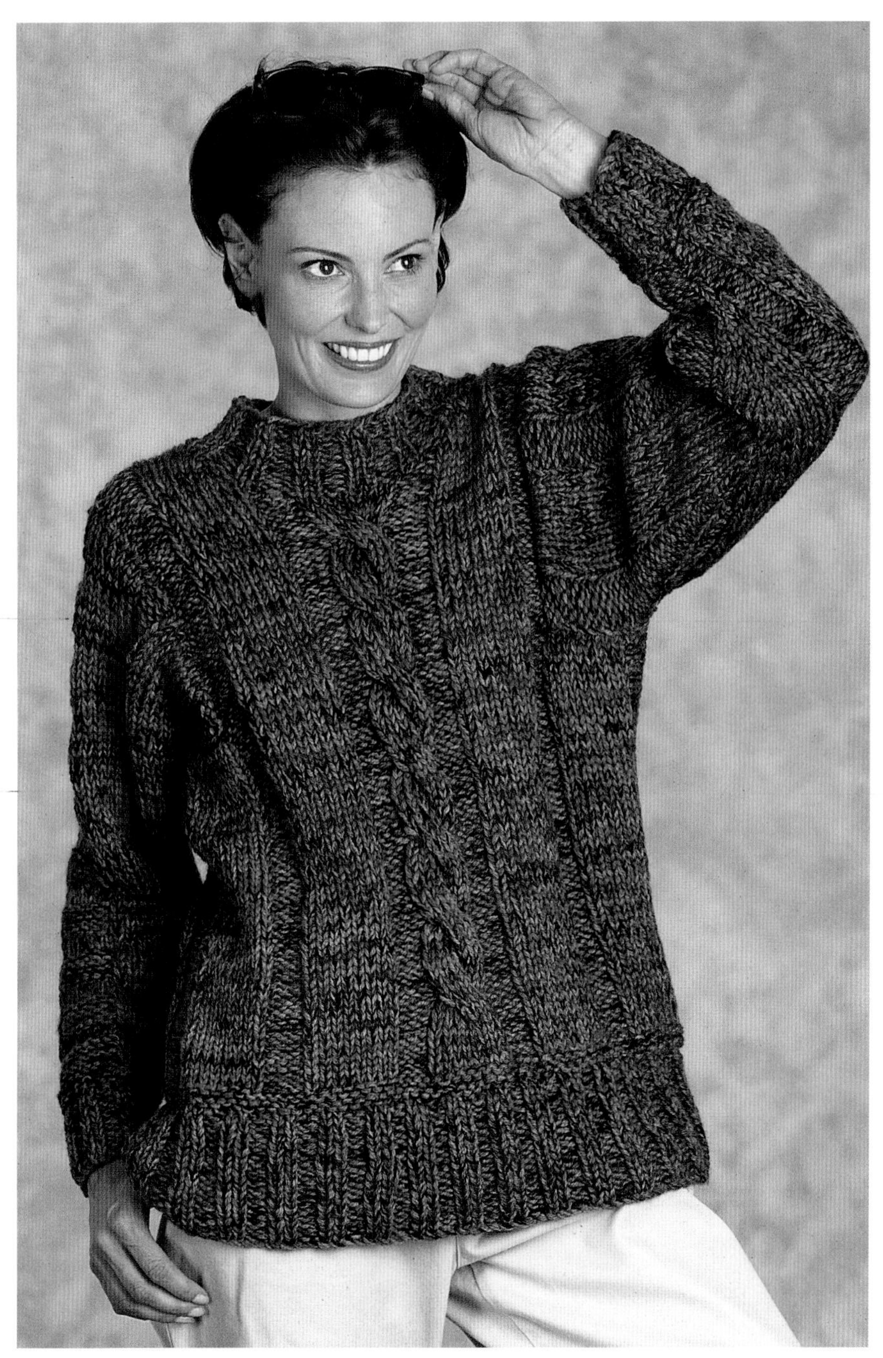

23
Center-Cable Pullover
(pattern on p. 243)

Bias Hat
(pattern on p. 247)

24
Luxury Shawl and Scarf
(pattern on p. 246)

donating her time communicating with knitters across the country about knitting charities. "I have been dealing with charity knitting for almost ten years now and it is a very rewarding experience, not only for the person who receives a gift, but for the knitter," she says. "Like many people, I just want to give something back to others."

Joan has seen the ways in which people who knit for charities can become frustrated. "Many charitable organizations are run by volunteers, or by one person with a limited amount of time to devote to this work." She says that when the amount of donations is substantial, it takes a good chunk of time and money to respond to each giver individually. "Sometimes this is simply not possible. This doesn't mean that the gifts were not appreciated." To ensure that the experience of knitting for charity is satisfying to both the giver and receiver, Joan offers this list of tips for charity knitters.

1. Contact the charity before you begin to work. Make sure that it is still in existence, that the address is current. Find out about the organization's needs. Some charities, like Children in Common and Caps for Nepal, prefer garments made with wool. Others, like Christmas-at-Sea, prefer acrylics or washable blends that can survive industrial washing machines. Be careful to knit for the charity in mind by using appropriate fibers and colors. For example, bright or pastel colors are perfect for babies and children; dark colors may be more suitable for those in the military or homeless people trying not to draw attention to themselves. In addition, by contacting the organization, you will find out if their needs have changed or whether those needs fluctuate with the season. You can also get specific deadlines for items. This is especially important for holiday-driven charities.

2. Look in your own community for ways to help. Because knitted throws and garments are bulky and expensive to ship, many people donate their work at the local level to nearby charities. Contact hospitals, battered women's shelters, and organizations dealing with the homeless to see if you can donate directly to local groups. Donating directly to a local center in need also has its benefits: you can help your own community. Many charities, like Warm Up America!, encourage people to make donations in their own communities because it saves shipping and distribution costs. The charity itself offers project guidelines, patterns, and information about what volunteers are doing.

3. Provide a way for the organization to acknowledge your donation. Enclose a self-addressed, stamped postcard that the charity's organizer can just drop in the mail. Even if you aren't waiting for a pat on the back, you'll know the package reached its destination. You might also put a hang-tag on the item with your name and address so that recipients can write to you if they choose.

4. If you are personally delivering a donation, find out who at the organization should receive it. Get in touch with the director or find the appropriate contact person at the charity and deliver your goods directly to him or her. Joan tells of a time when hand-knitted baby items were delivered to the information desk of the hospital without instructions and the mystified employee handed them over to the gift shop for resale.

There are hundreds of organizations that collect and distribute hand-knitted and crocheted gifts. Most of the charities were started when one individual, moved by the needs of a group of people, organized fellow crafters to work on projects that could be distributed to those who could use them. Here are the stories of a few of those organizations and the individuals who run them.

Care Wear

Every day, in hospitals throughout the country, babies are born whose weight is more likely to be measured in ounces than pounds. Approximately half a million babies are born at 24–36 weeks of gestation or earlier each year. These premature babies, or "preemies," require special medical care and equipment, but one challenge—that of finding clothing small enough for these tiny babies—is met by volunteer knitters. It's nearly impossible to find clothing in stores that fits these babies, whose heads can be as small as a lemon and arms so thin that they fit through their father's wedding band (pattern page 149).

Care Wear, a charity that donates clothing for premature babies, was started by Bonnie Hagerman, a professor of home economics at Hood College in Maryland. She was inspired by a magazine article she read in 1991 about a group of women in Ohio who provided preemie clothing for a local hospital. Contacting hospitals in the Washington-Baltimore area where she lived, she discovered a pressing need for such garments. Before Care Wear, makeshift hats were made from cut-up socks, and the sleeves of ill-fitting garments had to be rolled up several times.

As a graduate of the Fashion Institute of Technology, Bonnie was able to design clothing and write patterns for hats that could fit babies too tiny for standard newborn sizes. Volunteers added special touches like pompoms to the hats and blankets designed with the colors of the local football team. The caps and booties not only provide the important health benefit of keeping the delicate babies warm, but they give the worried parents a lift by adding a whimsical and warm touch in an otherwise frightening environment of tubes and machines. In response to the need for a garment that could accommodate the tubes that are attached to so many preemies, Bonnie designed a kimono that closes and adjusts with a Velcro tab. Volunteers also make tiny mittens that help keep infants from pulling out stitches.

One particularly poignant need is burial gowns for premature babies. "In the past," Bonnie points out, "parents had to go to a local toy store to buy doll clothes to bury their baby in, passing by bassinettes and baby toys to find something appropriate. It only made the tragedy more difficult." Recognizing this, Care Wear provides handmade burial gowns as part of its donation.

The items that Care Wear provides have expanded beyond garments for preemies over the years. Finger puppets were developed for children who had to take finger-stick blood tests. Although some blood tests no longer require finger-sticks, children in hospitals still find the finger puppets comforting. Hand-knitted sweaters for stuffed animals are also offered to cheer up young children in the hospital.

Christmas-at-Sea

Barbara Clauson is the director of this program at the Seamen's Church Institute, which provides gift boxes to merchant seafarers who are out at sea on Christmas Day. There is a particular loneliness to being at sea at Christmas; the Christmas-at-Sea program aims to alleviate some of that loneliness. It was founded in 1917 as a program of the Seamen's Church Institute, a not-for-profit organization, and collects and distributes about 13,000 gifts each year to mariners from all over the world who pass through the ports of New York and New Jersey.

A ship will get a delivery of gift boxes only if there are enough gifts to hand out to the entire crew. Each of these boxes also contains personal items, such as a mirror, stationery, a sewing kit, or pen, along with the hand-knitted garment. The institute provides patterns, collects contributions, and sets standards for garments, including the requirement that they be washable in the industrial washers and dryers on the ships. Garments include a vest, watch cap and scarf set, or a pair of socks. River mariners receive a checkerboard pattern Mariner's Scarf (patterns pages 153–154). The Seafarer's Scarf is always given with a cap and is distributed to the mariners calling at the International Seafarers' Center in Port Newark.

Thousands of knitters in every state work throughout the year and volunteers at the institute assemble, inspect, count, acknowledge, store, and then pack the garments. Beginning in October, when a ship arrives in port, a ship visitor delivers packages for each member of the crew. They are stowed away until Christmas Day, where they are distributed as an important part of the Christmas festivities on the ship.

In one of the many thank-you notes written by recipients of the scarves, a captain writes:

> Crossing oceans, especially stormy ones at Christmas, can be depressing. We received our packages of presents, including your lovely knitting, from Seamen's Church Institute on the 13th of November and here we are more than halfway across the Pacific en route from Yokohama to Long Beach on Christmas. There is a loneliness in 40-knot winds and 35-foot seas that is difficult to express to those who have never experienced it. With this in mind, I would like to tell you how much we appreciated, at our little Christmas dinner, the knitted articles you made for us. The best gift is always the one you make yourself, and the fact that there are people in the world who will sit down and make things like these for merchant seamen they have never met is truly moving.

To knit a garment for the Christmas-at-Sea program, use one of the institute's approved patterns and machine-washable and dryable worsted-weight yarn, preferably in a dark, solid color. This type of yarn will hold up well in the industrial-sized washers and dryers on board a ship and will appeal to the recipients, who are usually men. Colors may be striped so that odds and ends of yarn can be used.

Warm Up America!

Started by Evie Rosen, this program has given over 70,000 afghans to people in crisis, from homeless people to communities devastated by floods or snow storms. To contribute to a Warm Up America! afghan, a knitter or crocheter creates a 7" x 9" square. A group of people from a religious or community organization may work together to make an afghan from the squares; they sew them together and then donate the afghan locally.

Warming Families

Started by a handful of volunteers in April 2000, Warming Families has donated hundreds of knitted garments to homeless and domestic-violence shelters. Volunteers contribute their work to local shelters for people who have been displaced from their homes. Dee Chouinard, the director of Warming Families, also works with a group of domestic-violence shelters that are considered "safe houses." Because their locations are kept confidential, Dee does not visit the shelters; instead she meets a staff person at a designated place to drop off the items. The Warming Families Web site, http://www.thefamily.com/charity/oneheartblankets.html, offers information about the foundation, which is a project under the umbrella of the One Heart Foundation, started by Alan Osmond (of the Osmond family).

Preemie Cap Patterns

The circumference of a premature baby's head varies from approximately 5½" to 10". All sizes within this range will fit most of the babies in a neonatal unit. Washable yarn of acrylic or blended fibers should be used in finer weights from lightweight to sportweight. Double-pointed needles are ideal, but not essential, because they avoid seams that could irritate the delicate skin of premature babies. If the hat is washed before donating, a mild hypoallergenic soap is recommended. Pack donations in plastic to keep them clean.

Basic Hat

MATERIALS

- 1 partial ball of light to medium weight yarn in one or more colors
- Size 6 (4 mm) needles (straight or double-pointed)
- Large-eyed yarn needle

NOTE

1. One skein of yarn will make a number of hats.

2. When working with double-pointed needles, join after casting on, taking care not to twist stitches.

HAT

Cast on the desired number of stitches. Work in knit 1, purl 1 ribbing for 1". Work in stockinette stitch (knit on right side; purl on wrong side) to suggested length.

Finishing

Cut yarn and draw through all stitches on needle with a tapestry needle and pull tightly. Knot to secure. Sew seam if using straight needles.

Optional

Make a small pompom or bow for the top. Secure well.

REGULAR INFANT SIZE

Cast on 74 stitches.
Rib for 1" and work in stockinette stitch for 6" to 6½".
Total length of hat: 7" to 7½".

FULL TERM

Cast on 66 stitches.
Rib for 1" and work in stockinette stitch for 5" to 5½". Total length of hat: 6" to 6½".

X-LARGE PREEMIE

Cast on 58 stitches.
Rib for 1" and work in stockinette stitch for 4½".
Total length of hat: 5½".

LARGE PREEMIE

Cast on 50 stitches.
Rib for 1" and work in stockinette stitch for 3½" to 4".
Total length of hat: 4½" to 5".

MEDIUM PREEMIE

Cast on 44 stitches.
Rib for 1" and work in stockinette stitch for 3" to 3½".
Total length of hat: 4" to 4½".

SMALL PREEMIE

Cast on 40 stitches.
Rib for 1" and work in stockinette stitch for 2½" to 3".
Total length of hat: 3½" to 4".

X-SMALL PREEMIE

Cast on 36 stitches.
Rib for 1" and work in stockinette stitch for 2½".
Total length of hat: 3½".

Preemie Caps

SIZE

Preemie caps should fit over an orange to be the correct size. For full-term newborns, the cap should fit over a grapefruit.

MATERIALS

- 1 skein Lion Brand *Jamie*® in #200 White (1¾ oz, 196 yds; 100% acrylic)
- Size 4 (3.5 mm) needles, or size to get gauge

GAUGE

30 stitches = 4" (10 cm) in stockinette stitch (knit on right side; purl on wrong side) using size 4 needles.

Be sure to check your gauge.

NOTES

1. See abbreviations on page 71.
2. One skein of yarn will make a number of hats.

RIBBED CAP

Cast on 72 sts. **Row 1** *K2, p2; repeat from * to end. Repeat last row until piece measures 2". Work even in stockinette stitch for 2½", ending with a wrong side row.

Work decreases

Row 1 (right side) *K4, k2tog; repeat from * to end. **Row 2 and all wrong-side rows** Purl. **Row 3** *K3, k2tog; repeat from * to end. **Row 5** *K2, k2tog; repeat from * to end. **Row 7** *K2tog; repeat from * to end. Cut yarn long enough to sew back seam and run through stitches on needle, pull up tight and sew seam. Add pompom if desired.

BASKETWEAVE HAT

Cast on 65 stitches.

Row 1 (right side) Knit. **Row 2** K5, *p5, k5; repeat from * to end. **Rows 3, 4, 7, 9, 11** Knit. **Rows 4 and 6** Repeat row 2. **Rows 8, 10, 12** P5, *k5, p5; repeat from * to end. Continue in pattern until piece measures 2½" from beginning, increasing 1 stitch on last row—66 stitches.

Work Decreases

Row 1 (right side) *K4, k2tog; repeat from * to end. **Row 2 and all wrong-side rows** Purl. **Row 3** *K3, k2tog; repeat from * to end. **Row 5** *K2, k2tog; repeat from * to end. **Row 7** *K1, k2tog; repeat from * to end. **Row 9** *K2tog; repeat from * to end. **Row 11** K1, *k2tog; repeat from * to end—6 stitches. **Row 12** P2tog, p2, p2tog. Sew side seam leaving remaining 4 stitches on needle.

Topknot

Note: You'll need one double-pointed needle to work top knot.

Next row Knit 4, slip sts back to left needle and bring yarn back across stitches to beginning of row. Repeat last row until cord measures approximately 1" or desired length. K2tog twice, then k2tog again. Fasten off last stitch.

Baby Soft 'n' Seamless Cardigan

Designed by Lynda Ward

SIZE

6 months

FINISHED MEASUREMENTS

Chest at underarm 21"

MATERIALS

- 2 skeins Lion Brand *Jiffy* in #157 Pale Yellow (3 oz, 135 yds; 100% acrylic)
- Size 9 (5.5 mm) circular knitting needle, or size to get gauge
- One set of size 9 (5.5 mm) doubled-pointed needles (for sleeves)
- Stitch markers and stitch holders
- Five ¾" (20 mm) buttons

GAUGE

15 stitches and 22 rows = 4" (10 cm) in stockinette stitch (knit on right side; purl on wrong side) using size 9 needles.

Be sure to check your gauge.

NOTES

1. See abbreviations page 71.
2. This sweater is worked from the top down. Body is worked with circular needle worked back and forth as with straight needles.

BODY

Neckband

Loosely cast on 57 sts. Work even in garter stitch (knit every row) until there are 2 garter ridges on the right side, ending with a wrong side row.

First Buttonhole

Buttonhole row (right side) Boy's sweater: K2, yarn over (yo), k2tog, knit to end. Girl's sweater: Knit to last 4 stitches, k2tog, yo, k2. Repeat this buttonhole row approximately every 2" (about 7 ridges apart). Continue in garter stitch until there are 4 garter ridges on right side, ending with a wrong side row.

Shape Raglan Armholes

Set-up row (right side) K4, place marker (front band), k9 (front), mark next stitch and then (k1, yo, k1) into that stitch, k5 (sleeve), mark next stitch and then (k1, yo, k1), k17 (back), mark next stitch and then (k1, yo, k1) into that stitch, k5 (sleeve), mark next stitch and then (k1, yo, k1) into that stitch, k9 (front), place marker, k4 (front band)—65 stitches. **Row 1 (wrong side)** K4, slip marker, purl to last 4 stitches, slip marker, k4. **Row 2 (right side)** Slipping markers for front bands, *knit to marked stitch (k1, yo, k1) into that stitch 4 times, k to end. (**Note** To keep raglan increases aligned, remember to increase directly above yarn over of the previous increase row.) Repeat last 2 rows 10 times more. Repeat row 1 once more—153 stitches. Remove markers for marked stitches.

Divide for Sleeves

Next row (right side) Knit 26, slip next 29 stitches onto a holder; cast on 4 stitches by looping yarn around needle, knit 43, slip next 29 stitches onto holder, cast on 4 stitches by looping yarn around needle, knit 26—103 stitches remain on needle. On next right side

Baby Soft 'n' Seamless Cardigan *(continued)*

row, knit 49, place marker, k5, place marker, knit 49. Keeping 4 border stitches in garter stitch and continuing to place buttonholes at regular intervals, work even in stockinette stitch until body measures 1¼" from sleeve division, ending with a wrong-side row.

Body Increases

Increase row 1 (right side) Knit to 2nd marker, work M1 increase, slip marker, k5, slip marker, work M1 increase, knit to end. Continue to work even, repeating increase twice more at 1¼" intervals. (These increases add a bit of flare to the back of the sweater, making it fit more easily over diapers.) Work even until piece measures 4½" from sleeve division, ending with a wrong-side row.

Lower Band

Work even in garter stitch until there are 4 purl ridges on right side. Ideally the last buttonhole should be placed two ridges above the bottom edge to match the neckband. Loosely bind off all sts.

SLEEVES

With double-pointed needles, divide 29 sleeve stitches onto 3 needles, plus pick up 4 stitches along cast-on of underarm—33 stitches. Mark center underarm stitch and have that stitch be the beginning round. Attach yarn and knit 1 round, joining stitches. **Decrease round** K1 (marked stitch), ssk, knit to last 2 stitches, k2tog—31 stitches. *Knit 4 rounds even, then repeat decrease round. Repeat from * once more—27 stitches. Work even until sleeve measures 4" from beg. Work garter-stitch border as follows: (purl 1 round, knit 1 round) 3 times, then purl 1 round (4 garter ridges). Bind off loosely with a larger needle if necessary.

FINISHING

Sew on buttons and work in ends.

For color images of these items see color insert, photo numbers 18 and 19

Christmas-at-Sea Patterns

Mariner's Scarf

FINISHED MEASUREMENTS
10" x 40"

MATERIALS
- 2 balls Lion Brand *Wool-Ease®* (3 oz, 197 yds; 80% acrylic, 20% wool) or washable/dryable worsted-weight yarn
- Size 9 (5.5 mm) knitting needles, or size to get gauge

GAUGE
12 stitches and 24 rows = 4" (10 cm) in stockinette stitch (knit on right side; purl on wrong side) using size 9 needles.
Be sure to check your gauge.

SCARF
Beginning at narrow end, cast on 40 sts. Knit 8 rows (4 ridges on right and wrong sides).
Rows 1–6 K2, (k6, p6) 3 times, k2. **Rows 7–8** Knit. **Rows 9–14** K2, (p6, k6) 3 times, k2. **Rows 15–16** Knit. Repeat rows 1–16 for pattern until scarf measures approximately 39" (about 32 rows of pattern blocks), ending with either a row 6 or 14. Knit 8 rows (4 ridges on right and wrong sides). Bind off. Do not block.

Watch Cap

Can be made as a set to give with the Seafarer's Scarf.

FINISHED MEASUREMENTS
Circumference 17–18"

MATERIALS
- 1 ball Lion Brand *Wool-Ease®* (3 oz, 197 yds; 80% acrylic, 20% wool) or washable/dryable worsted-weight yarn
- Size 8 (5 mm) knitting needles, or size to get gauge
- Large-eyed yarn needle

NOTE
Do not make this cap with double-pointed needles.

GAUGE
20 stitches and 28 rows = 4" (10 cm) in garter stitch (knit every row) using size 8 needles.
Be sure to check your gauge.

HAT
Cast on 40 sts. Work in knit 2, purl 2 ribbing for 4".
Work even in garter stitch for 40 rows (20 ridges).

Crown

Row 1 *K10, k2tog; rep from * to end. **Row 2 and all wrong-side rows** Knit. **Row 3** *K9, k2tog; rep from * to end. **Row 5** *K8, k2tog; rep from * to end. **Row 7** *K7, k2tog; rep from * to end. **Row 9** *K6, k2tog; rep from * to end. **Row 11** *K5, k2tog; rep from * to end. **Row 13** *K4, k2tog; rep from * to end. **Row 15** *K3, k2tog; rep from * to end. **Row 17** *K2, k2tog; rep from * to end. **Row 19** *K1, k2tog; rep from * to end—14 stitches remain. **Next row** Knit 7 and then join crown.

Join Crown

With half the stitches on each needle, break the yarn, leaving a 15" length, and thread it into a large-eyed yarn needle. Fold the cap so that both needles are even and parallel (one in back of the other). While working, always keep yarn under the needles. With free yarn extending from right-hand end of back needle (or the farthest from you), graft stitches (making garter-stitch pattern) from the front and back needles together as follows.

Grafting

Beginning on front needle, *pass yarn needle through first stitch on needle (entering from left to right) as if to knit. Slip the stitch off the needle. Pass the yarn needle through the second stitch on the same needle (enter from right to left) as if to purl. Pull yarn through, but leave the stitch on the needle. Repeat from * on the first two stitches on the back needle. Continue to graft the stitches together, alternating from front to back until all the stitches are off both needles. Pull yarn through last stitch and fasten securely, leaving yarn to sew side seam.

Sewing Seam

Place edges of cap adjacent to each other with the patterns matching. Secure edges with pins. Picking up outside loop of stitch from each side, sew back and forth, drawing two edges securely together from crown to bottom of ribbed cuff. Do not sew through double thickness. Do not block cap.

Seafarer's Scarf

FINISHED MEASUREMENTS

6½" x 46"

MATERIALS

- 2 balls Lion Brand *Wool-Ease*® (3 oz, 197 yds; 80% acrylic, 20% wool) or washable/dryable worsted-weight yarn
- Size 8 (5 mm) knitting needles, or size to get gauge

GAUGE

20 stitches and 28 rows = 4" (10 cm) in garter stitch (knit every row) using size 8 needles. *Be sure to check your gauge.*

SCARF

Loosely cast on 32 sts. Knit every row for 14". Work in k4, p4 ribbing for 18". Knit every row for 14". Bind off loosely. Do not block.

WARM UP AMERICA! PATTERNS

Use any of the following patterns or ones of your choice. They can be combined in one blanket. Non-rolling stitches work best. If you are using scraps of yarn, squares can be worked in stripes.

MATERIALS

- Worsted-weight yarn
- Size 7 or 8 (4.5 or 5 mm) knitting needles, or size to get gauge

GAUGE

20 stitches = 4" (10 cm)

Be sure to check your gauge.

GARTER STITCH

Cast on 35 stitches. Knit every row until piece measures 9". Bind off.

SEED STITCH

Cast on 35 stitches.

Row 1 *Knit 1, purl 1; repeat from * to end. Repeat this row until piece measures 9". Bind off.

DOUBLE SEED STITCH

Cast on 35 stitches. **Row 1** *Knit 1, purl 1; repeat from * to end. **Row 2** *Purl 1, knit 1; repeat from * to end. **Row 3** Repeat row 2. **Row 4** Repeat row 1. Repeat rows 1–4 until piece measures 9". Bind off.

LINES

Cast on 35 stitches.

Rows 1 and 3 Knit. **Rows 2 and 4** Purl. **Rows 5 and 6** Knit. Repeat rows 1–6 until piece measures 9". Bind off.

14

Collecting and Storing Yarn

Barbara K., a passionate yarn collector who lives in Cupertino, California, tells of a dream that her daughter had. In the dream, her daughter came to visit her. After knocking on the door repeatedly to no response, her daughter walked around to the side of the house where she saw the windows breaking out as yarn poured from them. She ran frantically back and forced open the front door to find the entire house filled with yarn, leaving only about two feet of space near the ceiling in which her mother was "swimming" across the top of the yarn.

Knitting and a love of yarn are often inextricably linked. On the KnitList (see Chapter 18 "Knitting on the Web" p. 189), shopping for yarn is known by the acronym SEX, which stands for Stash Enrichment eXpedition. Because knitting is such an important part of most knitters' lives, the paraphernalia of the craft are important as well. Knitters often feel compelled to purchase all manner of objects related to knitting including yarn, patterns, books, needles, knitting totes, and bumper stickers. But of all of these items, yarn occupies the most important place in both their hearts and their homes.

A passionate knitter's collection is a vital part of his or her life, and often in the lives of his or her family members. Wherever a collector goes, whether surfing the Internet, traveling, or visiting a local town, he or she is probably on the lookout for something special to add to the collection. While some may shop for yarn to knit a particular pattern, many buy yarn because they fall in love with it. "I see a purple mohair," says one such yarn buyer, "and it makes my fingers itch to get going."

"A real knitter collects yarn and doesn't feel she has to use it all. There is a pleasure in owning a ball of yarn," says Barbara S., a knitter from California. "Many knitters feel guilty about all the yarn they own but my philosophy is that everything about knitting should be enjoyable. If I knit something I don't like, I allow myself to ditch it. Knitting for me is totally pleasurable. I collect yarn because I love being surrounded by yarns that have texture, bright colors, are soft and cuddly, and that present possibilities of what they can become with a little imagination. I am quite comfortable owning yarn and never knitting with it. I also collect teapots and never brew tea in them. Yarn is my motivation and my joy," says Barbara.

Barbara has two close friends who are also knowledgeable and passionate collectors of everything yarn-related, including novelty accessories—from mugs with pictures of people knitting, to the scores of tote bags each friend owns. Although they live hundreds of miles apart, they speak to each other about knitting several times a week and hold conference calls every month or whenever a new issue of a knitting magazine or catalog arrives in the mail. They review every pattern, analyze new yarns for their color range, fiber content, and cost per yard, and discuss exciting new gadgets.

While some people plan their collections to fit within the framework of their lives, many admit (with a sly smile) that it would be truer to say that their lives are shaped by their collections. When searching for a new home, one yarn collector mentally measured the closets to see how many 32-gallon bins of yarn would fit and how many closets could be allocated for the yarn collection. The house with the best storage space won over the one with the eat-in kitchen.

The cost and space requirements of storing yarn can become an issue for knitters' partners. Minding one's collection may provide shared projects or create strife, depending upon the relationship. Some spouses are willing accomplices, like Barbara's husband, who used his carpentry skills to build a shelving unit to organize her yarns. Others may simply tolerate the collection good-naturedly. Knitters with less tolerant spouses describe a source of constant conflict, requiring covert operations like hiding purchases or keeping collections behind closed doors. The compulsion to collect yarn may drive decisions about the relationship itself. As one knitter quipped, "I live with my significant other, who's so sweet. I once had a husband, but he complained about the yarn . . ."

Even the language used by yarn collectors reflects the addictive nature of the habit. They refer to themselves as "yarnaholics" and their collection as a "stash." They may become infatuated with a particular yarn, believing that they "cannot live without it." In fact, the urge to acquire yarn is often unrelated to the practical needs of current or future projects. "Often, the yarn just grabs me," says one yarnaholic, "or the price is just too good to ignore."

One yarn collector believes that there are many people like her, who have memories of poverty or who felt deprived or at risk as children and who "are probably more interested in owning the stuff than knitting with it. We spend more time managing it than using it," she says. For these knitters, surrounding themselves with yarn provides a sense of control, comfort, and security.

The desire to accumulate yarn and knitting accessories may also be motivated by a love of color, texture, and design—a creative urge. A growing collection raises the inevitable questions of how to store, organize, manage, and make use of it. The way you organize your collection both reflects and directs your style of knitting. The major organizing principle of a yarn collection is usually fiber, weight, or color. Your standard of organization will depend on what aspect of the yarn is primary in your imagination. Are you enamored of the fiber, swooning over the feel of silk or cotton, or is it a color—purple, red or blue—that moves you?

Organizing a Collection

Yarn collections are purchased, organized, inventoried, and stored in ways as personal and distinctive as the individual collector. A yarn collection may be stored randomly in a few boxes or it may be organized in a way that would be the envy of the Library of Congress. As one knitter counsels, "Whatever system you choose needs to work for you and only you."

Knitters differ on whether the ideal collection is neatly tucked away or kept out in the open. Neil and Susan of Indiana, a husband and wife who both knit, believe that keeping some yarn out at all times is important to the creative process. Neil describes the process that keeps them motivated. "My wife and I both have containers beside our chairs with projects in them. After about a month, we empty out the container and put in new projects. If we start one of the projects but don't finish by month's end, it can be put in for the next month. This way you can rotate through what you have and the change of 'scenery' motivates you to do something with the yarn." Susan agrees: "I like to keep my yarn exposed on open bookshelves. I have a great chair and lamp in the room and I sit amongst it all. I get the most wonderful ideas as my gaze goes around the room."

Yarn lovers have improvised a variety of solutions for storing their yarns. The collection may be kept in an old chest of drawers in the attic, on open bookshelves, or in bins. Clear or solid plastic storage bins can be purchased from discount chain stores such as Wal-Mart, Target, or Kmart in a variety of sizes and may be used with or without lids. Corrugated cardboard boxes with removable lids or hatboxes may be an even less expensive solution, but don't have the advantage of being see-through. Plastic bags of all sizes are also popular for smaller groupings of yarn, but be sure to leave some opening so the yarn can breathe. Bags can be suspended from clothespins on hangers, and the hangers can be bent so that some bags hang higher than others, which utilizes more of the space of the closet.

Storing odds and ends is also an important consideration, because collectors by their nature don't discard these small leftover pieces. "I have a container labeled 'Kaffe Fassett Wannabe,' " says Jackie of Michigan. "When I have odd balls or leftover pieces of yarn, I toss them in this container." Kaffe Fassett is a designer known for knitting, needlepoint, and quilting designs that have revolutionized color work in these crafts (see Chapter 24, "The Literature of Knitting").

Those who choose to organize their collection by color are often inspired to design by looking at the colors, the way an artist may select a palette before painting a picture. "When I grouped my yarns by color, out jumped an idea for a lovely sweater using five different shades of rose, red, and pink," says one knitter. The problem with designing by color is that a pleasing selection of colors may have different weights or fibers. This may be overcome by doubling thin yarns so that they knit up well with thicker yarns (see yarn weights, p. 15), but you need to feel comfortable improvising in this manner. Fibers that have the same gauge are easily mixed, which offers potentially interesting and surprising results for the adventurous knitter.

Sally, who describes herself as a highly organized person, orders her yarns alphabetically by color and from heaviest to lightest, using plastic photograph negative holders. These are plastic sheets with pockets that have holes on one side to fit into a three-ring binder. She puts a note card in a slot with all the information about the yarn. In an adjacent slot she puts a 3" piece of the yarn. She can pull the cards out to compare yarns and quickly know what other colors she has in each yarn and whether the fibers are compatible. This way, she keeps a miniature palette handy, and the yarn can be put away in a closet.

Those who sort by weight—sportweight, DK, chunky, bulky, or worsted—often keep compatible or contrasting colors together within each weight. That way, when they find a pattern they want to work with, they know where to look for the yarn that will be compatible with the gauge in that pattern.

Knitters who prefer to plan projects ahead of time often organize their yarn collections by project. Kathryn of Portland, Oregon, explains, "I lay out my yarn by color and, in some cases, by brand name, then begin going through all my patterns, and create kits: pattern and yarn together in one bag. Then I divide these kits into four categories: small projects, mindless, fun, and challenging. Next, I make a numbered list of all the kits and put them in plastic tubs with lids, labeling each tub by category and listing the numbers on the kits I put inside. Any fiber that doesn't make it into a kit is snipped and tied onto a small card with all its details. Now my whole stash is on little cards in a little plastic bag that I can take when I go shopping. The thought is that my shopping will now be more directed and I can grab a kit to fit my mood and needs."

Some collectors prefer a less methodical system than organizing the collection by concept, color, or thickness, and simply store the yarn in an available container as it is purchased. Yet, even then, there can be a system for locating the yarn. Each container or drawer may be labeled with a number that refers to a corresponding list describing its contents.

The system that you use for referencing and searching for yarn may be maintained on a sheet of paper, in a notebook, or on simple computer software. Most collectors look upon this process not as a tedious exercise, but as a way to let the pleasurable experience of buying yarn linger as they savor the new stash and think about possible uses for it.

One self-confessed yarnaholic suggests a simple system that allows you to store your collection anywhere in your home and move it as necessary. She uses a loose-leaf notebook. Each page is labeled with the number of the container. First, note the location of the container (for example, under the bed, in a corner of the guest room, or the top of the hall closet) and then list what is in the container. Note each time you move the yarn or change a container's contents. If there are too many changes on a page and it begins to look sloppy, simply replace it with a new page, and rewrite the current contents. For this reason, it is advisable not to list the yarns directly on the box, shelf, or bin; in the course of working through your collection, the changes will probably outpace the space on the label.

How much information you record on each ball or skein of yarn depends on how much you want to know about it without actually looking at the yarn. It may also depend on whether you are concerned about losing the ball band, which has the yarn specifications. Some people like to record when and where they purchased the yarn, as well as the brand, color, fiber, weight, yardage, washing instructions, and dye lot. More involved notations are easier to maintain and search on a computer file.

Most basic computer programs, such as word processing, database, or spreadsheet, offer practical solutions to maintaining a yarn archive. All three can be easily searched using any word, combination of words, or numbers. In a spreadsheet program like Excel, lists can be sorted so that you see your yarn organized by brand, fiber, color or thickness, no matter how you actually store it. The ability to sort information in several ways is an invaluable tool in planning projects and purchasing additional yarn.

A spreadsheet program may also be useful in developing an index of patterns. Although patterns don't present the storage problems that yarn does, a collection of patterns will be more useful if it is archived in a way that puts the pattern you are looking for at your fingertips. Patterns also may be in several formats, so separate purchases and those included in knitting books and magazines. To make it easier to locate a specific pattern from your collection, list the patterns on a spreadsheet with the name, page, and issue of the book or magazine. You'll always be able to find the pattern you are looking for without having to leaf through everything in your pattern library.

Adina Klein—A Passionate Yarn Collector

"If I knit 24 hours a day and live to be 95 years old, I won't go through my stash. Once I get to a yarn store, my urge to buy yarn is very hard to control," says Adina Klein, who had to move to a larger apartment to accommodate her collection of yarn, needles, books, and knitting collectibles. Adina, the daughter and granddaughter of knitters, first learned to knit when she was six years old but did not take it seriously until college. At about the same time, she was introduced to her first yarn shop, the Yarn Company in New York. Eventually she worked in that shop and went on to work in various capacities in the world of knitting. "For me, building a collection is an occupational hazard," she says, but she can also identify a number of reasons why knitters become unwitting collectors of yarn and other knitting needs.

Novice knitters, she points out, can fall into yarn collecting by accident, since they may abandon projects they are not happy with and save the leftover yarn for future use. A driving force of her growing collection is what her friend Charlotte has identified as the search for "the perfect stash." "You are always trying to achieve the right balance of lace weight to bulky-weight yarn or light colors or dark colors, or the perfectly designed knitting bag."

Another stash builder is the "mainstay gift." Adina knits a cabled, seed-stitch afghan for the important events in the lives of her friends and family and will always pick up yarn to make an afghan if she comes across it, accumulating about four to five projects' worth of yarn at any one time. The other impetus to buy yarn is that she has just found the newest thing, like muskox yarn or a beautiful hand-dyed wool in her favorite color. Mostly, she says, the reason for accumulating so much yarn is simple: "I shop much quicker than I knit."

What else does she collect? Knitting tote bags, books, and needles, her favorites being those made of ebony. "Lately I have developed a fetish for tacky tchotchkes," she says. These include snowmen knitting, cats knitting, and the ultimate kitsch item: a schoolhouse that lights up and says "knitting school" on the top. All of these were located on eBay.

"I don't really intend to buy anything and I don't have a shopping list when I go into a store," she says, "but then my heart starts to race because I see what looks like the perfect hand-dyed color of yarn and I just have to have it."

15

Knitting Traditions

To discuss knitting in a historical sense, you have to envision the evolution of the world as a whole. Keep in mind that the earliest roots of this craft are most likely not to be the same craft as we know it today. The beginning of knitting was more likely to have been some form of interlocked looping that formed fabric that was unlike woven fabric formed by crossed interwoven strands. The most written-about looping technique is called *Nålbinding* (Norwegian spelling) or *Nålbindning* (Swedish spelling).

Why is so little documented history of knitting available? Mary Thomas says it best when she states, "Knitting, because of its practical use, made its appeal in the new world, as it did in the old, to all classes, and perhaps why so little remains of all this activity is because of its too-general acceptance and obvious utility." Knitted pieces of yesteryear were used, worn out and discarded. They were not made to be museum pieces.

The other reason that so little remains of knitted pieces has to do with the fact that fiber doesn't last over time except in the driest climates. Eventually most fabric and fiber disintegrate unless attempts are made to preserve and retain pieces. Perhaps this accounts for why the oldest samples were discovered in Egypt.

As a brief overview, it's good to know about the origins of a number of regions throughout the world. It should be noted that the longer you study knitting and look at deviations of knitting, the more you will see that many of the same types of patterns are used in completely different parts of the world. A symbol or pattern from a Nordic country may appear in a South American design. A lace technique from Scotland can be found in parts of Russia. The world of knitting techniques and pattern has clearly traveled far and wide. Unfortunately, most of the actual people who dispersed the legacy we have come to love will never be known to us. We can only thank them by carrying on a cherished tradition and copying patterns that have been around for thousands of years.

Keep in mind that most of the early knitters were men, and that knitting was an occupation and source of income rather than a leisure activity. Even when women began to knit, many knitters were adding to their family's pocketbook and helping to bring in much-needed pay.

The discussion here is meant merely as an introduction to knitting and its heritage and a jumping-off point for further exploration and study. The books that follow will enable you to find out more about specific historical periods and regions.

Knitting from the British Isles

Many of the more popularly known knitting traditions have roots in Britain. How knitting got there is open to speculation. Some say that knitting originated in Egypt or somewhere in the Middle East and traveled to Spain. From Spain, it was brought to England. Some believe that islands such as Shetland got their input from Scandinavian countries like Norway. At any rate, knitting was established in England by the fifteenth century and, as throughout Europe, was done by guilds of men as an occupation rather than as a hobby. Even back in the days of Henry VIII, knitted stockings brought from Spain were popular. In a move to be independent of Spain, Elizabeth I (who reigned from 1558–1603) had her silk stockings copied and knitted in England. Knitting had such a political standing that an act was passed to control the price of felt and knitted hats in 1571.

Much of the traditions from Britain come from windswept, rugged islands and coastal areas where knits were not optional clothing but a necessity. The many fishermen who lived there needed warm wool sweaters to fight the elements. There is a long-held legend that sweaters were knitted with specific patterns to identify men who drowned at sea, but some knitting historians feel that this is a romantic and unproven view invented to embellish what little was really proven history. Knitters may have used or devised patterns in their knitting, but not specifically for that purpose.

FAIR ISLE

High in the North Sea, the Shetland island of Fair Isle has popularized the multicolor knitting that bears its name. The speedy knitters of Fair Isle work intricate designs circularly on long, double-pointed needles using no more than two colors per row. Shetlanders have made socks, hats, gloves, mittens, and sweaters using this technique, knitting with the warm coat of Shetland sheep. Although this knitting tradition had been in practice for many years, a portrait of the Prince of Wales wearing a Fair Isle pullover in the 1920s popularized this form of knitting. For many in Shetland, knitting was their chief income source. While there are still knitters and knitting, since the discovery of oil in the North Sea there is less need to knit for a livelihood.

ARAN

Another rough-weather set of islands are the three Aran Islands Inishmore, Inishmaan, and Inisheer, that lie off western Ireland. The men of this rugged region were mainly fishermen. The sweaters knitted in the Aran tradition are highly textured, using a combination of cables and other dimensional stitches and are done in a natural color (off-white or fisherman) called Bainin by natives. Noted Scots author and designer Alice Starmore believes that the origins of Aran knitting were similar to those of fishermen's ganseys, except that Arans have cables in addition to knit-and-purl patterning. In the 1930s they are brought to the public's attention in Robert Flaherty's film *Man of Aran,* which showed life on the island. The highly cabled sweaters became popular around the time of World War II, and they were primarily made fashionable as commercial garments.

FISHERMEN'S GUERNSEYS (ALSO KNOWN AS GANSEYS)

Fishermen's gansey sweaters are traditional garb from the late nineteenth century that migrated to Scotland via the Netherlands. Although ganseys from various regions were different, they had some similarities. As this sweater style was prominently known in the Channel Islands, specifically in the island of Guernsey, it became known by that name. These sweaters were utilitarian, warm garments worn by fishermen and most often knitted by female family members. The islands of Guernsey and Jersey have two famous knitting terms named for them. Guernsey describes a type of sweater, and jersey is sometimes used to describe a sweater and is also another term for stockinette stitch. Guernseys are traditionally dark, tightly knit sweaters made in the round, with a stockinette-stitch body and yoke created with designs using only knit-and-purl stitches.

SHETLAND SHAWLS (LACE KNITTING FROM UNST)

Noted for their finely knit lace shawls, the knitters of the Unst region are best known for creating shawls that are so lightweight that one will fit through a wedding ring. These intricate lace pieces are usually made in natural colors and have a wide lace edging. For full effect, they are blocked on large wooden racks.

Iceland and the Faroe Islands; Sweden; Norway

Many of the knitting traditions brought to Britain came from countries with borders along the North Sea. Many have suggested that these designs and techniques traveled on the sea with sailors.

ICELAND AND THE FAROE ISLANDS

These islands, both originally under Danish control, have always had a heritage that included knitting and the exporting of their knitted products. Iceland is known for making a soft, untwisted wool called Lopi that has been exported for many years. The motifs and patterns are done in simple geometric designs. The typical Icelandic sweater is knitted circularly in one piece that has a colorful, patterned yoke. Faroe is also known for patterned designs and for shawls with a distinctive gore in the back, which are made to sit on the shoulders. These shawls, originally worn by working women, have points that are tied around the back of the wearer.

SWEDEN

While Bohus knitting is the style of knitting most often identified with Sweden, it was actually a commercial enterprise. The traditional knitting designs of the country are worked in motifs of red and blue on a cream background. Much like designs known as Fair Isle, many of the motifs have floral or nature-inspired aspects. Sweden is also known for a one-color, double-knitting technique called Tvåändssticking.

NORWAY

One can't think of Norway without thinking about the beautiful Luskofte ski sweaters knitted and worn by Norwegians for years and popularized around the world because of the Olympics. The traditional colors for these masterpieces are black and white (or cream), but colors have also been added to the patterning (notably red and blue).

Books Tell the Tale

There have been many books written that delve into the beginnings of knitting. After you read a few, you'll soon learn that not everyone agrees about the historical accuracy of how knitting traveled throughout the world. However, to get glimpses into the roots of knitting, these 20 books (in alphabetical order) are certainly worthwhile. Many of these books (originally published in the 1980s) are out of print, but can occasionally be found second-hand or on eBay. Another shorter list of titles follows that you may also find of interest.

1. *Andean Folk Knitting: Traditions and Techniques from Peru and Bolivia* by Cynthia Gravelle LeCount (Interweave Press, 1990)

   While much has been written about the history of knitting in northern European countries, little has been documented about the craft in South America. Cynthia LeCount, art historian, artist and photographer, has spent a great deal of time in both Bolivia and Peru and is well qualified to tell the story of knitting in the Andes. Much of this book documents "chullo" hats of the region—there are directions for making the patterns at the end of the book—and focuses on the symbols and colors typical of this region.

2. *Aran Knitting* by Alice Starmore (Interweave Press, 1997)

   Alice is a great modern-day authority on traditional knitting, and a list of books wouldn't be complete without one of hers. Also excellent: *Alice Starmore's Book of Fair Isle Knitting* (The Taunton Press, 1988). Any book you can find with her name as author is worth purchasing. In the Aran book she discusses myths and legends of the Aran tradition. Several historical garments from the region are photographed, and each one's history and patterning are discussed at length. Also included are a number of Alice's beautifully designed and photographed sweaters. For both history and sweater designs, this one is a treasure.

3. *The Art of Fair Isle Knitting—History, Technique, Color and Patterns* by Ann Feitelson (Interweave Press, 1996)

   A good historical study plus a wealth of pattern designs and technique are included in this nicely done book. The extensive history chapter includes old black-and-white photos and a nice grouping of full-color shots of Fair Isle sweaters. American Ann Feitelson did exhaustive research on this book, and it really shows. She spent time interviewing knitters of all ages in Shetland and has put this legacy into a very understandable form.

4. *Canada Knits* by Shirley A. Scott (McGraw-Hill Ryerson Ltd, 1990)

   An exploration of the history of knitting in Canada, from the first British and French colonials to the current knitter-of-leisure. Of special note is the chapter on Cowichan

(continued on next page)

knitting of the Pacific Northwest, an indigenous hand-knitting industry that continues today.

5. *The Complete Book of Traditional Knitting* by Rae Compton Charles (Scribner's Sons, 1983)

   This far-reaching volume not only covers the traditions of Britain, but also encompasses Iceland, the Faroe Islands, Norway, and much more. From the Shetland Islands to Finland, Rae examines the rich past of knitting. The scope of the knitting includes dramatic color knitting, rich one-color patterning, and fine lace originating from Unst, the northernmost island in Shetland. She even includes two brief pages on South American knitting.

6. *Folk Knitting in Estonia* by Nancy Bush (Interweave Press, 1999)

   Estonia is one of the three Baltic States (the other two are Latvia and Lithuania), and it has a rich history of knitting. Nancy Bush begins the book with a history of Estonia and devotes a chapter each to the country's culture, day-to-day life, and popular customs. The next chapter discusses how knitting fits into this background, and in it we learn that some of the earliest known knitted artifacts have been found on Estonian soil. Estonian patterns, like those of many Scandinavian countries, are colorful and use symbolic motifs. This book, full of color photos, incorporates instructions and techniques for making 26 gloves, mittens, and socks along with photos of period examples.

7. *Gossamer Webs—the History and Techniques of Orenburg Lace Shawls* by Galina Khmeleva and Carol R. Noble (Interweave Press, 1998)

   Galina, a native Russian, tells the fascinating story of knitting in Orenburg, located on the steppes of the southern Ural mountain range. Orenburg shawl knitting dates back before the 1760s and the reign of Catherine the Great. The book discusses the earliest knitting in the region to the present day. There are also techniques and patterns for making your own Orenburg shawl as well as a discussion about the fine goat hair that gives these shawls their special loftiness and warmth.

8. *A History of Hand Knitting* by Richard Rutt (B. T. Interweave Press, 1989)

   Richard Rutt, otherwise known as the Bishop of Leicester, knitted since he was a young boy and became somewhat of an authority on the subject. Rather than concentrating on specific traditions, his book is set up by periods in history, starting with a chapter titled "Before 1500." The introduction talks at length about the origin of the word knitting and its historical meaning. An early chapter shows (in words and illustrations) interlocking methods that are the knitting we know today and the Nålbinding (an ancient method of making looped fabric) of bygone eras. Other chapters include "First World War and After," "Some Local Traditions," "The Americas" and "Eastern Knitting." By and large the book is mostly devoted to the British knitting history—of which there is much to say—and is full of wonderful black-and-white photos.

9. *The Illustrated Dictionary of Knitting* by Rae Compton (Interweave Press, 1988)

   This book is, as it says, a dictionary of all sorts of knitting techniques, methods, and terms. While the various types of traditional knitting around the world are not covered in detail, you'll find a very nice overview, from Aran knitting to Turkish knitting.

10. *Knitting Ganseys* by Beth Brown-Reinsel (Interweave Press, 1993)

    This book is devoted to the knit-and-purl garments worn by fishermen in nineteenth-century Britain. It begins with the gansey sweater's history and teaches you how to construct your very own gansey by making a mini-sampler. Also included are six full-sized garments.

11. *Latvian Mittens* by Lizbeth Upitis (Schoolhouse Press, 1997)

    For a good perspective on the traditional knitting of the Baltic countries of Latvia and Lithuania, this book can't be beat. Lizbeth covers the rich patterning and colors used by the people of this region. One of the more interesting sections talks about the mittens that were knitted by young brides-to-be to prove themselves worthy of marriage. There are instructions and patterns for a wealth of mittens.

12. *Mary Thomas's Knitting Book* by Mary Thomas (Dover Publications, 1972)

    When there were barely any knitting books on the market, everyone relied on Mary Thomas for basic information. Her book begins with a good fourteen-page historical overview. The frontispiece has a black-and-white reproduction of *The Visit of the Angels* (the Knitting Madonna) by the Master Bertram, dated approximately 1390. Because of its significance, this painting is shown in a number of other knitting volumes, such as *Vogue Knitting, The Ultimate Knitting Book.*

(continued on next page)

13. Michael Pearson's *Traditional Knitting—Aran, Fair Isle and Fisher Ganseys* by Michael Pearson (Van Nostrand Reinhold, 1984)

    Many of our current knitting traditions have come to us from Britain. Michael covers the roots of these traditions, examining in depth the financial implications of the craft and its importance to those who depended on it for their livelihood. Also included are sweater instructions, a number of traditional patterns for one-color cables and knit-and-purl stitches as well as several richly colored Fair Isle patterns.

14. *No Idle Hands—The Social History of American Knitting* by Anne L. Macdonald (Ballantine Books, 1988)

    Historian Anne Macdonald covers knitting from Colonial times to the present. With over 400 pages and many black-and-white photos, this well-documented and researched book gives great insight into how knitting has woven a road through American history.

15. *Patterns for Guernseys, Jerseys and Arans—Fishermen's Sweaters from the British Isles* by Gladys Thompson (Dover Publications, 1971)

    More than half of this book is devoted to knit-and-purl fisherman sweater patterns. It features period photos of the fishermen, photos of swatches of knit-and-purl stitches, knitting instructions, and charted patterns. The rest of the book reviews cabled designs from the three Aran Islands, off the west coast of Ireland.

16. *Poems of Color—Knitting in the Bohus Tradition* by Wendy Keele (Interweave Press, 1995)

    The story of Swedish Bohus knitting is a powerful one and certainly makes an interesting read. This style of knitting gets its name from Bohus Stickning, a 1930s relief organization for financially stressed women led by Emma Jacobsson. The book includes an in-depth study of Bohus, known for its fine gauges and beautiful, subtly colored yokes, as well as a discussion of color choices and techniques for making these garments.

17. *Salish Indian Sweaters, A Pacific Northwest Tradition* by Priscilla A. Gibson-Roberts (Adventure Publications, 1989)

    A history of Salish Indian—also known as Cowichan—sweaters from the Pacific Northwest. Also included are exhaustive details on the techniques and geometric animal patterns used in these (usually zippered) thick shawl-collared sweaters.

18. *Traditional Knitting* by Sheila McGregor (B. T. Batsford Ltd., 1983)

    Sheila has some interesting theories on the origins and evolution of knitting. This small volume is a wealth of information and includes full-color photos.

19. *Traditional Knitting—Patterns of Ireland, Scotland and England* by Gwyn Morgan (St. Martin's Press, 1981)

    The first chapter of this book, which features traditional sweater designs, gives a good overview of the historical significance of knitting.

20. *Twined Knitting* by Birgitta Dandanell and Ulla Danielsson (Interweave Press, 1989)

    Twined knitting (Tvåändssticking), a method of knitting with two ends of yarn, first took hold in the Dalarna region of Sweden. It was an ingenious way of creating clothing—particularly mittens, gloves, and hats—that was impervious to the bitter weather outside. This book is replete with photographs and instructions for knitting in this unique style.

ADDITIONAL BOOKS

- *The Art of Shetland Lace* by Sarah Don (Lacis, 1995)
- *The Complete Book of Traditional Fair Isle Knitting* by Sheila McGregor (Charles Scribner's Sons, 1982)
- *The Complete Book of Traditional Scandinavian Knitting* by Sheila McGregor (St. Martin's Press, 1984)
- *Knitting in the Nordic Tradition* by Vibeke Lind (Lark Books, 1984)
- *Knitting in the Old Way* by Priscilla A. Gibson-Roberts (Interweave Press, 1985)
- *The Loving Stitch, A History of Knitting and Spinning in New Zealand* by Heather Nicholson (Auckland University Press, 1998)
- *Nordic Knitting* by Susanne Pagoldh (Interweave Press, 1991)

16

Fashion Trends in Knitting

By Trisha Malcolm

Fashion and knitting have always been closely intertwined, and since most of what we knit we wear, it stands to reason that we want to knit garments that add to our personal fashion expression. Though we often think of fashion influencing knitting styles and trends, knitting has also had its fifteen minutes, influencing the catwalk creations of many notable designers.

The oldest surviving pieces of true knitting have been found in Egypt, and since many of the examples were not found by trained archeologists, the exact dates and provenance of many of the pieces are unknown; however, most can be roughly dated to between 1000 and 1400 C.E. Later depictions include European paintings of a woman, known as the Knitting Madonna, sitting with her needles in her lap, which began to appear in the fourteenth century and seem to be the first documented evidence of knitting in Europe.

We know very little about the evolution of knitting in the next few centuries, other than from small regions that developed their own esoteric styles. Fair Isle, the Channel Islands, Ireland and other areas of the British Isles all produced unique styles of knitting, as did Iceland and other Scandinavian countries, Northern Europe, and the countries on the perimeter of the Mediterranean. While we often hear about the history and peculiarities of these particular styles of knitting, their influence on the fashion world is also readily apparent. Knitted lace, Fair Isle patterning, trailing cables and intarsia work have all evolved into the modern knitting vernacular and are the basis of the knitting styles that have been a major part of the fashion arena of the twentieth century.

Fashion reveals a great deal about the social values of an era, and the evolving style of dress documents the evolution of society and culture. In reviewing the major fashion styles of the twentieth century we are able to trace the influence these have had on knitting and on sweater styles in particular.

Early Art Deco (1911–1929)

This era saw clothing become less structured, less restrictive, less fitted and more flowing—a direct reflection of the social upheaval of the day, particularly in the women's movement. The automation of the knitting machine at the end of the previous century had brought knits into the fashion arena; however, knits were more influential at this time in the sporting field. Wool was touted as having health properties, and woolen sweaters were worn primarily as sporting wear for golf and tennis, with pullovers and knitted sports coats the most significant pieces. The most influential garment of the era was a traditional Fair Isle pullover worn by the Prince of Wales in 1922 for a game of golf—the ensuing trend was so big it is credited with having revived the flagging Scottish woolen industry.

Other notable events took place around 1918, with the end of the era of the Victorian corset, when knitted one-piece bathing suits began to appear, and in 1927 when Elsa Schiaparelli dazzled the world and launched her design career with her famous black-and-white trompe l'oeil bow sweater.

Late Art Deco (1930–1945)

During the depression years of the 1930s, the glamour of Hollywood ushered in a more traditionally feminine image for women. Evening knits were hugely popular at this time, often lavishly embellished with beading, feathers and embroidery. Marlene Dietrich and Katharine Hepburn, the darlings of the movie world, helped make it acceptable for women to wear trousers, and this provided the opportunity for American designers to establish themselves—until then the influence of the French designers had prevailed. The twinset was born in this time, perfect for pairing with trousers, and in the 1940s the short to-the-waist finely knit sweater was all the rage.

During the Second World War, knitting took on new popularity as women took up their needles for the war effort. In more economically depressed countries knitting became a means for money saving, a way to make warm clothes for those at home. Everywhere, sweaters, socks, and caps were knitted for soldiers. Some of the items of this era, like the balaclava, were introduced into the fashions of the time.

Postwar (1946–1963)

Once the war was ended and soldiers returned to take up careers and marry, women were expected to give up their wartime work efforts to become homemakers and mothers. This new domesticity, embodied in the growing middle class of America in the 1950s, kept fashion on the path of the decidedly feminine. Christian Dior led the New Look with longer hemlines, narrow shoulders, closely fitted bodices, and full, crinolined skirts, and then later, the narrow long skirt. These were topped with pretty fitted cardigans in small-gauge stockinette accented with bands of Fair Isle, allover small cables, fine stitch patterning, or small, feminine lace patterns. Structured jackets and coats were also knitted, but the biggest hits were the tightly fitted "sweater girl" look, or its antithesis, the big, baggy Sloppy Joe pullover, a look derived from women wearing oversized men's sweaters over fitted skirts or pants.

This era saw the introduction of the Aran influence in American knitting, as well as the revival of traditional motifs, such as argyles and herringbones—all patterning that had a rich, well-bred look in keeping with the burgeoning wealth of postwar industrialization. During this time, other fibers were added to wool as the technology in the textile industry grew, making yarns softer and more appealing to the hand knitter. Angora and mohair became popular, with the luxurious "fluffiness" adding to the soft, feminine mystique of the time.

At the end of this era, the biggest influence in fashion was designer Yves Saint-Laurent, whose less fitted styles engineered in modern materials permitted him to sculpt shapes that stood away from the body. It was also the era of Jackie Kennedy and Audrey Hepburn, in which there was a distinctly tailored, dressed-up approach to fashion. Knitted coats and pullovers featured all-over surface stitches as knit designers sought to mimic the textured wools created in the new suiting technology.

Youth and Change (1964–1973)

The Civil Rights movement, the Vietnam War, the women's movement and the cultural revolution of the youth movement dominated this era, in which there were probably more changes to society and fashion than at any other time in our recent history. Revolution was in the air, and it was very apparent in the fashions of the day. Old values, old looks, and traditional views of femininity were tossed aside as clothing became anti-structure and anti-Establishment—long and flowing, with skirt lengths swinging from mini to floor length. New musical trends influenced mod and rocker fashions, and then there were the hippies, with their homespun, folkloric look. This era also saw the beginning of thrift-shop style, which gained prominence again in the '90s as retro dressing became suddenly hip.

The Boom Years (1974–1996)

After the influences of the past era were incorporated into the dress codes of the day, there was an eventual settling down, but not before the best aspects of the change were highlighted in the new fashions of the '70s. The leaning toward the handmade look was one of the main reasons for the subsequent revival of hand knitting and hand-knitted looks. As well, updated technology was responsible for the engineering of much more creative yarns, often made from the combination of synthetics with wool and other natural fibers.

The Brit pack, consisting mainly of Edina Ronay (known for making traditional Fair Isles fashionable), Kaffe Fassett (with an artist's approach to color knitting), and Patricia Roberts (whose chunky, brightly colored sweaters drew international interest), were largely responsible for the rise in popularity of hand knits in England. The British influence took the American market by storm as designers incorporated knits into their lines, and hand knitting was suddenly incredibly popular. The late '70s saw a revival in knitting at home—with new technology in yarns and a much more creative approach to writing knitting patterns, and their availability to so many more people. Runways were featuring knits of an entirely different style as designers pushed the limits to use yarn and knitting stitches, as well as crochet, in entirely innovative and creative ways. From enlarged stitches, chunky yarns, and bold colorblocking to unstructured looks, ponchos, and wraps to oversized crochet, anything was possible and readily accepted. Brightly colored tank tops worn over psychedelic-print shirts were de rigueur for all as denim jeans became the backdrop for knits, smock tops, embroidered cheesecloth, and granny-square ponchos.

Sonia Rykiel's trademark striped, tight mod sweaters were a major force, especially when paired with fitted knit caps sporting her signature bunch of faux foliage and fruit. In Italy, the Missoni family began creating knitted garments in unusual color mixes and stripes over interesting stitch patterning, ushering in a timeless look that has lasted to this day. In the United States, the way was paved by the most talented and lasting designers of the latter part of the twentieth century. Perhaps the biggest influence at the time was Perry Ellis—Mr. Pop of American fashion—who designed young fun knits with graphic images (think signature playing-card pullover or scenes of the New York City skyline at night). He even sold kits of his designs to knitters who wanted to create their own versions. Adrienne Vittadini's sculptural cables and intarsia pullovers that featured wonderful images drawn from pop culture, as well as more traditional looks, were at the core of her very successful line. Joan Vass, a popular designer of classic clothes with an interesting twist, was known for her innovative shapes, combinations of interesting yarns, and clever construction techniques.

As the hippie look began to appear a little tired, Americans were calling for a new way to dress. In direct opposition evolved the dressed-up casuals of the early '80s that became the uniform of the American preppy and the British "Sloane Ranger." Calvin Klein created more sedate hand-knitted looks that worked with his classic approach to designing for the American public, as did Ralph Lauren, who made '30s-style Scottish knits popular, the biggest look of the time being the Fair Isle round yoke pullover. The '80s also ushered in power dressing with the menswear-inspired suit a major player in the wardrobes of working women, causing a decline in the importance of knits in everyday wear. The converse of this masculine look was after-five disco glamour. Knits were either fabulous with accentuated shoulders and glitz, or were more relaxed weekend pullovers.

Hand-knitted sweaters were primarily the domain of knitters as there was a decline in interest at the designer level. However, it was at this time that the basic shaped pullover, slightly oversized with straight sides and dropped shoulders, was introduced, making knits very easy for most women to wear. As the '90s progressed, there were still wonderful examples of knits in the lines of the more important designers. One of the most innovative and influential designers of this time was Donna Karan. She continued to show knits in both her Signature line and her incredibly successful and more casual DKNY line. They ranged from highly textural artwork in the early '90s to much simpler, yet still groundbreaking pieces as the century drew to a close. Miuccia Prada swept the world by storm during these years also, as she approached fashion from a more ladylike, slightly dressy viewpoint, showing a variety of knits that perfectly accented her very influential collections.

Perhaps the biggest influence on our dress during this era was the evolution from the dressed-up times of the '50s and '60s finally to the relaxed casuals of the '90s. The dressed-down mood began to prevail in our entire society—even Wall Street embraced the new look as the power suit was replaced with business casuals. Women no longer needed to prove themselves at work—they no longer needed to dress the part to be a player in a traditionally male world. The extreme of it all was the grunge look, but most people found their own level of comfort in their own approach to casual attire.

The New Millennium (1997–2000)

As the century drew to a close, a gentle mood of nostalgia took most of us by the hand and led us back through our past, as we prepared to enter a new century and a new millennium of unknowns. In the early years of the '90s there was a definite interest in the fashions of the '60s and '70s as a source of inspiration. In the late '90s, subtle aspects of '80s style made their way back into our wardrobes. Perhaps the best aspect of this retro/nostalgia approach to design was the swing back to knits—to their comfort just as much as their style. Better yet, there was a new, young generation that had been raised in the sweatshirt era but had not yet experienced the joys of being wrapped in (or seen in) a wonderful sweater. In the words of Valentino, "I believe that every piece of a wardrobe today can be made in knit," and this was the general tone as knits showed up everywhere, in every major collection on the planet. Not only were there incredible sweaters, cardigans, scarves, wraps, and coats, but handbags, tank tops, shells, and sleeveless turtlenecks. Knits began to show up in home fashions as well—in luscious throws and pillows, lampshades and chair covers in every fiber imaginable.

So many trends were evident at this time. Global looks ruled, as the melding of many looks came to be cool, from wonderful folkloric to urban hip. There was Stella McCartney for Chloe with her glam rock-chick chic. Knitter extraordinaire Julien MacDonald at Chanel spun his beautiful cobweb-inspired creations, and Michael

Kors created new classics, with traditional stitches reinterpreted into very wearable pieces. Longtime knitter Marc Jacobs, once of Perry Ellis, was the new darling of the younger set, creating interesting pieces for both his own and the Louis Vuitton label. Isaac Mizrahi and Todd Oldham, also longtime knitters, included groundbreaking pieces in their collections. Again, mainstays Donna Karan, Ralph Lauren, and Calvin Klein continued to create innovative knits that set the trends for the urban fashionista both in their collections and in their diffusion lines of more affordable clothing. Easy shapes, lightweight but chunky yarns, self-finished edges, cowls and turtlenecks, shrugs and—for a brief moment—ponchos, were all very strong looks, easy to wear, and easy for the new breed of young knitters to make in a reasonably short amount of time. No-fuss knits in easy stitches were created for the no-fuss woman of the late '90s.

The economic-boom years fueled spending on all luxury items; knits and knitting yarns were no exception. Coupled with a glut in the cashmere market and the driving force of the runway, the cashmere craze was born, showing up in the usual knitted pieces, as well as home accents. Cashmere yarns were suddenly available to the knitter to create the same luxurious looks at home, and the cost of the yarn gave knitting a new cachet. At cashmere house Malo, knit kits were selling for over $900, and knitting acquired a new image as the pastime of the wealthy. It became the new Hollywood craze and was *the* activity of choice for Julia Roberts, Sandra Bullock, Cameron Diaz, Daryl Hannah, and many others, and articles began appearing in every fashion magazine and on TV newsmagazine shows.

In the new millennium there is still a yen for traditional knit styles, and now the trend is to look back to the wonderful craftsmanship of times gone by, as we are developing a new appreciation for originality, fine work, and incredible detail.

TRISHA MALCOLM is the editor-in-chief of *Vogue Knitting* and *Family Circle Easy Knitting* and the editor of over 20 books about knitting.

17

Knitting on the Go—Events and Travel

Spending time with fellow knitters at a retreat, camp, festival, or tour enhances the relaxation and deepens the pleasure of knitting. What a knitting class or lunchtime club offers in small servings of learning, camaraderie, and relaxation, a retreat or tour serves up in long, leisurely expanses of time.

Events that span two or more days include camps and retreats, conventions, national and international travel, fiber festivals, and country fairs. For a complete, annually updated list of events, see the *Interweave Knits* annual *Traveling Knitter's Sourcebook,* published in the September issue and available on the *Interweave Knits* Web site year-round at www.interweave.com.

Camps and Retreats

In beautiful settings, from the Adirondack Mountains of New York to the Black Forest of Colorado, knitters on retreat have the opportunity to immerse themselves in the experience of knitting. For several days, the focus is on learning new techniques, sharing stories about projects, and being around others who are also passionate about the craft. The beauty of nature enhances the peaceful atmosphere of a retreat where knitting takes center stage.

Camp Stitches, a retreat sponsored by *Knitter's Magazine,* takes place annually at rustic locations such as Silver Bay, New York and Lake Junaluska, North Carolina. For four days, knitters fill the chairs on the porch of the main building. They knit and talk about their projects and their families, and share helpful hints as the porch becomes abuzz with fluttering movements and clicking needles. Classes during the day help knitters learn new techniques and chat with experienced professionals, authors, and designers while they compare notes with fellow campers, who represent all levels of experience and talent. At night needles are left in the bungalows for activities like English line dancing and boat trips on the lake. Last year the most popular classes sold out months in advance. One of them was taught by Sally Melville, author and designer. In her class, Knitting as a Metaphor for Life, she spoke about how patience, attention to detail, creativity, and setting appropriate goals are all principles learned while practicing knitting.

The Green Mountain Spinnery, a Vermont yarn shop, sponsors an event each year in mid-September in New England. The weekend event moves to different locations but is always in a cozy setting where meals reflect the local cuisine. In addition to classes, people who attend the retreat take a tour of the Spinnery's plant, where a private yarn sale is held for them. "The rural beauty and distinctive culture of southeastern Vermont give attendees the feeling that they have really been able to get away from it all, while stretching the boundaries of their knitting knowledge," says Margaret Wilson, one of the owners of the Spinnery.

On the opposite side of the country, in the romantic Victorian town of Port Townsend, Washington, Helga McDonald, a designer, teacher, writer, and yarn-shop owner, runs Knitting by the Sea. After twenty years of hosting the retreat five times a year, Helga has noticed an increase in the number of younger guests who are just learning to knit. "The most wonderful knitting groups are a mixture of beginning, intermediate, and advanced students," says Helga, "where the sharing, learning and knitting friendships soar."

The sessions are five days long and the fee, about $900, covers tuition, lodging, food, and class materials. Guests stay in a rambling post-Victorian house with formal gardens. They gather to knit on wrap-around porches with views of the ferries and pleasure boats cruising the Strait of Juan de Fuca with the snow-capped Cascade Range in the distance. Helga limits the retreats to twelve people, to create a feeling of a knitting family and to offer individual attention and help. Knitting by the Sea members live together in the house, share home-cooked meals, and become part of the family atmosphere created by "mother" Helga. When guests are not sharing their craft with other knitters, they visit the town or roam the trails and bluffs along the seaport.

Knitting Travel and Tours

Knitting tours are a chance to explore the varieties of ways in which knitters around the world work and design. These tours focus on places that have a long history of locale-specific knitting traditions. Tourists have an opportunity to shop for yarns they cannot find at home while enhancing their yarn collections. The itinerary of a tour typically includes visits to museums that feature the fiber arts, trips to the homes of internationally known designers, and of course, shopping expeditions. From Alaska to the British Isles to South America, knitting tours offer a combination of cultural awakenings and knitting experiences that inspire participants and bring learning to life with the scenery, language, clothing, and traditions of knitters around the world. The cost of one- to two-week tours typically runs from about $1800 to $2500.

One popular tour to South America is called Behind the Scenes Adventures. The guide, Cynthia LeCount, explains that the name of the tour is derived from the purpose of the trips, which is to go behind the scenes to meet the artists and craftspeople—to visit their studios, homes, workshops, and factories. Cynthia, who has been to Bolivia twenty-two times in as many years, has developed a network of friends among the local artisans, who produce indigenous, traditional crafts. Travelers on Cynthia's tours enjoy a family-like intimacy with the Andean knitters in each of the small villages they visit. Unlike tourists who typically see local residents from a distance, members of the group are welcomed into the village and the homes of the men and women who demonstrate their craft. These villagers work with hand-spun hand-dyed, brightly colored wool, spun from the animals raised in their community.

A typical two-week trip starts with a flight to La Paz, Bolivia. When the group arrives, they are given a chance to settle into the hotel and explore the town and the textile market, which overflows with woven and knitted treasures. Day trips include a visit to a designer-sweater factory where knitters produce alpaca sweaters in radiant colors, and an exploration of pre-Incan ruins. As the tour continues, they visit the Cuzco region, composed of small rural highland communities where a weaving expert accompanies the group as they learn about indigenous knitting and weaving specific to each community. While visiting remote villages in the mountains, the travelers are treated to a lunch of local cuisine at the home of one of Cynthia's friends. Finally the group flies over the Andes to Lima, Peru, where they survey pre-Columbian textiles at several museums and visit the local crafts markets.

Vogue Knitting sponsors cruises and trips throughout the year to destinations around the world. *Vogue*'s offers include a Baltic knitting cruise and trips to Australia, Ireland, and England. Renowned knitting experts and authors such as Alice Starmore, Debbie Bliss, Hanne Falkenberg, Sasha Kagan, and Jean Moss have accompanied the groups, offering their insights on local design and techniques. Tour members have an opportunity to meet some of the stars of the knitting world, to be inspired by their work, to benefit from their experience, and to learn about the place that knitting has in their lives and their countries.

Alaska, the Yukon, and the Northwest Territories are the scenes for summer tours run by Jane Button of Dolly Varden Tours. The week-long trips include sightseeing at a bald eagle preserve, watching bears feasting on salmon, and visiting fiber artists at the Great Northern Arts Festival. The trip starts in Juneau, Alaska, where the group takes a ferry to Haines, Alaska. Jane introduces the knitters to native fiber artists in the Yukon town of Whitehorse, where the culture, lifestyle, and knitting traditions have remained unchanged for centuries because they are in a remote area, far from foreign influences. During one leg of the trip, the group travels 460 miles in Canada, from Dawson City to Inuvik through undeveloped land. There is only one place to stop and spend the night, with little else in between. But, no one complains about the vast expanses of undisturbed time. In July it is light for almost twenty-four hours, and the travelers happily knit until 2:00 a.m. without realizing it is the middle of the night. Button, who has been guiding knitters through the wilderness for several years, believes that at the end of the tour, each person has gained an appreciation of how vast North America is, while observing the multitude of knitting styles and creative use of colors and design of native peoples.

Knit shops on this tour offer indigenous yarns that are found virtually nowhere else in the world. Several years ago beaver, with an extremely soft feel, was the group's favorite. This past year, the preferred fiber was muskox, an animal that looks like a buffalo with a crown on its head. The inner fur of the muskox is called qiviut, which is softer than cashmere. Qiviut can be purchased only in Alaska and Canada and is so rare that a hand-knitted scarf made with this fiber can cost $300 or more.

Knitters have the unique opportunity to experience, firsthand, the cultural context of knitting in different corners of the world. In addition to learning more about knitting with others passionate about the craft, travelers can understand the ways that knitting traditions evolve from the local fibers, cultures, and history of the people who develop these traditions.

Fiber Festivals and Country Fairs

In the United States, where not long ago a significant portion of the population lived on or within hailing distance of a farm, most Americans are tourists when it comes to rural scenery and the activities surrounding breeding, raising, and utilizing farm animals. Even fewer of us have ever seen a shepherd.

Sheep and wool festivals are run by organizations that are dedicated to promoting sheep and wool products and to educating the public about these activities. Admission is free or nominal and visitors enjoy country music, local food, and demonstrations of the farming life and arts. It is an opportunity not only for knitters but for adults and children of all ages interested in the many facets of sheep farming and fiber arts to see a purely American tradition.

The Maryland Sheep and Wool Festival is organized by the Maryland Sheep Breeders Association. During the festival, about 1000 sheep are sheared and judged. Attendees at the award ceremonies learn the fine points of distinguishing a blue-ribbon animal from an average one and how to assess the herding abilities of sheepdogs. One of the competitions, a sheep-to-shawl event, pits teams of shearers, spinners, and weavers against each other in an all-day event that gives visitors a rare glimpse into the complete process from shearing to finished garment. Shopping is one of the most entertaining parts of the festival. Visitors can choose from local crafts and food booths, or attend an auction of animals or weaving equipment. Yarn lovers will find it particularly enjoyable to shop in this authentic atmosphere, where natural fibers abound.

Another such event is the Taos Sheep and Wool Festival, which draws about six thousand visitors each year. The most popular attractions, according to organizer Mary Stabolesky, are the vendor booths with wool items, demonstrations of wool spinning, weaving and knitting, and the silent and live auctions of crafts and animals such as Angora goats. The mission of the festival is to spotlight and promote wool grown in Colorado, New Mexico, and Texas, as well as alpaca, cashmere, angora, and mohair. Navajo churro sheep were brought to the area by the Spaniards and raised by the Navajo Indians. They had become rare until the local farmers began raising them, bringing them back from near extinction. These sheep have a hairy outer coat and a downy undercoat that make the wool both soft and durable. Other sheep featured are Wensleydale and Teeswater breeds with long, shiny, curly wool, brought over from England and still endangered. Vendors are local residents dealing exclusively in fibers produced in the Southwest.

Sheep and wool festivals are one way for knitters to invite spouses and children to share in their love of knitting fibers and crafting. At these events there is something for everyone in the family to enjoy from live music to local food and demonstrations of the farming lifestyle.

18

Knitting on the Web

When knitting sites first appeared on the Web in the early '90s, the popularity of knitting was at a low point in the United States as a generation of knitters moved into retirement and the younger generation showed little interest in the craft. The online knitting community has been a crucial factor in the resurgence of knitting. Kim Salazar, webmaster of wiseNeedle.com, says the support and information provided by online knitters has increased her knowledge, interest, and motivation to knit and made her feel more comfortable knitting in public.

The virtual online world helped motivate people to knit in public, which helped spread the popularity of this relaxing and creative craft and dispel the myth that only grandmothers knit. When people began to communicate and commiserate online about their experiences knitting in public, they often spoke of their embarrassment when knitting on trains and in waiting rooms and encountering people who made critical remarks. Knitters e-mailed responses sharing their indignation and offering support and encouragement. Once the issue was brought out into the open, people were emboldened to knit in public again. This, says Salazar, illustrates the impact of the online knitting community: "Knitters who use Internet resources are more adventurous, teach more, and, in general, are more confident about pursuing their hobby, thereby attracting others to do the same."

Today, a few short years after knitting took root on the Internet, the resources available to knitters there are almost limitless. You can obtain hundreds of free patterns, develop and enhance your skills, ask a question about any knitting-related matter, and form friendships.

E-commerce has become part of the knitting world as well. The number of yarn shops, small fiber farms, and craft catalogs that sell yarn, needles, patterns, books, and other knitting-related items on the Internet is astounding. Many have taken their sites a step further and offer not just goods for sale and information about their products, but teaching tools and free patterns as well. A good place to start your hunt is at a search engine such as Google at www.google.com. Type in the word "yarn" or enter the specific name of the yarn or accessory you're interested in purchasing. The search engine will return thousands of results, or "hits," which you can click on to go to. (Hint: On a Windows PC, right-clicking your mouse opens the site you've selected in a new window so that your list of search results is also still open.) The more specific your search is, the more accurate your results will be.

Although many knitters consider buying yarn to be a tactile experience, people who are familiar with a specific yarn often opt to purchase online for more comprehensive selection and convenience. In a typical 50-mile radius of anyone's home, there may be few or no places to buy yarns, and rarely are there more than 50 different types of yarn in any single yarn shop or discount chain. Purchasing online allows a customer to choose from many hundreds of yarns, thousands of colors, and is an opportunity to find a significant quantity of one dye lot—rarely found in a store. There is also the added convenience of having the yarn delivered right to your door.

One of the most interesting and valuable aspects of the Internet is the way it facilitates communication with other knitters around the world on bulletin boards, Listservs (or e-mail lists), and in chatrooms. It wasn't that long ago that the only way to reach others who shared your love of knitting was to go to your local yarn shop or perhaps a guild meeting. Asking for help with that problem you were having with a pattern simply had to wait until you had time to drive down to the shop. Knitters now disseminate information via the Internet about patterns and styles of knitting. Active online discussions can catapult a new yarn or popular pattern into nationwide popularity. Knitters also commonly form very strong bonds online, occasionally resulting in off-line meetings and friendships that last a lifetime.

Remember that Web sites, like home addresses, are not static, so what is here today may be gone tomorrow. The Web site addresses, or URLs (uniform resource locators), provided in this chapter were accurate at the time of publication. If the URL listed here doesn't take you to the site, try typing the name of the site into a search engine to get the updated address. Accessing the sites and downloading patterns may be more time-consuming if you have a slower modem or an older computer, although many sites try to keep their graphics small for faster downloading.

Here, culled from the vast array of knitting-related Web sites, are the best and most useful sites categorized by their purpose and strengths.

Web sites That Teach Knitting and Enhance Skills

The best Web sites for instructional information not only have excellent illustrations, but also use Web technology to add animation or film. The people behind these sites have developed them as a labor of love and are motivated by a generous desire to teach.

The Craft Yarn Council (www.craftyarncouncil.com) has links to pages on their site (www.learntoknit.com) that offer excellent knitting lessons. The council also offers a program that certifies knitting instructors. The site includes general information about knitting in the news, locations and times of Knit-Outs and the charity Warm Up America!

Caryl and Nancy Nelson own a shop called Common Threads in Encinitas, California. The goal of this mother-daughter team is to offer products and training in many of the time-honored fiber arts to people who might not have the opportunity to have these skills passed down to them from family members. Free videos of the basics of learning to knit are available at their site (www.fiberartshop.com/index.htm) on streaming video. It's easy to use and much like watching a movie on your computer. As you advance, you can join their Video Knitting Club for a small annual fee and view a wide variety of videos teaching additional skills.

Borealis Sweaterscapes (www.sweaterscapes.com/index.htm) is

a small mail-order company located high atop a hill in rural Maine and owned by Doug and Lynne Barr. They have been in business since 1989, when they created their first sweater design for L. L. Bean. They specialize in intarsia landscape designs, and sell kits and books. "I studied painting privately as a child and in college, and Doug studied at Rhode Island School of Design. The landscape designs have been a true collaboration and it has been wonderful working with him," says Lynne. Currently Doug also works as a mechanical engineer and Lynne homeschools their two sons.

Their helpful site includes excellent tutorials on intarsia knitting as well as seaming, picking up stitches, and short rows. "Obviously, we enjoy and like to encourage the arts," Lynne states. "Knitting is generally classified as a craft, but it is also a creative endeavor which, for many knitters, is their personal foray into an art form. It's a useful art that also satisfies the wonderful qualities of giving and sharing. Just ask some recipients of knitted items how it feels to be on the receiving end, and also look at today's charitable knitting. Bravo knitters! So if anyone benefits from our help section then we feel grateful to be able to do our very small part and to you for helping to make the connection."

Annette Roennow, who has been making three-dimensional toys and dolls since 1994 using basic knitting techniques, runs the DnT, Inc. Web site, which offers animated knitting techniques (www.dnt-inc.com/barhtmls/knittech.html), unique animations illustrating skills such as yarn-overs, casting on, and binding off. She is motivated to teach knitting on her site because of her belief in the value of knitting. "I thoroughly enjoy exercising this wonderful craft, because it offers such indescribable tranquillity," Annette says. "You can always create something quite unique which cannot be purchased anywhere and it is made in your country instead of being imported. To keep knitting alive has now become the main interest in my life."

Vardhman Knitting Yarn (www.cuddlesvardhman.com/how/index.htm) has been a leading producer of yarn in India since

1978. In addition to information on their company and lots of free patterns, they provide a wide variety of illustrated instructions on the basics of knitting as well as seams, joining new yarn, decreases, and increases.

A Wealth of Free Patterns

There are more free patterns available on the Internet than one can knit in a lifetime. They can be found on sites run by yarn manufacturers, shops, designers, and everyday knitters who just want to share their patterns with others. A desirable pattern can motivate people to purchase a yarn they might not otherwise have on their shopping list. In 1999, for example, Joan Hamer, publisher of the newsletter *Pine Meadow Knitting News,* posted a sock pattern on an Internet KnitList (see "The Knitting Community Online" on page 198) that called for Lion Brand Wool-Ease. The pattern became so popular that it created a resurgence of sock knitting and increased the sales of Wool-Ease.

Sarah Bradberry runs knitting-and.com (www.knitting-and.com), notable for over 500 free patterns from afghans to a Barbie G-string (www.knitting-and.com/knitting/allpatterns.htm). Some of the patterns are Sarah's original designs and some are designed by others and available there with the designer's permission. She started her site "because there were no publishing opportunities for knitting designers in Australia at the time (early '90s). I had mailed proposals to every magazine and knitting publisher I could find in Australia, only to receive their standard reply: 'We get our patterns free from our advertisers.' I thought it was a waste to design something and only knit it once," she says, "so I put my patterns on a Web site in case anyone else might like to make them. I think I started with two patterns and some pictures of various things I had made." Sarah is a freelance knitwear designer, pattern writer, author, and Web site designer for fiber-related sites. "None of these manage to pay the bills at the moment," she says, "but I'm working on concentrating on the things I like best and making a go of those as a business."

Yarn Forward (www.yarnforward.com/index.html) started as a mail-order company on the Internet in 1996. They have since expanded and now have two stores in Ontario, Canada, selling yarn, kits, patterns, and books. This family-owned and -operated company of active and knowledgeable knitters is headed up by Helen Gunther, who is assisted in various roles by her sister-in-law, Louise Manship, her parents Roger and Carol Manship, and family friend Jo-Ann Raven. The Web site includes almost 20 free patterns for everything from sweaters to slippers and a beautiful christening gown and shawl not to be missed. "The free patterns have been put on the Web as a service to knitters and as a method of attracting people to the site," says Roger. "The patterns have been derived from a variety of sources including staff, family members, and friends." Roger, with his mathematical background as an engineer, has recently begun creating patterns.

Frugal Knitting Haus (www.frugalhaus.com/home.htm) is owned by Ruth Braatz and is based in Woodbridge, California. She offers more than 30 free knitting patterns, many of which are very simple and good for beginners. They are primarily for projects that you don't commonly find patterns for, such as placemats, hair scrunchies, and a dishpan scrubber. There is a strong emphasis on patterns using leftover yarn, hence the name Frugal Knitting Haus. How did she get started? Ruth's statement on her site explains, "When I married, I was on a very tight budget, and I made sweaters for the children using leftover yarn from my mother. After the children got bigger, I started knitting little things like potholders for gifts. I thought about selling my things at craft fairs, but no one wants to pay you the money you've put into it. I wanted to work at home, so I started advertising by mail order."

Flor's Homepage (flor.freeservers.com/handknit.htm) has a wide variety of free patterns for sweaters, hats, and motifs, all designed by the webmaster, Flor. It also contains tips for advanced knitters, including shaping options for drop shoulders, Norwegian steek techniques for armholes, and a gallery of beautiful garments she has knitted from commercial projects over the years. Flor was born and lives in southern Brazil in a city called Florianópolis, where the downtown area is located on an island surrounded by 42 beaches. A lovely feature of the site is a collection of pictures of the beautiful, little-known town where Flor finds inspiration for her designs (www.flor.freeservers.com/home.htm).

Lion Brand (www.lionbrand.com), established in 1878, is a family-owned business that markets yarn throughout the United States and Canada. Their site contains over 200 free knitting patterns for throws, sweaters, baby blankets, and garments for children; new patterns are added monthly. A high school–age member of the family set up the site, one of the earlier entries to the Internet, in 1995. The company's current webmaster connected with Lion Brand when she was searching the Internet for a ball of cotton yarn to make potholders. As a graduate of Stanford who had been programming since she was a child, Nancy Miracle welcomed the opportunity to combine two of her loves—knitting and programming—and offered to develop the site. In addition to free patterns, the site offers free screensavers related to knitting and yarn as well as hints and tips for knitters.

The prevalence of free patterns on the Web has raised interesting issues regarding copyright. Some people have the mistaken belief that since the patterns are on the Internet, they can be copied and distributed freely. In fact, each pattern is copyrighted and it is a violation of copyright law to distribute them without permission. Jennifer Tocker, with the assistance of others, has put together a guide to copyright law that should answer most questions and lays out what is and is not permissible in easy-to-understand language. The Copyright FAQs (frequently asked questions) for Knitters (www.geocities.com/jbtocker/copyright) is well worth a visit.

All-Encompassing Sites That Collect and Organize Valuable Information

Knitting.About.com (www.knitting.about.com), one of the topic-driven sites of the About.com project, is arguably the most extensive Web site with practical content about knitting. The "expert guide," as About.com calls the host of each specialized area, is Barbara Breiter. A former geriatric social worker with a degree in creative writing and a master's in social work, Barbara put up her own site in the mid-'90s to try to organize some of the content on the Web aimed at knitters. As with most webmasters who start private sites, it was a labor of love. She was a self-taught knitter, who found a book in the library to teach her how to knit once she found herself out of wall space to display her needlepoint. She also learned HTML (hypertext markup language) to create her Web site. About.com contacted her to run their knitting site and she went live in March 1997 with about 50 pages. She singlehandedly runs the site, which has ballooned to over 2000 pages of free patterns and information on every conceivable aspect of knitting, from instructions on basic and advanced knitting techniques to knitting-software reviews. "Just when I think I've covered everything there is to cover," Barbara says, "someone will send me a terrific idea." The Local Yarn Shop Review section was one such idea. "The person suggested that reviews of yarn shops by real knitters would be a reference that people could use before they traveled to see which shops in that area were must-visits." She asked for submissions from people who use her site and there are now scores of reviews for shops throughout the United States and Canada along with addresses and phone numbers.

Wool Works (www.woolworks.org), run by Emily Way, was started in 1994 by this English major and was impressive from its inception. Emily is an American who immigrated to Canada in 1992 and works as a technical writer. The site offers free patterns, discussion groups, reviews of knitting books, and help with everything from spinning to making socks and information about buying yarn around the world.

Kim Salazar heads up wiseNeedle.com (www.wiseneedle.com/home.asp). Kim is a Web production manager for companies that make high-capacity data networks and Intranet infrastructure hardware. She finds knitting to be "a refuge from the high-stress world of inflexible deadlines and intangible results." She describes herself as a "lone wolf" knitter until she discovered the Web, where she found other professional women and men who shared a passion for yarn and knitting. Kim's range of knitting interests is broad—from lace to stranded colorwork to socks—and she does most of her own designing.

The Internet has enhanced her knitting, she believes, because it "has given me a sense of connection and place, the ability to wait until I have the time to participate . . . then to welcome me back seamlessly and without guilt. I have found new friends around the world, a ready-made family at the other end when we relocated from D.C. to Boston, and the confidence to begin teaching formal classes." She says, "I was having so much fun just hanging out with other knitters that I wanted to do something useful for them in return." As a result, she compiled an international glossary of knitting terms in English, French, Italian, and German, and founded an extensive, interactive, online collection of yarn reviews. Her site also boasts a searchable list of over 1000 yarns, including fiber content, yardage, gauge, manufacturer, and other key information.

Those interested in lace knitting will find a wealth of information at Knitted-Lace List (www.knittedlace.com/index.htm). You can join their mailing-list discussions, find free lace patterns, view photos of finished projects, and read reviews of books specifically on lace knitting. The site and list are run by Helen Eisler with assistance of others who help to coordinate exchanges and welcome new list members. "I only got interested in lace in the mid-'90s," says Helen. "My first project in lace knitting was an edging, but I just couldn't get the hang of it. I put it away for a while. Then one day I pulled it out and tried again and that time I got it. I have been knitting lace every since." Helen finds her contributions to the online knitting world both enjoyable and rewarding. "I love reading about what others are doing, what they are experimenting with, and what they are having problems with. And I have worked with computers for many years, so I enjoy that aspect of running the list and Web site too. Plus, the list is a means for persons serious about lace knitting to communicate, and I find being able to provide a 'place' for them rewarding."

Socknitters (www.socknitters.com) is a site and mailing list devoted exclusively to sock knitting. It's run by Linda Nelson with the able assistance of others. They have a very active mailing list, with over 3000 members. The site includes lessons on how to knit socks, free patterns, a huge gallery of photos, and lots of tips and help.

The Knitting Community Online

There are three primary ways to discuss knitting and make knitting friends on the Internet: Listservs (mailing lists), bulletin boards, and chatrooms. Mailing lists are e-mail messages that are sent to people who are subscribed to the group; you must join the group in order to send or receive these messages. Bulletin boards reside on the Web. You can post a question or an answer and your message is read by anyone with access to the board. Chatrooms also reside on the Web; either no special software is needed, or a simple downloadable program is provided on the room's site. You simply log on and can chat in real time with others who are in the room at the same moment by typing in messages.

MAILING LISTS

The scores of knitting mailing lists are as varied as the things we knit and the yarn we use. There are lists for discussing general knitting topics, Aran knitting, knitting for larger women, knitting for children, and knitting for charity. Each group has its own culture and its own set of rules. It's important when joining any new group to spend some time "lurking"; that is, reading messages in order to learn what the acceptable norms of the group are. Some groups encourage and allow OT (off-topic) chitchat, while others do not. Most groups have a formal set of rules that you are expected to abide by. When you're comfortable, jump in and start making friends or asking questions!

Within general interest sites, areas have been developed that serve the knitting community. Amazon.com, for example, has a lively and intelligent knitting community. They have good reviews of all the relevant books, comparisons with similar books, and quite a few knitters have posted their own lists of favorites on linked pages under the "Listmania" heading. Almost every book listed in Chapter 24, "The Literature of Knitting," whether it is in or out of print, is available used and at a bargain price on the site. Knitters can save time and money, and broaden their library by using the peer-to-peer reviews and second-hand buying available on Amazon, eBay, and Bibliofind.

Many lists are set up through a service that Yahoo! offers. It's a good place to see and join the varied groups that are available. At present, there are 197 mailing lists set up at www.dir.groups.yahoo.com/dir/Hobbies_Crafts/Crafts/Knitting.

For a peek into what knitters are currently talking about, join the KnitList (www.groups.yahoo.com/group/knitlist). This is one of the largest knitting lists, and it offers an opportunity to communicate with several thousand knitters. A wide range of knitting expertise is represented, from top New York designers and editors at the center of the knitting world to a beginning knitter in Juneau, Alaska. Topics include everything from the current trends in yarn to sharing the best response members have ever received from a knitted gift. During the holiday season, those who wish to participate present a gift to the list: an original pattern of their own design. These patterns have been archived on the Internet since 1995.

The KnitList was founded by Jill McAllister at the University of

Minnesota in 1994 and is currently moderated by three women affectionately known as ListMoms: Barb Burri, Ruth Schooley, and Mary Hunt. "It has been interesting to watch how the KnitList has evolved," says Ruth. "At first, it was composed of mostly academics because they had computers available at work. Then, as the cost of computers became more reasonable and Internet access available to more and more people, the character of the list changed to accommodate them. I like to think that the KnitList provided a safe place for people to learn about computers and the Internet."

The women rotate the responsibility of ListMom weekly, updating informational files on the list site, adding new members, and reminding folks to stick to their knitting, as off-topic posts are generally not allowed. "For the most part, I find it enjoyable," says Barb. "It's interesting getting to know different knitters online and following the ebb and flow of the trends in both knitting and posting. It gets maddening sometimes when the list gets off-topic and gentle ListMom reminders aren't serving well to put us back on track. The two weeks after September 11 in New York and Washington, D.C., were some of the most rewarding, seeing how the facility to share feelings and knitting all rolled into one helps folks deal with the attacks." Mary has been with the KnitList almost from the beginning. "There are times that the list is very difficult, when arguments start and reason is out the window," she says. "But there are the other times that make all the difference in the world. The caring on this list is phenomenal. I've met some wonderful people who have become close friends. I've learned so much from the list."

When they're not busy with their ListMom duties, Barb is a self-employed software engineer and computer consultant, Mary is employed as a secretary at Cornell University and has designed some patterns for small yarn companies, and Ruth is a librarian at the Honnold/Mudd Library of the Claremont Colleges in Southern California.

Another popular mailing list is called KnitU or Knitter's University. Sponsored by *Knitter's Magazine,* (www.knittinguniverse.

com), it is moderated and led by "KnitU dean David Xenakis and his Knitting Faculty," including Lily Chin, Joan Schrouder, Rick Mondragon, Meg Swansen, and Sally Melville. On this list, when you e-mail a message to be posted, it must first be approved by the moderator to be sure that it adheres to the rules of the list. You can ask (or answer) a question about an unfamiliar knitting term, a pattern you're having problems with, or any other number of knitting-related topics. The list has almost 3000 subscribers, and messages are archived from December 1998.

An online knitting magazine, entitled KnitNet (www.knitnet.com/current/toc.htm) offers a well-developed site with feature stories, useful information, and patterns.

BULLETIN BOARDS

Bulletin boards, sometimes referred to as forums, are another way of communicating with other knitters. As with mailing lists, there are numerous boards on the Internet. Many knitters are members of several of these communities. How you read and post messages differs from board to board, depending on the type of software used; some are easier and more user-friendly than others. Some have search functions that allow you to easily find messages of interest.

Wool Works (www.woolworks.org/cqi-bin/dcforum/dcboard.cgi) has discussion boards for topics including patterns, knitting techniques, contacting other knitters, knitting sources, and the Wool Works site. The Craft Yarn Council (www.craftyarncouncil.com/cyca-forum/) sponsors bulletin boards for knitting and another for tips to be shared by both knitters and crocheters.

You'll also find a board at the Knitting Guild of America (www.tkga.com/wwwboard/wwwboard.html), where knitters can ask questions and search for patterns.

MSN Communities (communities.msn.com/KnittingandCrochet) offers a board for those who knit and crochet, led by Gwen Butler. They often do exchanges of different types, where members exchange items with other members. Their Kitchen Exchange is popular. Each member who wishes to participate exchanges three handcrafted items for the kitchen with another member.

Knitting.About.com (knitting.about.com/mpboards.htm) has three forums: the Marketplace Forum, the Knitting Patterns Forum, and the Knitting Forum. Barbara Breiter, who moderates the boards, has watched as friendships have developed; some people visit religiously, every day, to check in with the current conversation in their favorite thread. "A new person will join us and ask a question and be amazed by how quickly they get multiple responses to their knitting dilemma. We have an amazing group of friendly people who are very knowledgeable knitters," Barbara says.

During a month-long period, those who wanted to learn to knit socks were invited to participate in the Great Sock Adventure at Knitting.About.com's forum. A free pattern on the Internet was chosen and the start date was announced in advance. New knitters and veterans alike all knitted the pattern at the same time, with the veterans stepping in to assist the new sock knitters with questions and problems they were having. "It was a great success. Many people learned to knit socks and wondered why they had been so intimidated by them before!"

CHATROOMS

Finally, another great way to meet other knitters and establish friendships is in interactive chatrooms. Like bulletin boards, they all work a little differently, but none are difficult to learn.

MSN Communities' Knitting and Crochet Board has a scheduled chat every Monday night at 6:00 p.m. Pacific time (9:00 p.m. Eastern time). They welcome new knitters to join in. The URL (communities.msn.com/KnittingandCrochet/chatroom.msnw) takes you to the sign-in screen. Knitting.About.com (knitting.about.com/mpchat.htm) has scheduled chats Monday, Tuesday, Wednesday, and Friday, and (knitting.about.com/library/blchatsched.htm) shows the chat schedule.

The offerings on the Internet for knitters are constantly expanding. Yarn companies continually develop their sites to include more content; charities offer updated information about what and where to contribute; magazines provide current lists of knitting events, and Listservs expand their communities. As a result, we enjoy more opportunities to learn, to broaden our experience, to share in knitting activities and events, and to enjoy the support of like-minded people. The alliance of two seemingly opposite worlds—the high-tech, virtual Internet and the low-tech, tactile knitting community—continues to power the growth and development of knitters and their craft.

19

The Healing Power of Knitting

Of all the reasons for knitting, its ability to soothe, comfort, and heal may be one of the most compelling. When airports tightened security after the attack on the World Trade Center, confiscating knitting needles along with knives, Internet knitting lists buzzed with concern about how people could travel without their knitting. This is not the response of people who use knitting as a mere diversion or hobby. For many, it is a safe, effective stress reducer; some even describe knitting as a lifesaver.

Meg Manning, a yarn-shop owner, expresses a common sentiment among knitters: "I know I'm a calmer person for knitting. The repetition, the soft caress of the yarn, the opportunity for reflection as I knit—all of these things soothe and pamper me as no trip to a spa (or a psychiatrist) could."

Knitting creates a body-mind feedback-loop effect. Knitters describe how the simple, repetitive motion recalibrates their breathing to more even, deeper breaths that induce emotional calm. They also note that the concentration needed to follow a pattern deflects the mind from worries that could otherwise spiral out of control. This soothing of the mind also enhances physical well-being.

Rosemary C. is one of those for whom knitting became a lifesaving activity. Rosemary, who had been a nurse for 15 years, changed professions after a work injury. Now 42, she works from her home doing medical transcription and computer graphics. For her, knitting is far more than a means of enhancing her wardrobe. Throughout her life, knitting has been an important part of the process of overcoming difficult times of stress or crisis.

She met her husband in 1997, and by 2000 was planning a wedding. The normal stress of making wedding plans, arguing over the details with family members, working out a difficult situation with a future stepdaughter, and trying to meet tight deadlines for clients upon whom she depended for income became overwhelming. One day, while making arrangements with the florist, she had a terrifying experience that made her fear for her life; her heart suddenly started pounding, she felt dizzy, and she started gasping for breath. She was certain she was having a heart attack. Her fiancé rushed her to the doctor, beginning a long process of diagnostic tests and various drug therapies to lessen the symptoms. Finally, she was diagnosed with anxiety/panic disorder. "It was during this time," she remembers, "that knitting really helped me cope with everything that was going on."

"Not being a person who likes taking medication anyway, I tried to find ways to wean myself off the drugs. I didn't like feeling goofy most of the day and didn't want to develop a dependence on the medication. That's when knitting became the focal point of my life." Terrified to leave the house for fear of having a panic attack or passing out in public, Rosemary felt isolated and "left behind." Knitting countered that feeling by giving her a useful way to spend her time and a sense of accomplishment.

Rosemary took on the most complicated projects possible. Her favorites were advanced and intricate lace patterns that required intense concentration. She says that the knitting helped to soothe her, to distract her from the thoughts that were causing her stress. Knitting claimed her attention, keeping panic attacks at bay.

In order to keep working, she often had to travel alone on public transportation, a situation she particularly feared. Rosemary was somewhat embarrassed to knit in public, and in any event, she found it physically difficult to carry her knitting when she traveled, laden with paperwork. She resourcefully devised a way of mentally "knitting."

"I would memorize a row or two of the pattern, and mentally 'knit' my entire trip. On the trip I visualized my needles doing the knit, yarn-overs, and k2tog (knit two together) stitches to make the pattern. The funny thing was that, even in my mind, I could make a mistake if I happened to look out the bus window, so I mentally unknit the stitches that weren't right. I concentrated as hard as I could and was actually able to 'see' my knitting needles making the stitches. I guess I shut myself out from the real world and totally focused on my knitting. I don't know how I would have made those trips otherwise." With each successive trip without a panic attack, her confidence grew, and eventually she was able to venture out again and again without an attack.

Shortly after her wedding, Rosemary realized that she had completely weaned herself off the medication by using her knitting needles. Whenever she feels like stress is getting the better of her, she goes into a "knitting frenzy" and creates intricate afghans, sweaters, and shawls that she usually gives as gifts to family and friends. "Not only is knitting therapeutic," she says, "but I have something beautiful to show for it."

Another knitter, Sue, tells how knitting helped her work through a period of grief. Her grandmother, an expert knitter who had taught Sue to knit when she was a child, was battling cancer. As long as she was able, in the long waits at doctors' offices and during chemotherapy treatments, Sue's grandmother worked on a complicated Norwegian ski sweater for Sue. When her grandmother passed away, Sue's grandfather handed her the bag with the unfinished sweater. Sue decided to finish the sweater, and she struggled to work the challenging pattern, trying to match the quality of her grandmother's work. Sue remarks that "the beauty of this sweater was that it made me feel like my grandmother was with me, helping me through this process."

By finishing a sweater that her grandmother had started, Sue experienced the continuity of her grandmother's life—and in some sense kept her grandmother with her until it was a little easier to let go. The sweater, a shared project, was a tangible connection between the two of them, and the lifelong gift of knitting has served Sue well. "Whenever I pick up my needles," she says, "I think of my grandmother and say 'thank you.' "

Diane S. was also able to use knitting to ease her grief. She didn't realize that her knitting was a source of comfort until she found herself without it during a difficult time. When her father died, she returned to her family's home in Texarkana, Texas, where she hadn't lived since college. The practice of the town was to "be at home" with the family of the deceased. For days after the funeral, friends and neighbors came to the home, fried chicken and Cokes in hand. Diane worked on a project the first day as she sat and tried to make conversation with people she barely knew. Concerned that the visitors would think it rude of her to work on a sweater during the period of mourning, she left her project in her room the second day. By the end of that day she was "a complete nervous wreck! It had become clear," she realized, "that some sort of handwork is necessary for my mental health, especially in times of stress." She says that, since then, she has never been without a project.

When asked how knitting has helped them through a difficult time, many knitters often use the phrase "it helped me maintain my sanity." For Pat Ashforth, a British mathematician who experienced health problems at several points in her life, it not only helped to maintain her equanimity, but also gave her an added career as a knitwear designer. "I would not be the knitter and designer I am today had I not experienced a serious illness," she says. She knitted through two difficult pregnancies that each required two months' bed rest, and later while going through dialysis for kidney failure. The time she spent knitting also helped her develop and express mathematical concepts in an easy-to-understand way—by displaying them in her knitting. Collaborating with a fellow mathematician, Steve Plummer, she designed colorful, geometrical afghans. She and Steve wrote a book entitled *Wooly Thoughts* about their theories of design, which included using simple garter stitch, creating squares, and experimenting with color. Long periods of time in isolation, recovering from a kidney transplant, and the inability to go shopping for yarn contributed to Pat's unique approach of using odds and ends of leftover yarn and thinking through math problems with her needles in hand.

Carol S. was a stay-at-home mom with a new house and two young children when financial problems shattered their comfortable lives. Her husband's health care company, threatened by a change in government regulations, was on the brink of bankruptcy. Sue had to get a full-time job and leave her children, ages five and two, in day care. Her new job was stressful and she found herself in the depths of a serious depression. When her doctor asked, "What do you do for *you*?" she almost laughed. Stretched to the limit both emotionally and physically, there was nothing she did for herself. But one day, while running errands, she passed a knitting shop and decided to buy some needles and yarn, a small luxury, even though she had not knitted in over ten years. "It was so relaxing and my projects actually looked good. I could feel my self-confidence coming back."

Her family got past the most difficult times, but whenever Carol feels stressed or down, she picks up her knitting. "I pull out my needles and can feel the tension leave my body. I also see the joy in my kids' faces when they say, 'You made that for me?' But knitting is something I do for me—it brings me so much joy."

Elaine D., a young mother of a three-year-old daughter, woke up from a nap one day with a horrible feeling of dizziness and vertigo. She was sick for two days and was eventually diagnosed with a virus that caused her to become completely deaf. "Most people can't understand true silence," she says. "We aren't talking a little hearing, like most people have when they are hard of hearing, but complete and total silence. I have stood next to a fire truck with the siren going full tilt and not been aware of it until I saw people running past covering their ears with their hands and grimacing." She also suffered balance problems that made it difficult to walk. Like others, the words she used were "knitting kept me sane." She felt less isolated when she knitted. "When I got frustrated with communicating with people who refused to write things down for me,

I would knit. When I realized that this was what the rest of my life would be like and I would never hear my daughter talk to me again, I knit. It kept me going, and it kept me strong." Today, with a cochlear implant, she can hear her daughter again. But she is certain it was the knitting that kept her going through the years when she heard nothing.

Elaine believes that knitting helped because it was "productive, creative, positive, and, at the same time, was a form of meditation" that helped her relax. She was mourning the loss of her ability to dance, walk, ski, swim—or even to perform simple household duties. She felt like a failure as a mother because she couldn't understand her daughter's simplest requests. But knitting gave her something she could do herself: "Most of my life seemed to be a shambles, but I could still knit and make beautiful things."

How is it that knitting can help someone overcome difficult emotional and even physical problems? Mihaly Czikszentmihalyi, a professor of psychology and author of several best-sellers, coined the term "flow" for the mental state of total engagement in an activity in which a person does not experience herself as being separate from the activity and time seems to pass unnoticed. While experiencing flow, a knitter is oblivious to her surroundings, feels in control of her actions, and experiences a sense of well-being. When people describe the pleasurable feeling that Czikszentmihalyi calls flow, they mention these seven facets of the experience.

1. There is a clear goal, with specific, visible markers of accomplishment on the path to that goal. Knitting is such an activity; a knitter always knows where she is within the pattern and how far she is from finishing. The knitted item itself provides tangible evidence of achievement.
2. Complete engagement in an activity that requires all of one's attention allows the experience of flow. The activity must be engaging and challenging, neither frustratingly difficult nor too simple. Some knitters require a complicated pattern to

help focus their mind on their knitting, but others may relax from the repetitive motion of a simple stitch pattern. When we are focused on what we are doing in the present, we don't have the psychic energy for anxious, distracting thoughts. The mental engagement eliminates boredom and the anxiety that often accompanies it.

3. Creativity and the sense of satisfaction achieved from performing a task that is a unique expression of ourselves are important elements of a flow state. Even when we follow the exact same pattern, no two sweaters will be exactly the same; the experience and result are unique each time.
4. One experiences a sense of control. No matter how out-of-control our environment or our emotions may feel, the knitter is in complete control of the needles and the resulting stitches.
5. The sense of time becomes subjective; clock time doesn't necessarily correspond to experienced time. Hours may fly by, or particularly intense moments may seem to stretch time itself.
6. Self-consciousness disappears when we are focused on a task such as knitting. Most of the time, when interacting with others, we are burdened by the need to satisfy or impress them. In a state of flow, we are too busy with the task at hand to worry about protecting our egos. As a result, we emerge more self-confident.
7. The altered state of awareness characteristic of flow makes people feel at one with the task. Athletes describe this feeling as being "in the zone." When a knitter is thoroughly absorbed in the work, it seems effortless, as if activity and awareness are perfectly synchronized.

The meditative quality of knitting is what keeps so many knitters calm in stressful situations like doctors' waiting rooms. In many ways, knitting is like prayer, the repetition of stitches like the phrases of psalms. In his book *The Relaxation Response,* Dr. Herbert Benson describes the calming physical reaction elicited by such activities, which helps counteract the fight-or-flight response.

The fight-or-flight response kicks in when we feel threatened. Our brain sends signals to the rest of our body that trigger chemical changes, like the secretion of epinephrine, also known as adrenaline. This makes our heart pump faster and our blood pressure rise. While this response is an innate protection from danger and useful when we have to run out of the way of an oncoming car, many of our contemporary fears take the form of persistent and long-term worries that wear on us mentally and physically. Perceived threat can come from a fear of impending job loss or, ironically, concerns about our own health.

We can alleviate the long-term stress caused by ongoing negative and worrisome thoughts by simply relieving the thoughts. People find personal and unique ways of doing this. Benson believes that activities that help elicit the relaxation response become part of a society's practices and are handed down from generation to generation. The relaxation response stimulates the sympathetic nervous system by way of a rhythmical activity such as chanting, praying, painting, and of course, knitting.

In *The Relaxation Response,* Dr. Benson suggests two specific activities to counter the physical reaction that assaults us when we are under stress. First, he suggests that you focus on the in-and-out of breathing, which brings your natural rhythms under control. When you are feeling stressed or in a state of panic, your breathing automatically increases and your breath is shallow. By using your breath as a sort of metronome, you bring your bodily responses into a smoother pattern. As your breath slows and becomes more even, your heart rate slows down and blood pressure is lowered. Benson also teaches patients to focus on the repetition of a word, a sound, a phrase, a prayer, or a movement. In knitting, the relaxation response can be triggered by the rhythm of the needles and the repetition of the stitches. Some people have described the feeling that their heart rate stays in synch with the movement of the needles.

Knitting does more than provide rhythmic movements that can be relaxing. It can provide a sense of accomplishment and control in the midst of life situations in which we feel helpless, hopeless, and very much out of control. And it can provide periods of contentment, even joy, in allowing us the experience of flow.

20

The Commerce of Knitting

The multitude of ways to shop for yarn and the wide array of yarns available to knitters can seem overwhelming. Yarn and other knitting supplies can be purchased at national and local chain stores, independent knit shops, catalogs, garage and yard sales, fiber farms, online shops, online auction sites, knitting lists and forums, and consumer shows. Even when your pattern limits your choice to yarns that match the pattern's gauge, there will still be a vast selection of yarns and colors to choose from.

While price is a consideration, your choice of yarns should be guided by both appropriateness and value. For example, a hand-knitted gift for a new baby should be machine washable and dryable and made of a fiber or blend that will not irritate a newborn. No matter how impressive you want the gift to be, it is not advisable to use cashmere or alpaca yarn, which cannot be machine-washed and might irritate the delicate skin of a newborn baby. That does not mean that you need to knit baby items from the lowest-price yarns. Several yarn companies make extremely soft, reasonably priced baby yarns of premium acrylic or blends in contemporary color palettes. On the other hand, if you are knitting a complex, multi-patterned throw as a wedding gift, you should consider the recipients' lifestyle and décor. You may or may not want it to be machine washable, but the yarn should be of enduring quality and beautiful coloration and texture.

To determine the true cost of the yarn you are buying, take the price and divide it by the yardage. This will level the field when you are comparing the costs of yarn, as the sizes of balls or skeins vary, as does the yardage per ounce of different yarns.

In the early part of the twentieth century most people who knitted did so because they could make something for less money than it would cost to buy it. With a few dollars' worth of yarn and a few weeks of time, a knitter could create a sweater or afghan for less than half the price of a store-bought item. However, when women first entered the workplace en masse in the late 1970s and early 1980s, their attitudes toward the value of their time changed drastically. For someone trying to balance the time spent on a career and a family, it made sense to use a yarn that would endure and to choose projects that would be worthy of the valuable expenditure of precious time. Knitters are motivated more today by a desire to create one-of-a-kind items for personal use or gifts that reflect the generosity of a handcrafted, loving effort. This attitude has changed both the types of yarns that knitters demand and the variety of yarns available in the marketplace.

Today, most of the yarn in the United States is sold in three chains: Wal-Mart, Michael's Arts and Crafts stores, and JoAnn Fabrics & Crafts. At one time these stores carried only 4-ply acrylic worsted-weight yarn, but today they offer a much wider variety, including natural fibers, natural fiber blends, and novelty, textured yarns such as Lion Brand Homespun. A number of regional chain stores, such as A. C. Moore in the Northeast; Hobby Lobby in the middle of the country, from North Dakota to Texas; and local fabric stores such as the Rag Shop, also sell a significant amount of the most widely purchased yarns. The price of most yarns in these stores ranges from one dollar a pound to over a dollar an ounce. Bargains can be found in chain stores during promotions, when selected yarns are sold close to or even below cost, and during periodic reorganizations or closeouts. The department manager can probably tell you when such promotions will occur. Chain stores also carry a wide selection of needles, tools, pattern books, and, occasionally, tote bags. Some offer knitting classes either free or for a nominal cost.

Your shopping experience in these stores will vary depending on the capability of the department manager or salesperson in the yarn department. Some stores have a policy, rarely publicized, which allows a department manager to special-order a color of yarn or more balls of an existing color they don't have in stock. This is particularly helpful, since it may be difficult to find enough of one color or dye lot to complete a pattern.

The second major source of knitting yarn is in the typically small, independent yarn shops, of which there are about 1200 around the country. Affectionately referred to as LYS, or local yarn shops, in the shorthand of Internet knitlists, each store is unique. Its stock may include hand-spun, hand-dyed yarn, luxury mixtures or cashmere, as well as more moderately priced blends of natural and acrylic yarns. Yarn shops can range in size from large, supermarket-style stores to tiny boutiques.

To locate a yarn or fiber shop, check in your local yellow pages or look at the *Interweave Knits* Web site's list of yarn shops by state (http://www.interweave.com/knit/sourcebook.htm) or the About.com knitting site's yarn-shop reviews (http://knitting.about.com/cs/yarnshopsreviews). Both *Knitter's Magazine* and *Interweave Knits* publish a yearly "ShopFinder" for subscribers.

Individually owned yarn shops reflect the flavor of the region as well as the philosophy, interests, and personality of the owner. You can often receive special services such as custom patterns and technical assistance. Although perhaps only about 15–20 percent of yarn sold in the United States is sold in these stores, they provide a shopping experience so personal and so permeated by the passions of their owners that they are worth special note. Here are examples of some of the different types of shops that offer knitting supplies.

Occasionally, stores known as mill stores will stock only the yarns produced and/or dyed by the owner. One such shop is Artfibers Yarns, which has been in business for six years and recently started a fine art textiles gallery. Located in downtown San Francisco, adjacent to the financial center (the Charles Schwab world headquarters is located next door), Artfibers draws traffic from local residents, business people, and international travelers staying at nearby hotels. Artfibers develops its own products in conjunction with spinners worldwide, and operates its own dyeworks and packaging operations. The staff have created fashion pattern collections appropriate for their yarns, some via computer software they helped to develop (which is also for sale). Patterns are offered free with the related yarn purchase. The store customizes patterns for their patrons, measuring them and showing them how to take their own measurements. Customers are encouraged to knit a gauge swatch for the pattern to check that the garment will fit perfectly.

The pricing philosophy at Artfibers is to provide good value. A kit for a women's medium long-sleeve pullover in mohair and silk costs about $84. A sweater kit in 70% angora in handpainted colors is about $72, but a sweater kit can be purchased for as little as $30. One of their more unusual yarns is from Nepal, produced from reclaimed sari silk.

Yarn Expressions is a 2000-square-foot store located in the Deep South in Huntsville, Alabama. Owner Meg Manning's goal is to provide a wide selection of yarns and materials and friendly, helpful service. "We are dedicated to our customers, whether we know them or not," she says. "My primary goal is to share the joy I derive from knitting with as many people as I can. That philosophy frees me to give help to anyone who walks in the door, regardless of where the project was purchased." The shop offers regular classes, and the demand to attend classes often exceeds the supply. This motivated Meg to create a video so students can learn at their own convenience. The store offers kits ranging in price from $30 to $260 and a variety of yarns from acrylic blends to rare, delicate fibers. "I would never belittle another person's choice of yarn, and happily send people to Wal-Mart, Hobby Lobby, or Michael's for the craft yarns they seek if we don't offer them.

"The knitting community today," Meg says, "is much more adventurous than when I learned to knit. Not only are novelty yarns incredibly popular, but we're exploring unconventional methods of creating garments. Mitered squares, strip knitting, new intarsia methods—these were all unheard-of for most of the '60s and '70s."

Playing with Yarn is located in Knife River, Minnesota, and

owned by Judy Casserberg. In Judy's 27 years' experience working in knit shops she has noticed a few changes. "The customer has become more hobby oriented. They are not knitting to clothe a family but for themselves. Customers are willing to pay more for special yarns. They want to knit something they would find in a boutique rather than a department or discount store. Knitters are getting younger and they love color and texture. They are more experimental. If they want a hood and the pattern doesn't have one, they add it. They are doing more than one project at a time. They are forming knitting groups with neighbors, coworkers, friends, and college roommates. The new knitters make time away from their families to travel and knit. They read and purchase books. As their skills improve, they want to learn finishing techniques rather than having sweaters put together for them. They feel that better tools are important and don't mind paying the price for high-quality implements."

Tara Jon Manning is the owner of Over the Moon, a combination knitting and coffee shop. Her love of design motivated her to have an outlet for her work and to share her love of hand knitting through instruction and support. She, also, notices an influx of new knitters; a large percentage of her client base is under age 40. Because the store is located in a high-tech area in Longmont, Colorado, many customers are computer programmers and scientists.

The Webs store in Northampton, Massachusetts, offers knitting supplies and discounts yarn purchases based on the size of the purchase, with specials available at their Web site (www.yarn.com, click on "specials"). The Webs store is organized into a main, warehouse-like room that has yarn in boxes and on shelves, as well as smaller rooms that include a room with only neutral-colored yarn, a mohair room, and a chenille room.

For those who prefer to shop from home, there are several catalogs (most of which have accompanying Web sites) that offer yarns, accessories, and information. Catalogs usually offer color cards or swatch cards that help a consumer shop from home by providing samples of yarn to allow a true sense of color, texture, and feel.

Patternworks is a catalog that offers a wide range of premium brands of yarn and a large color selection. In close to 100 pages, there are about 190 different types of yarn organized by weight, with patterns for each yarn. There is an extensive selection of needle brands and sizes, buttons, books, and accessories. Patternworks has perhaps the broadest overall selection of products for knitters, although it has a limited supply of more moderately priced yarns. The catalog is printed once a year with intermittent newsletters that provide information and offers.

Lion Brand Yarn Company's catalog is notable for the depth of selection in both price range and color (nearly 500) of their yarns. The nearly 125-year-old company started the catalog in 1996 in response to thousands of letters that often began, "I am desperate . . ." from customers who needed one or two more skeins to finish an ongoing project or customers who couldn't find enough of a color or a dye lot for a project in their local stores. The catalog includes a growing selection of knit and crochet patterns for the family as well as knitting needles, tote bags, and knitting-themed jewelry.

The Herrschner's Yarn Shoppe Catalog, published twice a year, offers a selection of yarns that includes both natural fibers such as alpaca, angora, mohair, and wool, and acrylic blends. They offer a range of colors in each yarn as well as patterns for sweaters and children's clothing and home décor patterns and accessories. Herrschner's also has a large-circulation crafts catalog, which offers everything from plastic canvas to rug hooking kits.

There are several other catalogs of interest to knitters. The Mary Maxim catalog carries a variety of craft supplies for rug hooking, cross-stitch, and quilting as well as knitting kits and yarns. The Stitchery specializes in needlepoint and has a continually improving selection of knitting kits. Cotton Clouds carries many varieties of cotton yarns. The Wool Connection has a selection of almost 60 different high quality yarns as well as kits and accessories.

Knitters also turn to the Internet to purchase yarn and knitting supplies. Many stores and catalogs have Web sites that allow online purchase with a credit card. The Web offers round-the-clock shopping from home, with no salespeople or checkout lines, which is ideal if you know what you are looking for or prefer to shop without assistance. One drawback is that the images of items are often not as good as those in a catalog and the colors on any given computer screen may vary. Many chain stores and local yarn shops have Web sites as well, although not all accommodate online purchasing. A few sites, such as eKnitting.com, sell exclusively on the Web, and *Knitter's Magazine* has a site, Stitchesmarket.com, which offers yarn, kits, tools, and accessories.

On any given day on eBay or Yahoo!, there are thousands of offers to sell yarn, knitting books (both current and out of print), and accessories of all sorts. These are excellent places to find discontinued yarn or out-of-print books. Another site for used or rare books is Bibliofind.com. A recent search for "knitting" yielded over 3000 widely varied titles. On Internet knitting lists or forums a knitter can offer unneeded yarn for sale, ask fellow knitters for help locating a hard-to-find yarn needed to finish a project, or even trade items. It may even be possible to find a long-discontinued dye lot by contacting yarn enthusiasts on Internet knitting lists. The knitting site of About.com provides a marketplace forum where knitters buy, sell, or barter for yarn.

Garage and estate sales may yield treasures such as brand-new yarn, partially completed projects, or yarn found in the back of a closet that has been discontinued for many years and is currently unavailable anywhere. Old hand-knitted sweaters found at garage sales can be pulled apart to supply a hard-to-find color for a project you are working on. To "harvest" the yarn from a sweater, carefully cut the seams with a seam ripper, lay out the pieces, and locate the bound-off row. Then cut the end and unravel the sweater slowly enough to avoid separating the yarn or creating knots. Since the yarn will be kinky, you may need to dampen it slightly and wind it around a large rectangular surface such as a loose-leaf notebook or large piece of cardboard to straighten it out before winding it into a ball. Sometimes it is necessary to wet or spray the yarn to straighten it out.

Other sources of yarn include the Stitches Markets that are held at the Stitches conventions around the country several times a year. Here yarn dyers, spinners, shops, and manufacturers' booths offer a spectacular selection of yarns from around the country. You can browse wares from a yarn shop in upstate New York, a shop in Atlanta, and a sheep farm in the Midwest all in one location. The booths at Stitches offer not only yarn and needles, but also every possible knitting-related item, from books (including out-of-print books) to jewelry, calendars, bags, and stuffed animals, all designed with the knitting enthusiast in mind. Yarn is also offered for sale at the various sheep and wool festivals around the country (see Chapter 17, "Knitting on the Go"), at country fairs, and farmers' markets.

For those who love the colors and textures of yarns, the problem will not be how to find a specific yarn, but how to maintain control when the options for purchasing yarn are so abundant. The most passionate purchasers of yarn do not limit themselves to one means of purchasing yarn. They buy to suit a particular need for convenience, price, and selection. Whether trying to find a yarn to fit a specific project or simply purchasing on impulse, a yarn buyer will find that using a combination of all of the buying methods—from shopping the wide variety of retail stores to the Internet to catalogs or knitting events—will satisfy every imaginable yarn desire.

21

The Chain of Knitting Instruction

You will always remember the person who taught you to knit. The generosity and patience that it takes to teach knitting, the physical closeness of a one-to-one lesson, and the opening of a new world of possibilities—all contribute to the enduring quality of the memory. Knitters relate vivid, detailed memories of learning to knit, marking it as an important moment in their lives. For those who embrace this craft for its many benefits and make it an ongoing and integral part of life, knitting is a treasured gift.

Knitting provides a link with others. Many knitters report that as children and young adults, they were able to bond with a family member with whom they might not otherwise have had an opportunity to feel close. Others find it a way to recapture a precious memory of watching loved ones knit. Rebecca, a Yale law student, decided to pick up knitting when she was in the middle of law school. "A few of my friends have recently taken up knitting," she says. "I think that we enjoy knitting because we think that it is a good way to unwind and it also has meaning because it serves as a connection with other generations. I remember watching my grandmother knit as a child."

When Jessica, a 37-year-old knitter, received the call that her grandmother had died, specific memories of her "Nana" flooded back to her. "My memories of times with Nana involved us knitting together," she recalls. "My Nana had a long and full life and I'm so thankful for the knitting legacy she left me."

For people of all ages, but for children in particular, the feeling that someone is taking the time to be present and patient while one works provides a sense of loving acceptance, warmth and security. "I am fourteen," says Becky, one young knitter, "and knitting is probably one of my favorite activities! My mom taught me to knit when I was about four. I remember every lunchtime I used to sit and knit this big old red scarf. Every time I had finished two rows, I'd give my piece to my mom to take out the mistakes, so as you could imagine, it took quite a while to finish."

Karen, a member of the KnitList, agrees. She remembers learning different styles of knitting from her mother and grandmother. "These are some of the most pleasant and enduring memories of my childhood and I never pick up my needles without thinking of my family."

Randy, a male knitter from the Midwest, recalls, "I learned to knit when I was about 11 years old. We lived in Michigan and the winters were always cold. My mom would sit by the fire in the living room and knit mittens, hats, scarves, slippers, you name it, for us nine children." One particular year she had a long list of garments she had promised to knit for her children before she could finish a pair of slippers she had promised to make for Randy. Impatient for his slippers, he asked her if she could show him how to knit. "When I finally became proficient at it," he says, "my mom was surprised at how closely my knitting matched the gauge of her knitting. Some of my fondest memories are of those evenings by the fire on those cold winter nights knitting with my mom."

Today Randy finds that when he knits, it evokes the same warm feeling he had when he sat with his mom. He has been teaching his daughter to knit and believes that spending this kind of quality time with a child is important and will provide his daughter with fond memories of him some day.

Both children and adults are motivated and enthralled by seeing the work materialize on the needles, and a new knitter is often eager to admire and to show her progress to others every few rows. To maintain interest, a new knitter should select a small project that creates something recognizable—a hat, a scarf, or a baby blanket. The sooner a project can be finished, the more powerful the motivation to continue to knit and to go beyond the basics. But young children are easily distracted and limited in their ability to follow patterns and advance in technique. People who learned as children often pick up knitting again at later points in their lives, like college or when they start a family.

Opinions vary on the best yarn and needles for beginners. We believe that it's easiest to begin with a thicker than worsted-weight yarn that is light in color so you can see your stitches more easily. A variable-colored yarn that is space-dyed or hand-dyed can also be good for early projects; the change of colors helps maintain interest and creates surprising results. Teachers usually start students with straight metal needles, but some believe that circular needles are best, to prevent dropping stitches.

It typically takes about 20 minutes to learn the basics of knitting, although people learn at different rates and prefer different routes—a teacher or book, video, or Web site (or combining bits and pieces of information from each). It will not be difficult to learn the basics of knitting from the first chapters of this book. If you want to proceed to the next steps, there are many opportunities and options for learning. Both independent yarn shops and some of the major retail craft chains offer knitting classes either free or for a nominal fee. Perhaps there is a friend or family member who can pass on his or her expertise. There are also knitting instructions, both advanced and basic, on the Internet (see Chapter 18) and learn-to-knit kits available in craft and yarn shops.

If you are curious and want to develop your skills further, you can avail yourself of any number of different methods. Once you know the basics, learning from a book is easier. To expand your choice of stitches, select a good knitting reference book (see Chapter 24, "The Literature of Knitting") and try some of the more advanced stitches in the stitch library section of the book. For a face-to-face knitting lesson, virtually all of the places where knitters meet offer opportunities to learn from others. Whether you go to one of the camps or conventions or take part in a knitting trip, your fellow knitters will almost certainly be happy to answer a question or demonstrate a technique when asked. Many of these events also offer knitting classes in all areas from Fair Isle to intarsia to finishing techniques.

In the beginning, you may find it easy or you may experience frustration, but if you are determined to knit, you will. Overcoming that frustration has its rewards, especially that of building confidence. Angel, who has her own online business, remembers her first attempts at knitting. "Practicing for hours and being so frustrated I wanted to poke my eye out with the needle. Then 'click'—all of a sudden it just worked. I don't know why, but it came together. My fingers worked like they were made for the task. Now I read every knitting book I can get my hands on. It's like the collective skills of all the wonderful women who've inspired me are being whispered in my ear."

Sally, a professional knitting instructor, first learned to knit as a child. She has chosen to pass on the craft to others and has observed initial frustration firsthand. "For a number of years I taught knitting at a friend's fiber shop," she says, "This was great. It was fun to experience the students' excitement at their newfound pastime. It was also interesting to occasionally see frustration—one person actually threw her knitting across the room! I encouraged her to take it less seriously, and she went on to become one of the best knitters I've known. Once she glimpsed the possibilities, she relaxed and her perfectionism served her well."

Bev, the director of Warming Families, a knitting charity, recalls, "My mother used to knit all the time and I remember her needles clicking gently and how comforting that sound was. But it was a lady who used to take care of us when my mom and dad went on trips who taught me to knit. Her name was Mrs. Plesner and she was originally from Norway. I have often thought of how many people have been influenced by her teaching me to knit. All the people who have received warm gifts, the homeless through Warming Families who benefit from my love for knitting and crochet too, and several people who I have taught to knit—who knows the good things they have done with this wonderful craft? Throw a pebble in a pond and watch it ripple outward. It's the same when you teach someone to knit."

22

Knitting Fellowship

One of the most compelling reasons to knit is the opportunity to work, create, learn from, and become friends with other knitters. Contemporary knitters easily find like-minded people with whom to share their passion for knitting because of faster transportation and communication—particularly on the Internet—as well as the proliferation of knitting conferences and events. The fellowship of knitters takes place wherever knitters gather: in the virtual space of the Internet, in knit shops, at knitting events like the Knit-Out or Stitches conventions, or at the meetings of knitting guilds. It takes only one person with a ball of yarn and a pair of needles to knit, yet knitters seek each other out for companionship, collaboration, information, and support.

Knitting Guilds

Knitting guilds have been in existence since the Middle Ages, when knitting workers (exclusively men) banded together to promote their profession, much like today's unions. Today's knitting guilds provide a place for knitters of all ages and levels of experience to gather to learn new techniques, to mobilize for charity work, and to make new friends. There's often a lively exchange of ideas about knitting, and members describe an opportunity to gain confidence while sharing their enthusiasm with other knitters. Even though the ages, occupations, and backgrounds of people in any given guild vary greatly, they are unified by their love of knitting.

The Knitting Guild of America lists hundreds of chapters on its Web site (http://www.tkga.com), and membership in each guild ranges from under 20 to hundreds of people. One of the country's largest and most active knitting guilds is located in Atlanta, Georgia. The first official meeting of the Atlanta Knitting Guild was attended by 52 people on February 6, 1985.

Whit Robbins, an artist, organized that meeting by putting notices in several local newspapers.

Her aim, she said, was to create relationships with local shops and to provide a network for knitters to learn, to stretch their skills, and to have fun together. "It is our little island of retreat and relaxation; refocusing on something creative and enjoying our craft and each other." Throughout the years they have helped each other with their knitting and supported one another through deaths, divorce, marriages, and the births of children and grandchildren. One charter member, Maggie Righetti, is the author of *Knitting in Plain English.*

The Atlanta guild has grown over the years to more than 140 members, including physicians, architects, lawyers, investment bankers, and an assistant district attorney who carries a gun in her bag along with her yarn and needles. "Our meetings are a welcome break from high-pressure jobs, talk of the markets, and forced deadlines," says one member.

Each monthly meeting of the guild has a planned program featuring a lecture or demonstration about knitting, often by a well-known figure in the knitting world. Out-of-town speakers fly in at the guild's expense, and members knit while learning from one of the country's most celebrated knitting teachers or designers. One of the most popular aspects of each meeting are show-and-tell sessions. Members bring projects that may or may not be complete, to share problems and work out solutions or simply to show off.

Charity work is an important part of most knitting guilds and as a large, active guild, the Atlanta Knitting Guild is busy year-round with fund-raising activities and donations to charitable organizations. The group works together on projects for local hospitals, knitting lap robes for hospice patients and hats for premature babies, as well as knitting in response to crises such as flooding in the Atlanta area. The Atlanta police distributed the several hundred teddy-bear sweaters they knitted for children who lost their homes during the flooding, and during a subsequent meeting, two police officers shared with the guild members how much the bears touched the children's lives. One of the guild's members from Bosnia helped organize members to work with the International Rescue Committee, which helps refugees from Bosnia, Vietnam, Croatia, and other countries resettle to the Atlanta area. The group teaches knitting to refugees and donates supplies.

Other benefits for guild members include a well-stocked, ever-expanding library of knitting books and videos, as well as trips and retreats. Once or twice a year the guild has a Knit Away retreat. For the past few years, they have been going to a retreat center in Highlands, North Carolina, called The Mountain, where members knit from dawn to dusk.

Carol Ogg, one of the guild's newer members, finds "inspiration and the confidence to tackle projects that a year earlier were only a dream." Linda Fetter, one of the guild's charter members, says that "all that creativity and energy feeds my enthusiasm."

The Big Apple Knitters in New York City boasts about 325 members and has grown steadily over the ten years since its inception. Former president Eve Ng estimates that, during the last two years, over 75 new members have joined, many of them in their twenties and thirties. The guild holds a general meeting once a month for which a speaker or workshop is the featured activity. Twice a year, guild member Michaela Schaeffer hosts informal meetings at her home in Brooklyn, where only charity knitting is permitted. The guild supplies the yarns, donated by yarn companies, the patterns, and the 50 or so participants bring their needles and food to share. "It's a relaxing, happy event with no stress, no lessons to focus on; just hanging out, laughing, and socializing," says Eve. There are also two annual events that take place in a popular New York restaurant. A recent event featured a runway fashion show of members' works. (Many well-known knitting designers are members of Big Apple Knitters.)

The guild holds a weekend camp in upstate New York in the spring. Attendees learn, shop, knit, and eat together in the scenic countryside. One of the activities is a pilgrimage to a local yarn shop, that offers special sales for the Big Apple Knitters'.

Because Eve wanted to meet with a smaller, less formal group, she organized a get-together the first Wednesday of every month to "sit, knit, and gossip." Fifteen to 20 people take over six or seven tables in the café of the Union Square Barnes & Noble during the fall and winter. Curious onlookers come to ask questions, new knitters stop to ask advice, and lapsed knitters offer to bring some of their stash to the next meeting. It's a relaxing, pleasurable atmosphere where the sound of laughter and clicking needles takes center stage in the midst of a bustling New York City café.

The Camaraderie of Knit Shops

For spontaneous, unstructured gatherings, local knit shops provide an intimate place for knitters. The quality of fellowship in a knit shop often depends on the personality of the owner and the neighborhood. Knit shops are places where knitters know they will find like-minded people with whom to exchange patterns, ideas, and solutions. A sociable and welcoming shop owner can create a home-away-from-home atmosphere for neighborhood knitters. Although not all shops have the space or staff to allow for social gatherings, they can still be an excellent source of inspiration for knitters.

At La Knitterie Parisienne in Studio City, California, owner Edith Eig presides over an upscale collection of yarns that caters to both the average neighborhood crafter and some of the most famous faces in the world. When knitting became a national trend in the late '90s, her shop became an inconspicuous gathering place for celebrity knitters. Television and movie actors found knitting a relaxing, creative, and productive way to spend downtime on the set between shots. While stars such as Jennie Garth, Tracey Gold, Julianne Moore, and Daryl Hannah stop by, knitting levels the playing field in the shop; everyone's primary concern is relaxing with current projects and sharing the companionship of other knitters.

Artfibers in San Francisco sponsors a quarterly show-and-tell party where attendees enjoy the recognition of having their work displayed on mannequins. Owner Nyle Seabright believes that daily courses, tutorials, and workshops are the core of the store's success. "We simply make sure that knitting becomes enjoyable and fulfilling for each person, on their own terms. When the customer gains confidence and gets compliments from friends, we do well. That is the basis of the Artfibers culture."

Playing with Yarn in Knife River, Minnesota, is a home away from home for its customers. The two-year-old shop is attached to owner Judy Casserberg's home, which overlooks Lake Superior and her gardens. In fine weather, the dyeing or knitting classes take place on the grounds. The store acts as a collection center for charity donations to the Salvation Army or chemo caps for the local oncology unit. "People feel that they have a caring place to come to," says Judy.

Stitches Conventions

Each year, *Knitter's Magazine* sponsors these conventions, which draw knitters from around the world. Stitches brings together under one roof, vendors of knitting supplies, both large and small, from across the country. The booths represent shops, yarn companies, companies that design and produce accessories such as bags and needles, hand dyers, craftspeople, and artists, all of whom provide products and services to knitters. They also have events including book signings, awards programs, classes, and speakers at the top of the knitting profession. The October Stitches East convention takes place in Pennsylvania. Stitches West is in February in Oakland, California, and Stitches Midwest is in August in Minnesota or Illinois. Over the years, Stitches has become a reunion for knitters who live all over the country.

A Knitting Encounter

As she scurried through airports on her way from one flight to another, flight attendant Pat Scott often scoured the scene for people knitting while they waited. One afternoon, with less time than usual to catch her next flight, she noticed a gentleman who was knitting a colorful sweater she recognized as a Kaffe Fassett design. Glancing at her watch, she realized she could spare exactly ten minutes and immediately struck up a conversation with the man, who was knitting the sweater for his wife. Pat asked him about Fassett, because this designer had been one of her inspirations, and they spoke urgently about yarn and what projects they were each working on. Pat wistfully mentioned a kit she thought fit his knitting style that she'd bought years ago but never had a chance to make. It was a hard-to-find kit made with a discontinued yarn, and he offered to buy it from her. With about three minutes left before her flight, she quickly decided to give up on the project, offering to sell it at her cost of $80. The man pulled out his checkbook and wrote out a check and handed it to her. "My address is on the check," he said. "Just send me the kit when you get home." They didn't even know each other's names until this moment, but a transaction involving trust and money had taken place inside of ten minutes. Later, when the man wrote Pat to thank her for the kit she sent him, he told her that his friends thought he was crazy for giving a stranger in an airport an $80 check with his name and address on it, although he never thought twice about it. Pat agreed that this event was unexceptional, remarking, "If knitters ran the world, it would be a much better place."

Barbara Selznick, a regular attendee, met her friends Dana and Pat 24 years ago, when they were flight attendants for Continental. Over the last 15 years, their primary connection has been their mutual interest in knitting. They speak almost every day on the phone, and once or twice a year the three friends, who live in California, Arizona, and Washington, meet at one of the Stitches Conventions. Each brings a gift to the convention for the others, like a knitting bag with the recipient's initials embroidered on it or a book in a gift-wrap featuring knitting designs. Over the years they have developed traditions surrounding their reunions at Stitches. When they enter the convention floor together, faced with rows of booths with every type of yarn and color combination imaginable, the first sentence Barbara utters is, "I can smell the yarn." Each year they pick an anthem for the convention they attend together—last year's was "Girls Just Want to Have Fun." And each time they meet, they commemorate the event with a group photo.

As a flight attendant, finding enough room in her suitcase for her yarn projects is a high priority for Barbara Selznick. "I would remove clothes before I removed yarn," she says, "because knitting offers me peace of mind. It's calming, methodical and creative." Barbara has often stopped to help passengers on her flights with their knitting and, in the process, has had an opportunity to talk to scores of others about her love of the craft.

The Knit-Outs

About 1000 people attended the first Knit-Out (officially Knit-Out & Crochet Too!!), held in New York City's Rockefeller Plaza in 1999. The Knit-Out was the brainchild of David Blumenthal, COO of Lion Brand Yarn Company. He was starting his first year as chairman of the Craft Yarn Council and wanted to find a way to bring knitting (a craft that at the time was considered passé) out into the open and encourage a new generation of knitters. His initial idea was to send knitters out across the city to knit in public spaces. After discussion, the council agreed to have one big event in a central location. Today major Knit-Outs in Los Angeles, Washington, Boston, and New York are attended by tens of thousands of people. They're unique, community-building events, without any commercial aspects (selling) allowed. The Craft Yarn Council Web site provides instructions on setting up a Knit-Out in your city (www.craftyarncouncil.com/knitoutbrochure.html), and several major cities have plans to start their own local events.

The Knit-Out is a festival of events and booths celebrating yarn crafts. Fashion shows feature garments, from simple to exquisitely complex and ornate. A recent New York Knit-Out even included a "doggie fashion show" where the dogs were outfitted in sweaters inspired by films like *Gone With the Wind* and *Jurassic Park*. The mood at the Knit-Out is celebratory as people mill through the crowd, talking, knitting or crocheting, meeting new friends, and catching up with old ones.

Corporate and College Knitting Clubs

Knitters were once told either directly or subtly that it was "unprofessional" to knit in a business situation, even when traveling; now they meet in corporate offices, conference rooms, and other professional settings to knit during their lunch breaks with the blessing, even sponsorship, of their companies. At Cadwalader, Wickersham & Taft, the oldest law firm in the United States, there is a weekly meeting of a group called the KnitWits. Rissa Piccar, the company's librarian, welcomes knitters each week through the French doors that open into the magnificent atrium of the Geoff Brown Reading Room. "The setting," she says, "encourages relaxation and an escape from stress. Our firm is filled with Type A individuals. They work all the time. When I give new attorneys a tour, I tell them that it is precisely because they will be so busy that they should join one of our clubs, but I think the KnitWits are the most lively group we've got. This group gets many passing smiles. I believe that when someone takes an hour out of a week to meet people they don't see all the time, and to do something other than their work, they become better employees."

Vita Ursina, who founded the group, says, "It was always my desire to share with others my love and knowledge of knitting and other crafts. As I instruct, I also learn from my fellow knitters. It gives me a great sense of satisfaction."

Many find the group to be a welcome respite from sometimes harsh realities. The Cadwalader offices are located only a few blocks from what once was the World Trade Center. Rose Flowers says, "This is good therapy for me. We are around good people. We laugh, we praise each other and joke about each other's mistakes.

For that one hour a week I'm not thinking about the attack." Joan Richter agrees: "The group is a great escape. As we do our crafts or talk about doing our crafts, we discuss life, work, and personal things, knowing it will not go any further. It's just looking at our lives with humor and warmth." Tyeisha Miller looks forward to the Wednesday meetings. "If I'm not having a good day, once I go to KnitWits, I feel better by the time I get back to my desk." Margarita Cortes concurs: "I actually come back to my desk refreshed."

The club also provides a way for people in a variety of positions to meet and become friends. Members include attorneys and people from many other areas of the firm: secretarial, administrative, bookkeeping. "You get to interact with so many different people on a personal level as opposed to a professional one," notes Miller. Joan Richter adds, "By laughing at craft mistakes and praising each other when the work is good, we all become equal."

Most members of the group speak about the way their knitting has improved, but it is clear that members also receive comfort, support, advice, a feeling of camaraderie among different professional levels, and a mini-vacation in the context of a high-pressure, newly frightening world. Jean Giammarina sums up the value of the club and the effect that the fellowship of knitting has on knitters whenever and wherever they gather: "If you have a problem that seems hopeless, there is always someone to help you along."

23

Showing Off

Now that you have the basics of knitting under your belt, you'll want to expand your horizons. In this chapter we feature a number of patterns that will allow you to show off your newfound skills.

Deep Rib Pullover

SIZES

XS (S, M, L, 1X, 2X)

FINISHED MEASUREMENTS

Chest at underarm 37 (40, 44, 48, 52, 56)"
Length from shoulder 24 (24, 24½, 25½, 26, 27)"

MATERIALS

- 5 (6, 6, 7, 7, 8) balls Lion Brand *Wool-Ease® Chunky* #139 Huckleberry (5 oz, 153 yds; 80% acrylic, 20% wool)
- Size 10.5 (6.5 mm) knitting needles, or size to get gauge
- Size 10.5 (6.5 mm) circular needle, 16" long
- Four stitch holders

GAUGE

13 sts and 18 rows = 4" (10 cm) in stockinette stitch. *Be sure to check your gauge.*
Stockinette stitch (St st) = knit on right-side rows; purl on wrong-side rows.

Deep Rib Pullover (continued)

NOTES

1. See abbreviations on page 71.
2. For ease in working, circle all numbers that pertain to your size.

BACK

With smaller needles, cast on 67 (72, 77, 82, 87, 92) sts. **Row 1 (RS)** *K2, p3; repeat from * across to last 2 sts, end K2. **Row 2 (WS)** *P2, k3; repeat from * across to last 2 sts, p2. Repeat rows 1 and 2 until piece measures 7", decreasing 7 (6, 5, 4, 3, 0) evenly spaced across last wrong-side row—60 (66, 72, 78, 84, 92) sts. Change to St st, and work even until piece measures 15" from beginning.

Shape raglan armholes

Bind off 3 (5, 5, 6, 7, 7) sts at beg of next 2 rows—54 (56, 62, 66, 70, 78) sts.
Next row (RS) K2, ssk, k to last 4 sts, k2tog, k2. **Next row** Purl. Repeat last 2 rows 18 (18, 20, 22, 23, 25) times more. **Last row** P2tog, p to last 2 sts, p2tog. Place remaining 14 (16, 18, 18, 20, 24) sts onto stitch holders for back neck.

FRONT

Cast on and work ribbing and decrease row as for back—60 (66, 72, 78, 84, 92) sts. Change to St st and work even until same length as back to beginning of armhole shaping.

Shape raglan armholes

Bind off 3 (5, 5, 6, 7, 7) sts at beg of next 2 rows—54 (56, 62, 66, 70, 78) sts.
Work 2 rows of raglan armhole shaping until front is 3 inches short of back, ending with a wrong-side row.

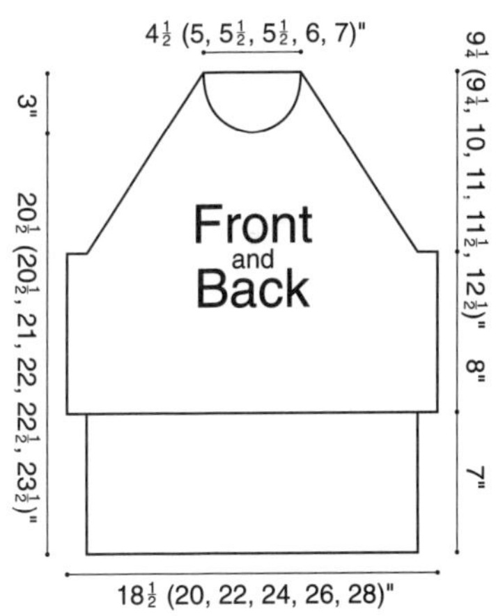

Shape neck

Mark center 10 (12, 14, 14, 16, 20) sts. **Next row (RS)** K2, ssk, knit to marked sts, place marked 10 (12, 14, 14, 16, 20) sts onto a holder for front neck, attach a separate strand of yarn and knit to last 4 sts, k2tog, k2. Working both sides of the piece at the same time and continuing armhole decreases, decrease 1 st from every RS neck edge 3 times. Continue raglan shaping as for back. Fasten off.

SLEEVES

Cast on 32 (32, 37, 37, 42, 42) sts. **Row 1 (RS)** *K2, p3; repeat from * across to last 2 sts,

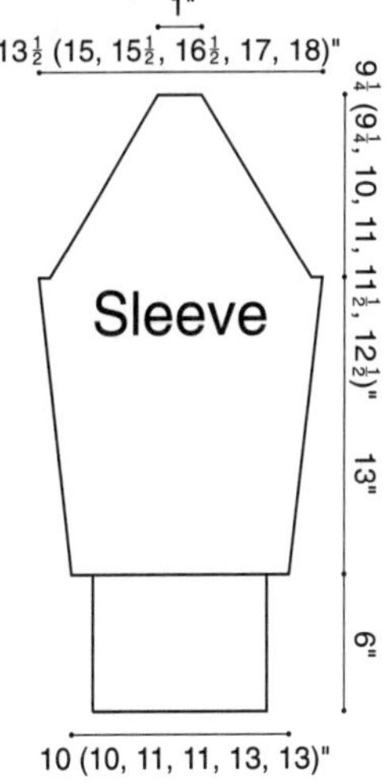

Deep Rib Pullover (continued)

end K2. **Row 2 (WS)** *P2, k3; repeat from * across to last 2 sts, p2. Repeat rows 1 and 2 until piece measures 6" from beginning, ending with a wrong-side row and dec 0 (0, 1, 1, 0, 0) sts on last row—32 (32, 36, 36, 42, 42) sts.

Inc row (RS) K1, inc 1 st in next st, knit to last 2 sts, inc 1 st in next st, k1. Repeat inc row every 4th row 0 (2, 2, 11, 8, 13) times, every 6th row 5 (7, 7, 1, 3, 0) times, and every 8th row 2 (0, 0, 0, 0, 0) times—48 (52, 56, 62, 66, 70) sts. Work even until piece measures 19" from beginning, ending with a wrong-side row.

Shape Raglan Armholes

Bind off 3 (5, 5, 6, 7, 7) sts at beg of next 2 rows.

Next row (RS) K2, ssk, k to last 4 sts, k2tog, k2. **Next row** Purl. Continue raglan decreases as for back. **Last row** P2tog, p2, p2tog. Place remaining 4 sts onto stitch holders.

FINISHING

Block pieces. Sew raglan armhole seams.

Neckband

With right side facing and circular needle, and beginning at back neck, knit 14 (16, 18, 18, 20, 24) sts from back neck holder, 4 sts from one sleeve holder, pick up 13 sts along left front neck, knit 10 (12, 14, 14, 16, 20) sts from front neck holder, pick up 13 sts from right front neck, 4 sts from 2nd sleeve holder—58 (62, 66, 66, 70, 78) sts. Join and work in k2, p3 rib in rounds, and AT SAME TIME, inc 2 (dec 2, dec 1, dec 1, inc 0, dec 3) evenly on first round—60 (60, 65, 65, 70, 75) sts. Continue in rib until neckband measures 4". Loosely bind off all sts in ribbing pattern. Sew sleeve and side seams.

A color photo of this item can be found in the color insert, photo number 20

Tips

Decreasing Evenly Across a Row

When you decrease more than one stitch at the beginning or end of a row, you should divide the number of decreases by the total number of stitches on the needle and then work two stitches together evenly spaced on one row. For example, if you have 72 stitches on the needle and want to make six decreases (72 divided by 6 = 12), you'd work 5 stitches, make the decrease over the next 2 stitches, *work 10, make the decrease over the next 2 sts; repeat from * 5 times, then work the last 5 stitches in order to evenly space the decreases between the seams.

What Is a Raglan?

A raglan armhole is one that slants from the underarm toward the neck in a diagonal line. It is a flattering shape for many figure types. Note that this type of armhole is shaped the same way on the front (or fronts), back and sleeves.

Shaping a Raglan Armhole

To make a neat raglan armhole, leave at least one stitch on each edge before working a decrease. This gives you a selvage for seaming. The reason for a different decrease at the beginning of a row and the end of a row is to create a slant in one direction (ssk to the left) and then in the opposite direction (k2tog to the right).

Placing Stitches on a Holder

When you are asked to place remaining stitches onto a holder, do so by slipping them from the needle onto the holder. Close the holder and cut off remaining yarn, leaving a 4–6" tail.

Marking Center Stitches for Front Neck

You can mark either side of a group of stitches by using safety pins or split ring markers.

Working a Neckband

A neckband such as the one in this pattern is worked with a circular needle. The first row is started with a combination of stitches on holders and by picking up stitches along an edge (either side of front neck). The first row is knitted as the stitches are slipped from the holders or picked up. When you get back to the place where you began, you join the circle and work in rounds. When you work in rounds, you are always working from the right side of the piece. Be sure to bind off loosely or the neck opening will become too tight to slip easily over your head.

Baby Guernsey Set

SIZES
6 months (1 year, 2 years)

FINISHED MEASUREMENTS
Sweater chest 22 (24, 26)"
Hat 16 (17, 18)"
Blanket 36" square

MATERIALS
• 8 (9, 10) balls Lion Brand *Microspun®* #100 Lily White (2½ oz, 168 yds; 100% microfiber acrylic)
• Size 5 (3.75 mm) knitting needles, or size to get gauge
• Size 5 (3.75 mm) circular needle, 24" or 29" long
• Stitch markers
• Four 1" buttons for sweater

GAUGE
20 sts and 28 rows = 4" (10cm) in stockinette stitch (knit on right side; purl on wrong side). *Be sure to check your gauge.*

PATTERN STITCHES
Garter Stitch
Knit every row (2 rows = 1 ridge. Count ridges on RS).

NOTE
See abbreviations on page 71.

Basket Stitch (multiple of 4 sts plus 2)
Row 1 (RS) *K2, p2; rep from * to last 2 sts, k2. **Rows 2 and 3** *P2, k2; rep from * to last 2 sts, p2. **Row 4** Rep row 1. Rep rows 1–4 for basket stitch, ending with row 2 or 4.

2 x 2 Rib (multiple of 4 sts plus 2)
Row 1 (RS) *K2, p2; rep from * to last 2 sts, k2. **Row 2** *P2, k2; rep from * to last 2 sts, p2. Rep rows 1 and 2 for 2 x 2 Rib.

Sweater

BACK
Cast on 55 (60, 65) sts. Work in garter st for 10 rows (5 ridges). Work in St st until piece measures 5 (6, 7)" from beg. Work 4 rows in garter st (2 ridges), dec 1 st (inc 2 sts, inc 1 st) across last row—54 (62, 66) sts. Work in basket stitch until piece measures 9 (11, 12)" from beg. Work in garter st for 4 rows (2 ridges), dec 2 sts across last row—52 (60, 64) sts.

Shoulder ribbing
Next row K3, p2, *k2, p2; rep from * to last 3 sts, k3. **Next**

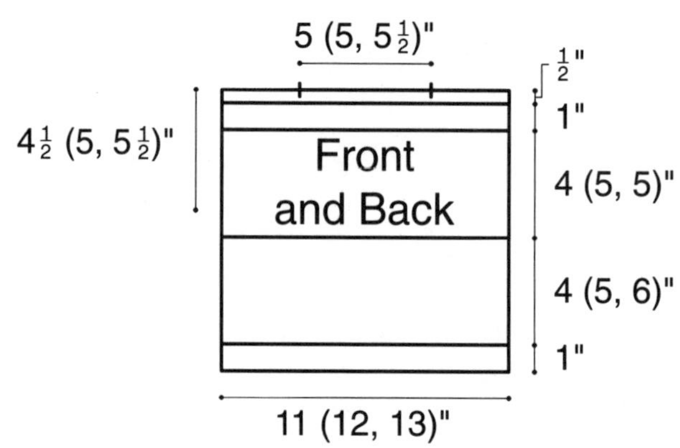

Baby Guernsey Set (continued)

row P3, *k2, p2; rep from * to last st, p1. Rep last 2 rows three more times (8 rows total). Work in garter st for 4 rows (2 ridges), binding off across last row.

FRONT

Work same as back to shoulder until 2 rows of ribbing have been completed. **Next row** Continue in ribbing, placing 2 buttonholes on each shoulder as follows: Rib, yo, k2tog, rib 14, yo, k2tog, rib to last 25 sts, yo, k2tog, rib 14, yo k2tog, rib 7. Continue in ribbing on all sts for 5 more rows, Work in garter st for 4 rows (2 ridges), binding off across last row.

SLEEVES

With straight needles, cast on 26 (30, 34) sts. Work in garter st for 4 rows (2 ridges).

Ribbing

Row 1 (RS) *K2, p2; rep from * to last 2 sts, k2. **Row 2** *P2, k2; rep from * to last 2 sts, p2. Rep these 2 rows 3 more times (8 rows total). Work in garter st for 4 rows, then continue in St st; AT SAME TIME, on second RS row, inc 1 st each end of this row, then every other row 9 (5, 5) more times, then every 4th row 0 (4, 5) times—46 (50, 56) sts. Work even in St st until sleeve measures 6 (7, 8)" from beg. Bind off.

FINISHING

Lightly block all pieces. Overlap shoulder ribbing and sew through both front and back to secure along last st of each side edge. Measure and mark 4½ (5, 5½)" from mid shoulder on front and back. Sew sleeves to sweater body between markers and through both thicknesses where shoulder rib overlaps. Sew sleeve and side seams, leaving lower body garter-edge side seams free for slit, if desired. Sew buttons to back opposite buttonholes. Weave in ends.

HAT

With straight needles, cast on 78 (86, 90) sts. Work in garter st for 4 rows (2 ridges). Work 12 rows of ribbing same as for sleeve ribbing. Work in garter st for 4 rows (2 ridges). Work in St st until piece measures 5 (5½, 6)" from beg. **Next row (RS)** K2tog across row—39 (43, 45) sts. **Next row** K even. **Next row (RS)** K2tog across to last st, k 1. Thread 18" length of yarn in tapestry needle and run thread through all sts on needles without removing sts from needles. Work 4 rows in garter st (2 ridges). Bind off.

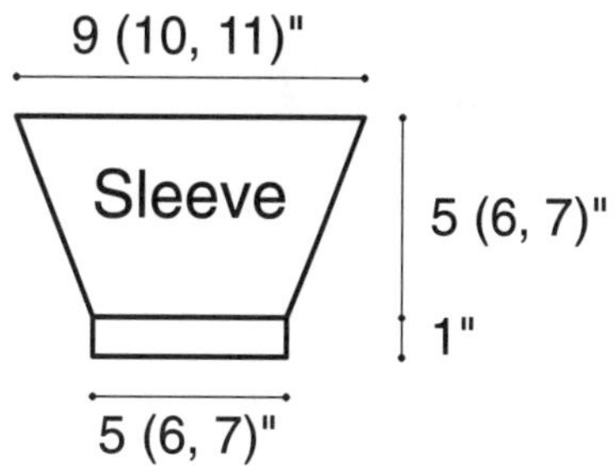

9 (10, 11)"
Sleeve
5 (6, 7)"
1"
5 (6, 7)"

Baby Guernsey Sec *(continued)*

Sew back seam. Pull thread tightly through top sts to create top garter roll and secure. Weave in ends.

BLANKET

With circular needle, cast on 180 sts. *Do not join.* Work back and forth on circular needle. Work in garter st for 20 rows (10 ridges). **Next row (RS)** K7, place marker, work in St st (knit) to last 7 sts, place marker, k7. **Next row (WS)** K7, sl marker, work in St st (purl) to next marker, sl marker, k7. Rep last 2 rows for 6", ending with a WS row. Work in garter st for 6 rows (3 ridges). **Next row (RS)** K7, sl marker, work in basket stitch to next marker, sl marker, k7. **Next row:** K7, sl marker, continue basket stitch to next marker, sl marker, k7. Rep last 2 rows for 6", ending with basket stitch row 2 or 4. Work in garter st for 6 rows (3 ridges). **Next row (RS)** K7, sl marker, 2 x 2 rib to next marker, sl marker, k7. **Next row** K7, sl marker, work 2 x 2 rib to next marker, sl marker, k7. Rep last 2 rows for 6", ending with a WS row. Work in garter st for 6 rows (3 ridges). **Next row (RS)** K7, sl marker, work 166 sts in basket stitch to next marker, sl marker, k7. **Next row** K7, sl marker, work basket stitch to next marker, sl marker, k7. Rep last 2 rows for 6", ending with basket stitch Row 2 or 4. Work in garter st for 6 rows (3 ridges). **Next row (RS)** K7, sl marker, work in St st to next marker, sl marker, k7. **Next row** K7, sl marker, work in St st to next marker, sl marker, k7. Rep last 2 rows for 6", ending with a WS row. Work in garter st for 20 rows (10 ridges). Bind off all sts very loosely.

A color photo of this item can be found in the color insert, photo number 21

V-neck Bicolor Tunic

SIZES

XXS (XS, S, M, L, 1X)

FINISHED MEASUREMENTS

Chest at underarm 37 (38½, 41, 42½, 45, 46½)"
Length from shoulder 23½ (23¾, 24, 24¼, 24½, 25)"

MATERIALS

- 2 (2, 2, 2, 3, 3) balls each Lion Brand *Microspun®* #149 Silver Gray (A) and #143 Lavender (B) (2½ oz, 168 yds; 100% microfiber acrylic)
- Size 6 (4 mm) knitting needles, or size to get gauge
- Large-eyed yarn needle

GAUGE

20 sts and 24 rows = 4" (10 cm) in stockinette stitch (knit on right side; purl on wrong side).
Be sure to check your gauge.

NOTE

See abbreviations on page 71.

Seed Stitch

Row 1 *K1, p1*, repeat to end.
Row 2 Knit the purl sts, purl the knit sts. Repeat row 2 for seed stitch.

BACK

With color A, cast on 98 (102, 108, 112, 118, 122) sts. Work in seed stitch for 6 rows. **Next row (RS)** Work 5 sts in seed st. work in stockinette stitch to last 5 sts, work 5 sts in seed st. Continue as established until piece measures 4" from beg, ending with WS row. Continue in stockinette stitch only as follows: **Decrease row (RS)** K2, k2tog, knit to last 4 sts, ssk, k2. Repeat decrease row every 22nd row twice more—92 (96, 102, 106, 112, 116) sts. Work even until piece measures 16" from beg, end with WS row. Place marker in center—after 46 (48, 51, 53, 56, 58) sts have been worked.

Shape Armholes and V-neck

Bind off 3 (3, 3, 4, 4, 4) sts at beg of next 2 rows. **Decrease row (RS)** Work 4 sts in seed st, k2tog, knit to last 6 sts, ssk, work last 4 sts in seed st. **Next row** Work 4 sts in seed st, purl to last 4 sts, work 4 sts in seed

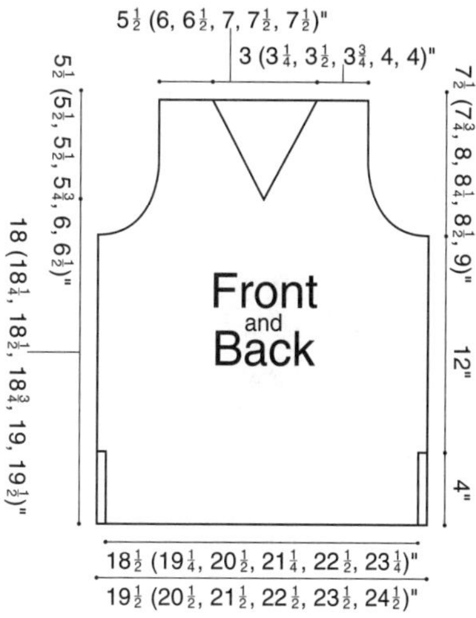

V-neck Bicolor Tunic *(continued)*

st. Repeat decreases 13 (13, 14, 13, 13, 14) times more. AT SAME TIME when armhole measures 2 (2¼, 2½, 2½, 2½, 2½)" begin V-neck shaping. Work as follows:

Next row (RS) Work to 5 sts before marker in center, ssk, work 3 sts in seed st; join a 2nd ball of yarn and work at other side: 3 sts in seed st, k2 tog, work to end of row. Working both sides at once, rep decrease at neck edge on right side 13 (14, 15, 16, 17, 18) times more. Work even until armhole measures 7½ (7¾, 8, 8¼, 8½, 9)".

Shoulder shaping

Bind off 7 (8, 8, 9, 9, 10) sts at beginning of 2 (4, 2, 4, 2, 4) rows, bind off 8 (0, 9, 0, 10, 0) sts at beg of 2 (0, 2, 0, 2, 0) rows.

FRONT

Work as for back, using color B.

FINISHING

Block pieces. Sew shoulder seams. Sew side seams. Weave in ends.

A color photo of this item can be found in the color insert, photo number 22

Center-Cable Pullover

SIZES

XS (S, M, L, XL)

FINISHED MEASUREMENTS

Chest at underarm 40 (43, 46, 49, 52)"
Length from shoulder 24½ (25½, 26½, 27½, 28½)"

MATERIALS

- 10 (11, 12, 14, 15) balls Bonkers Handmade Originals *Hand-dyed 2-Ply Wool* Burnt Amber MC (Main Color); 3 (4, 4, 5, 5) skeins Plum CC (Contrasting Color) (1¾ oz, 240 yds; 100% wool)
- Size 10 (6 mm) knitting needles, or size to get gauge
- Cable needle
- Stitch markers and holders
- Large-eyed yarn needle

GAUGE

11 sts and 18 rows = 4" (10 cm) in stockinette stitch.
Be sure to check your gauge.

SPECIAL ABBREVIATIONS

M1 (make 1) With tip of right needle, lift strand between stitch just worked and next stitch on left needle. Place on left needle and knit into back of it, twisting strand—1 stitch increased.
Rev St st (reverse stockinette stitch) Purl on right side, knit on wrong side. **St st (stockinette stitch)** Knit on right side; purl on wrong side.
4/4 LC (4/4 left cable) Slip next 4 sts to cable needle, k4, k4 from cable needle.

NOTES

1. See abbreviations on page 71.
2. Work with 3 strands MC and 1 strand CC held together as 1 throughout.
3. To begin a new skein of yarn, overlap ends approximately 4" from old and new skein and continue working.
4. On sleeves, work first and last stitches in St st for selvage. Work M1 on each side inside of selvage sts.
5. If there is only one number for a step, work that for all sizes.

Cable Panel Pat (over 16 sts)

Row 1 (RS) P4, k8, p4. **Row 2 (WS)** K4, p8, k4. **Rows 3–8** Rep rows 1–2 three times. **Row 9** P4, 4/4 LC, p4. **Row 10** K4, p8, k4. Rep rows 1–10 for cable panel pat.

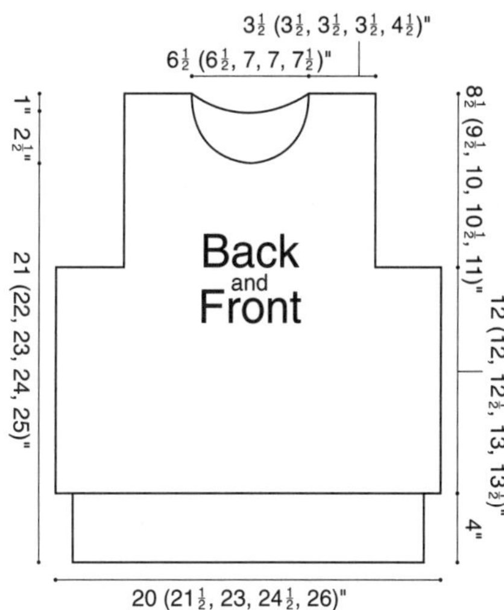

Center-Cable Pullover (continued)

Sleeve Panel Pat

Rows 1–4 Work in Rev St st. **Rows 5–8** Work in St st. Rep rows 1–8 for pat.

BACK

With 3 strands MC and 1 strand CC held tog as 1, cast on 60 (64, 68, 72, 76) sts.

Ribbing

Row 1 (RS) K1, *p2, k2; rep from * across to last 3 sts, p2, k1 **Row 2** P1, *k2, p2; rep from * across to last 3 sts, k2, p1. Rep rows 1–2 until piece measures 4" from beg, ending with a WS row. Knit 4 rows (2 garter ridges made).

Body

Next row (RS) Set up pat as follows: K1 selvage st, p1 (3, 0, 0, 0), k8 (8, 1, 3, 5), [p4, k8] 1 (1, 2, 2, 2) times, place marker (pm), work row 1 of cable panel pat over next 16 sts, pm, [k8, p4] 1 (1, 2, 2, 2] times, k8 (8, 1, 3, 5), p1 (3, 0, 0, 0), k1 selvage st. **Next row (WS)** P1 selvage st, k1 (3, 0, 0, 0), p8 (8, 1, 3, 5), [k4, p8] 1 (1, 2, 2, 2) times, work row 2 of cable panel pat to marker, [p8, k4] 1 (1, 2, 2, 2) times, p8 (8, 1, 3, 5), k1 (3, 0, 0, 0), p1 selvage st. Continue in rib pat as established, working the sts inside markers in cable panel pat until piece measures 16 (16, 16½, 17, 17 ½)" from beg, ending with a WS row.

Shape Armhole

Next row (RS) Bind off 10 (12, 14, 14, 14) sts at beg of next 2 rows—40 (40, 40, 44, 48) sts. Continue working even in pat until armhole measures 7½ (8½, 9, 9½, 10)", ending with a WS row.

Shape Neck

Next row (RS) Work 10 (10, 9, 11, 12) sts in pat, put next 20 (20, 22, 22, 24) sts on hold for back neck, turn. Continuing on left shoulder only, dec 1 st at neck edge once—9 (9, 8, 10, 11) sts remain for shoulder. Work even until armhole measures 8½ (9½, 10, 10½, 11)", ending with a WS row. Bind off shoulder sts.

Right shoulder

Beg with a RS row, work as for left shoulder, working dec at neck edge on 2nd RS row.

FRONT

Work as for back until armhole measures 5 (6, 6½, 7, 7½)", ending with a WS row.

Shape Neck

Next row (RS) Work 16 (16, 15, 17, 18) sts in pat, put next 8 (8, 10, 10, 12) sts on hold for front neck, turn. Continuing on left shoulder only, at neck edge bind off 2 sts twice, then dec 1 st every other row 3 times—9 (9, 8, 10, 11) sts remain for shoulder. Work even until armhole measures 8½ (9½, 10, 10½, 11)", end with a WS row. Bind off shoulder sts.

Right shoulder

Beg with a RS row, work as for left shoulder, working first bind-off on 2nd RS row.

SLEEVES

With 3 strands MC and 1 strand CC held tog as 1, cast on

Center-Cable Pullover *(continued)*

24 (24, 24, 28, 28) sts. Work ribbing as for back until piece measures 2½" from beg, end with a WS row. Knit 4 rows (2 garter ridges made).

Row 1 (RS) Set up rib pat and beg shaping as follows: K1 selvage, M1, p0 (0, 0, 1, 1), k7 (7, 7, 8, 8), pm, work row 1 of sleeve panel pat over next 8 sts, pm, k7 (7, 7, 8, 8), p0 (0, 0, 1, 1), M1, k1 selvage—26 (26, 26, 30, 30) sts. **Row 2 (WS)** P1 selvage, k0 (0, 0, 2, 2), p8, work row 2 of sleeve panel pat to marker, p8, k0 (0, 0, 2, 2), P1 selvage. **Row 3** K1 selvage, p0 (0, 0, 2, 2), k8, work row 3 of sleeve panel pat to marker, k8, p0 (0, 0, 2, 2), k1 selvage. **Row 4** P1 selvage, k0 (0, 0, 2, 2), p8, work row 4 of sleeve panel pat to marker, p8, k0 (0, 0, 2, 2), p1 selvage. **Next row** Keeping first and last st in St st for selvage and working sts inside markers in sleeve panel pat, continue in pat as established and at the same time, M1 each edge inside selvage st this row then every 4th row 2 (11, 14, 12, 14) times more, then every 6th row 7 (1, 0, 1, 0) times working new sts into k8, p4 rib pat—46 (52, 56, 58, 60) sts. Continue working even in pat until piece measures 20 (21, 22½, 22½, 22½)" from beg, end with a WS row. Bind off. Mark 3½ (4½, 5, 5, 5)" down from top of sleeve on each side.

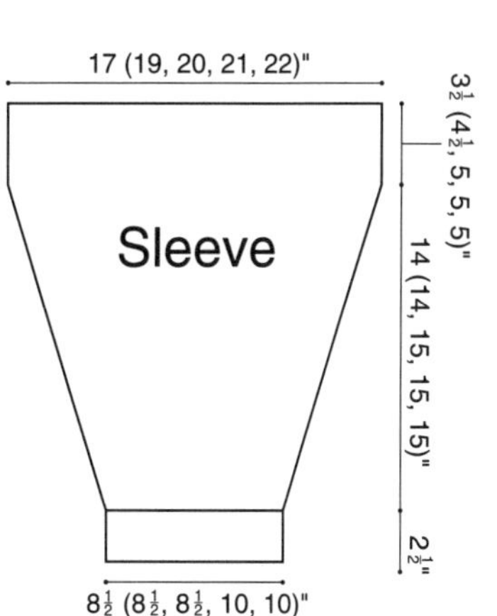

FINISHING

Sew right shoulder seam.

Neckband

Row 1 (RS) With 3 strands MC and 1 strand CC, pick up and k10 sts along left front neck, k8 (8, 10, 10, 12) sts from front neck holder, pick up and k10 sts along right front neck to shoulder, pick up and k4 sts to back neck, k20 (20, 22, 22, 24) sts from back neck holder, pick up and k4 sts to shoulder-56 (56, 60, 60, 64) sts. Beg with a WS row, work ribbing as for back for 2½". Bind off loosely. Sew left shoulder and neckband seam. Sew top of sleeves into armholes. Sew straight portion at top of sleeves (above markers) to bound-off armhole sts. Sew side and sleeve seams. Weave in all ends.

A color photo of this item can be found in the color insert, photo number 23

Luxury Shawl and Scarf

FINISHED MEASUREMENTS
Scarf 12" x 42"
Shawl 20" x 70"

MATERIALS

Scarf

- 4 balls Knit One Crochet Too *Richesse et Soie* #9512 Seafoam (1 oz, 145 yds; 65% cashmere, 35% silk)
- Size 6 (4 mm) knitting needles or size to get gauge

Shawl

- 8 balls Knit One Crochet Too *Douceur et Soie* #8512 Seafoam (1 oz, 225 yds; 70% baby mohair, 30% silk)
- Size 10 (6 mm) knitting needles or size to get gauge

GAUGE

Scarf

24 stitches and 53 rows = 4" (10 cm) with size 6 needles in pattern stitch.

Shawl

14 stitches and 28 rows = 4" (10 cm) with size 10 needles and 2 strands of yarn held together in pattern stitch.
Be sure to check your gauge.

A color photo of both items can be found in the color insert, photo number 24

NOTE
The shawl is worked with 2 strands of yarn held together.

Garter and Lace Pattern Stitch

Row 1 (wrong side) Knit. **Rows 2–10** Knit. **Eyelet row (wrong side)** Knit 1, *yarn over, knit 2 together; repeat from * to end. **Row 12** Knit. Repeat rows 1–12 for pattern stitch.

Scarf and Shawl

Cast on 71 stitches. Work in Garter and Lace Pattern until piece measures (scarf) 42" and (shawl) 70". End pattern after first 10 knit rows of pattern. Bind off stitches.

FINISHING
Weave in ends. Pin scarf or shawl onto towel placed on carpet or table. Spray with water and allow to dry.

Bias Hat

SIZE

Adjust size (see note below).

MATERIALS

- 1 skein Lion Brand *Wool-Ease® Chunky* #147 Boysenberry (5 oz, 153 yds; 80% acrylic, 20% wool)
- Size 10 (6 mm) knitting needles or size to get gauge
- Large-eyed yarn needle
- Beads for drawstring (optional)

GAUGE

10 stitches and 20 rows = 4" (10cm) in garter stitch (knit every row).

Be sure to check your gauge.

NOTE

Measure head size around the head, over the ears. The approximate head size for an adult is 21".

Make 1 increase (M1) Lift the horizontal bar between the needle tips and knit it without twisting.

HAT

Cast on 25 stitches. **Row 1** Slip 1 stitch, knit to end. **Row 2** Slip 2nd stitch, M1, knit to last 2 stitches, knit 2 together. Repeat last 2 rows until either long edge measures 1" less than desired head circumference. Bind off loosely, leaving a long tail.

FINISHING

Matching cast-on and bound-off edges, sew seam with tail yarn. You will have a tube with a 45-degree-angle seam. The increase edge (M1 edge) will be "holey." Take a double strand of yarn, a braid of yarn or ribbon and weave it in and out of the holes, beginning and ending at the seam. Draw up the crown of the hat to desired tightness and tie off in a bow. Decorate the drawstring with beads, tassels, or pompoms.

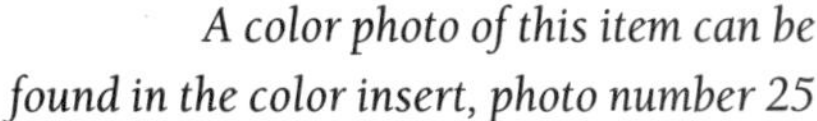

A color photo of this item can be found in the color insert, photo number 25

24

The Literature of Knitting

This collection of books is a suggested basic knitting library with a selection of important books in several categories. In compiling this list we chose books that are readily available, as a number of important books have gone out of print (but can sometimes be found used). One notable out-of-print book, for example, that knitters value highly is *Principles of Knitting* by June Hemmons Hiatt. It occasionally appears for sale on eBay and ends up selling for around $200.

Reference

Big Book of Knitting
By Katharina Buss
Sterling Publications, $19.95
Paperback, 240 pages

This oversized book with more than 950 color illustrations is an excellent reference for intermediate and experienced knitters. Basic information includes needles and stitches, cleaning and care, but the book really shines in its instructions for advanced patterns, complex cables, and color-knitting methods like intarsia, as well as its how-to sections on buttons and buttonholes, zippers, and finishing techniques. There are projects for each technique with excellent photographs and charts.

Meg Swansen's Knitting
By Meg Swansen
Interweave Press, $39.95
Hardcover, 144 pages

Meg Swansen is the daughter of famed knitter Elizabeth Zimmermann and has carried on her mother's work as a knitter, writer, and educator. Her book includes 21 designs for sweaters, vests, and socks. Swansen includes some of the more obscure knitting techniques such as steeking, as well as good tips and information to add designer touches to your knitting. The book is appropriate for intermediate and advanced knitters and is beautifully photographed.

Knitting Without Tears
By Elizabeth Zimmermann
Simon & Schuster, $16.00
Paperback, 128 pages

This classic knitting book is on many knitters' lists of the most important books to have in their libraries. Written in 1971, Zimmermann's book inspired a new generation of knitters with its homespun advice and a down-to-earth writing style, and is still in print. More guidance than instruction, this book is not necessarily for the beginner. Zimmermann implores knitters not to take the work too seriously and to experiment creatively without fear of mistakes. She offers an approach to designing that can take a knitter who understands the basics to a new level of creative expression. Zimmermann teaches the joy as well as the craft of knitting.

Reader's Digest Knitter's Handbook: A Comprehensive Guide to the Principles and Techniques of Handknitting
By Montse Stanley
Reader's Digest, $19.95
Hardcover, 318 pages

This oversized book is an excellent, straightforward knitting reference work that starts with the basics and includes comprehensive information for a knitter with at least some experience. It is annotated to indicate essential, useful, or specialty techniques. You can look up virtually any possible cast-on technique and a vast array of stitches. Stanley has put together excellent chapters on color work, finishing, blocking, and fixing errors. Most of the book is two-color with a wealth of stitch illustrations. Along with the basics, she includes some esoteric and more advanced techniques.

The Ultimate Knitter's Guide
By Kate Buller
Martingale & Company, $39.95
Hardcover/spiral-bound, 176 pages

This book is spiral-bound, to lie flat as you work. It includes 25 patterns for adults and children at difficulty levels from beginner to advanced. Most of the designs are by Kim Hargreaves, plus other well-known designers: Erika Knight, Louisa Harding, Kaffe Fassett, and Zoë Mellor. There is a well-done reference section with photographs illustrating techniques from basic to advanced.

Vogue Knitting: The Ultimate Knitting Book
By the editors of *Vogue Knitting* magazine
Pantheon Books, $38.50
Hardcover, 288 pages

This large, richly illustrated book (1600 full-color illustrations) is perhaps the most important reference book to have on your shelf of knitting books. It includes information about the history of knitting and knitting supplies as well as basic techniques and a stitch dictionary. As your learning progresses, you will be able to make use of a vast range of instructions from beginner to advanced. The organization of the book is practical and intuitive, with cross-references for each entry and color-coded chapters to help you find your place quickly. This is a classic that transcends reference and goes beyond how-to instructions, offering a design workshop with clear and simple guidance and inspiration to move beyond the basics.

Learning

How to Knit—The Definitive Knitting Course Complete with Step-by-Step Techniques, Stitch Library and Projects for Your Home and Family

By Debbie Bliss

Trafalgar Square, $29.95

Hardcover, 160 pages

Well-known designer Debbie Bliss's book is an excellent introduction to knitting. It is presented as nine workshops in which each lesson builds on the next. Each workshop includes instructions, techniques, tools, and then a practice project that builds confidence as you go. By the time you have completed the first course, you can knit a child's garter-stitch jacket and an adult tunic. The book starts with the basics and takes the new knitter through a range of knitting traditions, including Aran, intarsia, entrelac, Fair Isle, and lace knitting. Diagrams and illustrations are clear and accurate, and an excellent stitch library is provided for reference. Patterns illustrate each technique and include clothing for every member of the family, afghans, and other home-décor projects.

Kids Knitting: Projects for Kids of All Ages

By Melanie Falick

Workman Publishing, $17.95

Hardcover, 128 pages

Even adults will enjoy the fun approach to learning and colorful, whimsical projects in this book of richly illustrated patterns. These include yarn dying with Kool-Aid and making your own needles as well as knitting patterns like a scarf and hat or a beanbag. There are 15 projects, including a backpack, dolls, and an afghan as well as accessories that range from basic to a bit more advanced. The book is also physically beautiful, well designed, and exquisitely photographed.

Knitting in Plain English
By Maggie Righetti
St. Martin's Press, $14.95
Paperback, 241 pages

Righetti's writing style offers a casual and friendly approach to learning to knit. She shares anecdotes about knitters she has known, patterns she has designed, and the differences between yarns. While the book will not teach you to knit, it is filled with practical advice, tips, and suggestions about how to correct errors. It is humorous and enjoyable to read as a beginning course in design.

The Complete Idiot's Guide to Knitting & Crocheting
By Gail Diven and Cindy Kitchel
Alpha Books, $16.95
Paperback, 304 pages

This is a good book for beginning knitters and is written is a casual, friendly style that helps make knitting less intimidating. The book demystifies knitting and crocheting while making these crafts fun to learn. Step-by-step instructions with black-and-white illustrations and photos are punctuated with useful stories and helpful hints. Beginner projects like scarves and hats as well as more advanced techniques make this a useful reference book, even for intermediate knitters.

Designing

Designing Knitwear
By Deborah Newton
Taunton Press, $24.95
Paperback, 272 pages

This is an excellent resource for those who already have an understanding of basic design principles and want to learn more intricate details. Included are discussions of fiber (and resulting drape), bias, color, cables, and more. Of particular interest are the inspirational sources for many of Newton's designs and her many whimsical drawings. Patterns are included for 16 projects.

Sweater Design in Plain English
By Maggie Righetti
St. Martin's Press, $17.95
Paperback, 406 pages

Much of this book is devoted to determining your body type and finding a style of sweater that is best suited to you. Several chapters explore the mathematics involved in understanding design. The book concludes with a walk-through of how to develop patterns for various sweater styles.

The Advanced Knitting Architect
By Sion Elalouf
Knitting Fever, Inc., $12.95
Spiral-bound, 76 pages

This second book in the series discusses more advanced principles of design. Included are lessons on various necklines and garments knitted from the top down and from side to side. Some of the material is reprinted from the first book.

The Knitting Architect
By Sion Elalouf
Knitting Fever, Inc., $9.95
Spiral-bound, 49 pages

Packed with information, this is an excellent introduction to designing sweaters. It can be rather dry and doesn't offer fancy photographs, but it provides all the basic mathematical information you'll need to design basic sweaters in any gauge and any size.

Inspiration

Elizabeth Zimmermann's Knitters' Almanac
By Elizabeth Zimmermann
Dover Publications, $6.95
Paperback, 160 pages

The patterns in this book are arranged by season and include something for every member of the family. The instructions are often told in the form of a story and the knitter is encouraged to use the directions as a springboard rather than blindly following a pattern. Her writing style is charming and warm, and she welcomes knitters into a world where knitting is both craft and philosophy.

Other books of interest in the general category of inspiration include *Knitting in America,* by Melanie Falick, a virtual "art book" of beautifully photographed knitted garments, pictured on location with biographical profiles of their designers around the United States, and any one of the knitting books by Kaffe Fassett. Fassett's books are not for beginners, but offer a view into the world of colorwork, where this designer is in a category of his own.

Sally Melville Styles: A Unique and Elegant Approach for Your Yarn Collection
By Sally Melville
XRX Inc., $28.95
Hardcover, 128 pages

Exquisite designs and a variety of techniques offer a broad selection for intermediate to advanced knitters. Melville includes a chapter on organizing, protecting, and storing a yarn collection that is unique among knitting books and will inspire your knitting. She offers excellent instruction on working with color, useful in using up miscellaneous balls of yarn in appealing designs. Melville's suggestions of combining different yarn weight and colors are adventurous and inventive. This is an excellent guide for knitters willing to experiment with yarn using a pattern as a guide, as varying the yarns will mean your results may differ from those in the book. Includes patterns for sweaters and vests for the family.

Patterns

A Close-Knit Family

By Melissa Leapman
Taunton Press, $24.95
Hardcover, 153 pages

Knitters will enjoy this collection of classic sweater patterns for the entire family for years to come. There are many simple patterns in this book easy enough for beginning knitters as well as more challenging projects for advanced knitters. What's unique about this book is that all the patterns include variations for at least two members of the family. If you're interested in mother/daughter or father/son sweaters, this book is worth a look.

Family Album

By Kaffe Fassett and Zoë Hunt
Taunton Press, $24.95
Paperback, 200 pages

This wonderful collection of patterns for men, women, children, and infants features a rainbow of color in each garment. Exact "recipes" are provided to duplicate the patterns, but they will become uniquely your own if you use miscellaneous balls of yarn you already have on hand. The book is further enhanced by the beautiful photography of Steve Lovi.

Homespun, Handknit: Caps, Socks, Mittens and Gloves

Edited by Linda Ligon
Interweave Press, $19.95
Paperback, 160 pages

All the patterns in this book were designed by knitters for someone important in their lives. Garment and accessory patterns are included for babies, children, men, and women. The book also has a good reference section in the beginning about yarn equivalencies.

Patterns/Reference

A Treasury of Knitting Patterns
By Barbara G. Walker
Schoolhouse Press, $30.00
Paperback, 300 pages

The scope of stitch patterns covered in this book is astounding. Clear black-and-white photos show the patterns, which are well organized and extremely helpful for creating your own designs. Walker advises which patterns are ideal for specific uses such as a shawl or child's dress. Patterns, ranging from simple to complex, include basic stitches, cables, color work, lace, and Aran. This book, Volume I of a three-volume set by Walker previously published by Scribners in 1968, was out of print for some time.

Patterns/Learning

Knit It Your Way
By Cynthia Yanok Wise
Martingale & Company, $29.95
Paperback, 126 pages

Although this book offers a wide variety of patterns, the main point is to teach knitters how to substitute one yarn for another. Many times the specified yarn in a pattern is not available, too expensive, or not to our liking. All of the sweaters, socks, scarves, and more in this book are shown knitted in at least two different yarns to illustrate the differences.

Magazines

***Better Homes and Gardens* Knit It!**
Meredith Corporation
1716 Locust St.
Des Moines, IA 50309
www.bgh.com

The newest entry into the needlework magazine category is *Knit It!*. The first issue was sold exclusively on newstands and launched in December 2001. The magazine is for the new knitter but with the experienced knitter in mind. Like other Better Homes and Gardens' publications, it is written in a clear, concise style, is well photographed, and has a mix of designs and articles. The look and editorial focus of the magazine recognize the entrance of a new, younger knitter into the world of knitting.

Family Circle Easy Knitting
233 Spring St., 8th Floor
New York, NY 10013
http://www.fceasyknitting.com

This magazine includes approachable, practical knit and crochet designs for a general audience that tend to be easier than *Vogue Knitting* patterns. Family and home-decorating projects are included as well as sweater designs. Practical articles include subjects such as charity knitting or selling your finished garments.

Interweave Knits
Interweave Press
201 East Fourth St.
Loveland, CO 80537
http://www.interweave.com/knit/knits

The first thing one notices about this magazine is its beautiful, romantically styled lifestyle photography. Interweave has a more intellectual approach to knitting, with in-depth articles on fiber and profiles of designers. It offers sweater patterns for men, women, and children. *Interweave Knits* also offers an annual section about shopping for yarn, and information about knitting camps, conferences, and travel.

Knit 'n Style
All American Crafts
243 Newtown-Sparta Road

Newton, NJ 07860
www.knitnstyle.com

This magazine, formerly called *Fashion Knitting,* focuses primarily on patterns for garments and accessories for the whole family. While the difficulty level ranges from easy to experienced, the fashions are usually practical, with an occasional dramatic design included.

Knitter's Magazine
XRX Inc.
P.O. Box 1525
Sioux Falls, SD 57101-1525
http://www.knittinguniverse.com

Knitter's prides itself on its "Knitter's School" section, which includes well-illustrated instructions for a variety of knitting techniques. The magazine tends to be educationally oriented and concentrates on practical sweater designs with less emphasis on high style. The magazine produces an annual booklet called the ShopFinder to help locate knit shops around the country and has a well-developed Web site.

Vogue Knitting
233 Spring St., 8th Floor
New York, NY 10013
http://www.vogueknitting.com

The editorial focus of *Vogue Knitting* is high style with articles on cutting-edge fashion and design trends. *Vogue* is the only knitting magazine that has licenses with major fashion designers, including Donna Karan and Calvin Klein. Articles include fashion news and knitting techniques. The sweater designs range from very easy to experienced. Many serious knitters know the magazine's designs so well that when they see someone wearing a *Vogue Knitting* design, they can identify it as being from the Fall 1988 issue!

Resources

CHAPTER 13 KNITTING FOR CHARITY

Warm up America!
c/o Craft Yarn Council
2500 Lowell Road
Gastonia, NC 28054

Care Wear Volunteers, Inc.
Bonnie Hagerman
c/o Hood college
Frederick, MD 21701-8575

Pine Meadow Knitting News
131 Boxwood Road
Manchester, PA 17345-9652

Christmas-at-Sea
c/o Seamen's Church Institute
241 Water Street
New York, NY 10038

Warming Families
One Heart, Inc.
P.O. Box 757
Provo, UT 84603
www.warmingfamilies.org for local places to donate

CHAPTER 17 KNITTING ON THE GO-EVENTS AND TRAVEL

Camp Stitches
XRX, Inc.
231 S. Phillips Ave., Suite 400
Sioux Falls, SD 57104
www.knittinguniverse.com

The Green Mountain Spinnery
P.O. Box 568
Putney, VT 05346
www.spinnery.com

Behind the Scenes Adventures
18096 Poplar Street
Sonoma, CA 95476
www.btsadventures.com

Dolly Varden Tours
PO Box 758
Haines, AK 99827
www.dollyvardenalaska.com

Knitting by the Sea
c/o Helga McDonald
PO Box 1568
Port Hadlock, WA 98339
www.knittingbythesea.com

Maryland Sheep & Wool Festival
PO Box 99
Glenwood, MD 21738
www.sheepandwoolfestival.org

Taos Sheep & Wool Festival
PO Box 2754
Taos, NM 87571
www.taoswoolfestival.org

CHAPTER 19 THE HEALING POWER OF KNITTING

The Relaxation Response
By Herbert Benson, M.D.
Avon, $6.99
Mass market paperback, 240 pages

Flow: The Psychology of Optimal Experience
By Mihaly Caikszentmihalyi
HarperCollins, $14.00
Paperback, 320 pages

CHAPTER 20—COMMERCE OF KNITTING

Artfibers Gallery
124 Sutter St.
San Francisco, CA 94104
www.artfibers.com

Over the Moon Cafe & Mercantile
Meadow View Village
Ste #D
Longmont, CO 80503
www.over-the-moon.net

Playing with Yarn
276 Scenic Dr.
Knife River, MN 55609
www.playingwithyarn.com

Yarn Expressions
7914 Memorial Parkway SW
Huntsville, AL 35802
www.yarnexpressions.com

Mail Order

Cotton Clouds
5176 South 14th Ave.
Safford, AZ 85546-9252
www.cottonclouds.com

Herrschners
2800 Hoover Rd.
Stevens Point, WI 54492-0001
www.herrschners.com

Mary Maxim
2001 Holland Ave
PO Box 5019
Port Huron, MI 48061-5019
www.marymaxim.com

Patternworks
PO Box 1618
Center Harbor, NH 03226-1618
www.patternworks.com

The Stitchery
120 North Meadows Rd.
Medfield, MA 02052
www.thestitchery.com

Webs
PO Box 147
Service Center Rd.
Northampton, MA 01061
www.yarn.com

The Wool Connection
34 E. Main St.
Old Avon Village North
Avon, CT 06001
www.woolconnection.com

YARN COMPANY LISTING

Bonkers Handmade Originals
PO Box 442099
Lawrence, KS 66044
www.bonkersfibers.com

Classic Elite Yarns
300A Jackson St.
Lowell, MA 01852

Colinette/Unique Kolours
1428 Oak Lane
Downingtown, PA 19335

K1, C2
2220 Eastman Ave., #105
Ventura, CA 93003

Lion Brand Yarn Co.
34 West 15th St.
New York, NY 10011
www.lionbrand.com

Reynolds Yarn
JCA Inc.
35 Scales Lane
Townsend, MA 01469

List of Patterns

	Page Number
Cell Phone Holder	36
Tie Hat	37
Striped Stock Cap	40
Easy Bright Pullover	43
Bias Bicolor Scarf	49
Lengthwise Scarf	50
Tassel Scarf	51
Lace Rib Scarf	52
Double-Strand Scarf	53
Cabled Scarf	54
Increased/Decreased Baby Blanket	63
Garter Stitch Vest	80
Sleeveless T-neck	82
Roll-Neck Raglan Pullover with Hat	84
Easy Cardigan	87
Child's Cabled Cardigan	120
Cabled Pullover	123
Striped Sailor	125
Socks	127
Easy Strip Throw	129
Preemie Cap Patterns	149
Preemie Cap, Basketweave Hat	149
Baby Soft 'n' Seamless Cardigan	151
Christmas-at-Sea Patterns	153
Mariner's Scarf, Watch Cap	153
Seafarer's Scarf	154
Deep Rib Pullover	234
Baby Guernsey Set	238
V-neck Bicolor Tunic	241
Center-Cable Pullover	243
Luxury Shawl and Scarf	246
Bias Hat	247

Index

A.C. Moore, 214
Abbreviations, in knitting patterns, 71–72
Acrylic, 21–22
Advanced Knitting Architect, The (Elalouf), 253
Alice Starmore's Book of Fair Isle Knitting, 169
Alpaca, 19, 187
Amazon.com, 199
American technique, 32
Andean Folk Knitting: Traditions and Techniques from Peru and Bolivia (LeCount), 169
Angora, 19, 176, 187
Animal fibers, 18–20, 104
Aran Knitting (Starmore), 169
Aran tradition, 166, 176
Armhole shaping, 70
Artfibers Yarns, 215–216, 229, 260
Art of Fair Isle Knitting, The—History, Technique, Color and Patterns (Feitelson), 169
Art of Shetland Lace, The (Don), 173
As for back, 64
Ashforth, Pat, 207–208
AT SAME TIME, 64

Baby Guernsey Set, 238–240
Baby Soft 'n' Seamless Cardigan, 151–152
Baby yarns, 16
Back loops, 59
Ball band, 11
Barr, Doug, 192
Barr, Lynne, 192
Basketweave Hat, 150
Behind the Scenes Adventures, 184–185, 259
Benson, Herbert, 211, 260
Better Homes and Gardens Knit It!, 256–257
Bias Bicolor Scarf, 49
Bias Hat, 247
Big Apple Knitters, 227–228
Big Book of Knitting (Buss), 248
Binding off, 34–35
  in ribbing, 42
  three-needle, 99–100
Bind off from each neck edge, 64
Bind off in pattern (ribbing), 64
Bleach, 104
Bliss, Debbie, 185, 250–251
Blumenthal, David, 231
Bohus knitting, 168
Bonkers Handmade Originals, 261
Boom years (1974–1996), 177–180
Borealis Sweaterscapes, 191–192
Bouclé yarn, 23
Braatz, Ruth, 194
Bradberry, Sarah, 193–194
Breiter, Barbara, 196, 202
British Isles, 165–168, 174, 178
British technique, 32
Brown-Reinsel, Beth, 171
Buller, Kate, 250
Bullock, Sandra, 181
Burri, Barb, 200
Bush, Nancy, 170
Buss, Katharina, 248
Bust measurement, 91
Button, Jane, 185, 186
Buttonholes, 137

Cabled Pullover, 123–124
Cabled Scarf, 54
Cable needles, 9–10
Cabling, 107–110
Cadwalader, Wickersham & Taft, 232–233
Camel, 20
Camps, 182–184
Camp Stitches, 182, 259
Canada Knits (Scott), 169–170
Caps. *See* Hats and caps
Caps for Nepal, 143
Cardigans. *See also* Sweaters
  Baby Soft 'n' Seamless, 151–152
  Child's Cabled, 120–122
  Easy, 87–89
Care of knits:
  drying, 105, 106
  instructions, 12
  storing, 105–106
  washing, 103–106
Care Wear, 145–146, 259
Cashmere, 19, 181, 187
Casserberg, Judy, 217, 229
Casting on:
  defined, 30
  knitted-on, 31–32
Catalogs, 217–218
Cell Phone Holder, 36
Center-Cable Pullover, 243–245
Chanel, 180
Change to larger (or smaller) needles, 64
Charity, knitting for, 141–155, 226–227
Charts, reading, 73–72
Chenille yarn, 23
Children in Common, 132
Child's Cabled Cardigan, 120–122
Chin, Lily, 201
Chloe, 180
Chouinard, Dee, 148
Christmas-at-Sea, 143, 146–147, 259
  patterns, 153–154
Chunky or bulky yarns, 16
Churro sheep, 187
Circular needles, 3, 5–6
Classic Elite Yarns, 261
Clauson, Barbara, 146
Close-Knit Family, A (Leapman), 255
Colinette/Unique Kolours, 261
Color charts, 75
Color-fastness, 103
Color knitting, 134–136
Color name and number, 13
Company name, 11
Complete Book of Traditional Fair Isle Knitting, The (McGregor), 173
Complete Book of Traditional Knitting, The (Compton), 170
Complete Book of Traditional Scandinavian Knitting, The (McGregor), 173
Complete Idiot's Guide to Knitting & Crocheting, The (Diven and Kitchel), 252
Compton, Rae, 170, 171
Cont as establised (cont in the way/cont in this manner), 64
Continental technique, 32, 34
Copyright FAQs (frequently asked questions) for Knitters, 195
Cotton, 20–21
Cotton Clouds, 218–219, 260
Country fairs, 186–188
Craft Yarn Council, 191, 201, 231
Crochet:
  edges, 110–112, 136
  hooks, 10
  slip-stitch seam, 100
Curved stitch pickups, 103
Czikszentmihalyi, Mihaly, 209, 260

Dandanell, Birgitta, 173
Danielsson, Ulla, 173
Decreases, 59–61
Deep Rib Pullover, 234–237
Designing Knitwear (Newton), 252
Diaz, Cameron, 181
Dietrich, Marlene, 175
Dior, Christian, 176
Diven, Gail, 252
DnT, Inc., 192
Dolly Varden Tours, 185–186, 259
Don, Sarah, 173
Double crochet, 110
Double knitting yarns, 16
Double-pointed needles, 3, 6, 9, 113–114
Double Strand Scarf, 53
Dropping stitches, 45–46
Dry-cleaning, 106
Drying knits, 105, 106

Early Art Deco (1911–1929) era, 175
Ease, 90–91
Easy Bright Ribbed Pullover, 43–44
Easy Cardigan, 87–89
Easy Strip Throw, 129
Edges, 133
  crocheted, 110–112
  garter stitch, 134
  mock cable, 134
  rolled, 134
Edge stitches, 47–48, 71

Eig, Edith, 228
Eisler, Helen, 197–198
Elalouf, Sion, 253
Elizabeth I, Queen of England, 165
Elizabeth Zimmerman's Knitter's Almanac, 253–254
Ellis, Perry, 178
End(ing) with a wrong-side (or right-side) row, 65
Ends, weaving in, 101
Estonia, 170
Eyelash yarn, 23

Fair Isle, 135, 166, 171, 175, 179
Falick, Melanie, 251, 254
Falkenberg, Hanne, 185
Family Album (Fassett and Hunt), 255
Family Circle Easy Knitting, 257
Faroe Islands, 167, 168, 170
Fashion trends, 174–181
Fassett, Kaffe, 159, 178, 255
Feitelson, Ann, 169
Fetter, Linda, 227
Fiber content, 13
Fiber festivals, 186–188
Fight-or-flight response, 211
Fingering yarns, 16
Finger puppets, 146
Finished measurements, 67
Finishing, 70
  edges and bands, 101–102
  seaming, 97–100
  seam preparation (blocking), 95–96
  weaving in ends, 101
Flaherty, Robert, 166
Flor's Homepage, 194–95
Flow, 209–210, 212
Flow: The Psychology of Optimal Experience (Czikszentmihalyi), 209, 260
Flowers, Rose, 232–233
Folk Knitting in Estonia (Bush), 170
Fringes for scarves, 55
From beg (beginning), 65
Front loops, 59
Frugal Knitting Haus, 194

Garter stitch, 26, 33, 132
  edge, 134
  invisible seaming on, 98
  striping in, 118, 119
Garter Stitch Vest, 80–81
Garth, Jennifer, 228
Gauge, 13, 25–29, 68, 132
Giammarina, Jean, 233
Gibson-Roberts, Priscilla A., 172, 173
Glossary of knitting terms, 64–67
Gold, Tracey, 228
Gossamer Webs—the History and Techniques of Orenburg Lace Shawls (Khmeleva and Noble), 170
Greene, Lois, 142
Green Mountain Spinnery, 183, 259
Guernseys, 167
Guilds, 225–228
Gunther, Helen, 194

Hagerman, Bonnie, 145–146
Half double crochet, 110
Hamer, Joan, 142, 193
Hand spun yarn, 23
Hannah, Daryl, 181, 228
Hats and caps:
  Basketweave Hat, 150
  Bias Hat, 247
  Preemie Caps, 149–150
  Roll-Neck Raglan Pullover with Hat, 84–86
  Striped Stocking Cap, 40
  Tie Hat, 37
  Watch Cap, 153–154
Heathered yarn, 23
Hepburn, Audrey, 177
Hepburn, Katharine, 175
Herrschner's Yarn Shoppe Catalog, 218, 260
Hip measurement, 92
History of Hand Knitting, A (Rutt), 170–171
Hobby Lobby, 214, 216
Homespun, Handknit: Caps, Socks, Mittens and Gloves (Ligon), 255
Homespun yarn, 23
Horizontal buttonholes, 137
Horizontal seams, 98–99
Horizontal stitch pickups, 102
How to Knit—The Definitive Knitting Course Complete with Step-by-Step Techniques, Stitch Library and Projects for Your Home and Family, 250–251
Hunt, Mary, 200
Hunt, Zoë, 255

Iceland, 167–168, 170, 174
Illustrated Dictionary of Knitting, The (Compton), 171
Increase/Decrease Baby Blanket, 63
Increases, 57–59
Infants' sizing guidelines, 93
Intarsia, 135, 136
International Rescue Committee, 227

International Seafarer's Center, Port Newark, 146
Internet, 73, 143, 189–203, 219, 223
Interweave Knits magazine, 215, 257
Ireland, 174

Jacobs, Marc, 181
Jerseys, 167
Jersey stitch. *See* Stockinette stitch
JoAnn Fabrics & Crafts, 214

K1, C2, 261
Kagan, Sasha, 185
Karan, Donna, 179, 181, 258
Keele, Wendy, 172
Kennedy, Jackie, 177
Khmeleva, Galina, 170
Kids Knitting: Projects for Kids of All Ages (Falick), 251
Kids' sizing guidelines, 93
Kitchel, Cindy, 252
Klein, Adina, 163, 181, 258
Klein, Calvin, 179
Knit It Your Way (Wise), 256
KnitList, 156, 199–200
KnitNet, 201
Knit 'n Style magazine, 257–258
Knit-Outs, 231–232
Knits, care of. *See* Care of knits
Knit shops, 228–229
Knit stitch, 30–37
Knitted-Lace List, 197–198
Knitterie Parisienne, La, 228
Knitter's Magazine, 215, 219, 229, 258
Knitting:
  camps and retreats, 182–184
  chain of instruction, 221–224
  for charity, 141–155, 226–227
  commerce of, 213–220
  fashion trends in, 174–181
  fiber festivals and country fairs, 186–188
  gauge, 13, 25–29, 68, 132
  glossary of terms, 64–67
  guilds, 225–228
  healing power of, 204–212
  Internet and, 189–203
  left-handed knitters, 34
  needles, 3–7
  patterns. *See* Patterns
  stitches. *See* Stitches
  traditions, 164–173
  travel and tours, 184–186
  yarns. *See* Yarns
Knitting.About.com, 196, 202, 219
Knitting Architect, The (Elalouf), 253
Knitting by the Sea, 183–184, 259
Knitting clubs, 232–233
Knitting Ganseys (Brown-Reinsel), 171
Knitting Guild of America, The, 201, 225
Knitting in America (Falick), 254
Knitting in Plain English (Righetti), 226, 251–252
Knitting in the Nordic Tradition (Lind), 173
Knitting in the Old Way (Gibson-Roberts), 173
Knitting Without Tears (Zimmerman), 249
KnitU (Knitter's University), 200–201
Knitwise, 65
KnitWits, 232–233
Kors, Michael, 180–181

Lace Rib Scarf, 52
Lamb's wool, 18
Lamé, 22
Large-eyed needles, 9
Late Art Deco (1930–1945) era, 175–176
Latvia, 171
Latvian Mittens (Upitis), 171
Lauren, Ralph, 179, 181
Leapman, Melissa, 255
LeCount, Cynthia Gravelle, 169, 184
Left-handed knitters, 34
Length from back neck to waist measurement, 92
Lengthwise Scarf, 50
Ligon, Linda, 255
Lind, Vibeke, 173
Linen, 21
Lion Brand Yarn Company, 195, 218, 261
Lithuania, 171
Llama, 19
Lopi, 168
Lot, or dye-lot, number, 14
Loving Stitch, A History of Knitting and Spinning in New Zealand (Nicholson), 173
Lurex, 22
Luskofte ski sweaters, 168
Luxury Shawl and Scarf, 246

Macdonald, Anne L., 172
MacDonald, Julien, 180
Malcolm, Trisha, 174–181
Manning, Meg, 204, 216
Manning, Tara Jon, 217
Man of Aran (film), 166
Manship family, 194

Mariner's Scarf, 146, 153
Maryland Sheep and Wool Festival, 187, 260
Mary Maxim catalog, 218, 260
Mary Thomas's Knitting Book, 171
Matte cotton, 20–21
McAllister, Jill, 199–200
McCartney, Stella, 180
McDonald, Helga, 183
McGregor, Sheila, 173
Measurements, 67
  taking, 91–92
Measures and weights, 72
Measuring tape, 7–8, 10, 48
Meg Swansen's Knitting, 248–249
Melville, Sally, 183, 201, 254
Men's sizing guidelines, 93
Mercerized cotton, 20, 21
Merino sheep, 18
Metallic yarns, 22
Michael's Arts and Crafts stores, 214, 216
Microfiber, 21
Miller, Tyeisha, 233
Mill stores, 215
Miracle, Nancy, 195
Missoni family, 178
Mizrahi, Isaac, 181
M1 (make 1), 65
Mock cable edge, 134
Mohair, 18, 176, 187
Mondragon, Rick, 201
Moore, Julianne, 228
Morgan, Gwyn, 173
Moss, Jean, 185
Moth preventive, 105
MSN Communities, 201–202

Nålbinding, 164, 171
Necklines, 136
Neck shaping, 70
Needle cases, 7
Needles, 3–7
Nelson, Caryl, 191
Nelson, Linda, 198
Nelson, Nancy, 191
New millennium (1997–2000), 180–181
Newton, Deborah, 252
Next row (WS) or (RS), 65
Ng, Eve, 227–228
Nicholson, Heather, 173
Noble, Carol R., 170
No Idle Hands—The Social History of American Knitting (Macdonald), 172
Nordic Knitting (Pagoldh), 173
Norway, 164, 168, 170
Nylon, 21, 22

Ogg, Carol, 227
Oldham, Todd, 181
Ombré, 24
One Heart Foundation, 148
Orenburg shawl knitting, 170
Osmond, Alan, 148
Over the Moon, 217, 260

Pagoldh, Susanne, 173
Patch pockets, 137
Pattern on yarn label, 11
Patterns:
  abbreviations, 71–72
  alterations to, 131
  Baby Guernsey Set, 238–240
  Baby Soft 'n' Seamless Cardigan, 151–152
  Basketweave Hat, 150
  Bias Bicolor Scarf, 49
  Bias Hat, 247
  Cabled Pullover, 123–124
  Cabled Scarf, 54
  Cell Phone Holder, 36
  Center-Cable Pullover, 243–245
  changing stitch patterns, 132–133
  changing yarns, 131–132
  Child's Cabled Cardigan, 120–122
  Deep Rib Pullover, 234–237
  Double Strand Scarf, 53
  Easy Bright Ribbed Pullover, 43–44
  Easy Cardigan, 87–89
  Easy Strip Throw, 129
  Garter Stitch Vest, 80–81
  Increase/Decrease Baby Blanket, 63
  Lace Rib Scarf, 52
  Lengthwise Scarf, 50
  Luxury Shawl and Scarf, 246
  Mariner's Scarf, 153
  measures and weights, 72
  online purchasing, 193–195
  Preemie Caps, 149–150
  reading charts, 73–77
  reading instructions, 67–72
  reading schematic drawings, 77–79
  Roll-Neck Raglan Pullover with Hat, 84–86
  Seafarer's Scarf, 154
  skill levels and, 69–70
  Sleeveless T-neck, 82–83
  socks, 127–128
  Striped Sailor Pullover, 125–126
  Striped Stocking Cap, 40
  symbols, 72–73

Patterns (*cont.*)
- Tassel Scarf, 51
- Tie Hat, 37
- using as jumping-off point, 130
- V-neck Bicolor Tunic, 241–242
- Watch Cap, 153–154

Patterns for Guernseys, Jerseys and Arans—Fishermen's Sweaters from the British Isles (Thompson), 172
Patternworks, 218, 260
Pearson, Michael, 172
Piccar, Rissa, 232
Pick up and k (knit), 65
Pine Meadow Knitting News, 142, 259
Pins, 9
Place a marker, 65
Plant fibers, 20–21, 104
Playing with Yarn, 216–217, 229, 260
Plummer, Steve, 207
Ply, 24
Pockets, 137–138
Poems of Color—Knitting in the Bohus Tradition (Keele), 172
Point protectors, 10, 48
Polyamide, 22
Polyester, 21, 22
Possum, 20
Postwar (1946–1963) era, 176–177
Prada, Miuccia, 179
Preemie Caps, 149–150
Premature babies, 144–145
Printed yarn, 24
Pullovers. *See* Sweaters
Purl stitch, 38–40
Purlwise, 65

Qiviut, 20, 186

Rag, 24
Rag Shop, 214
Raven, Jo-Ann, 194
Rayon, 22
Reader's Digest Knitters Handbook: A Comprehensive Guide to the Principles and Techniques of Handknitting (Montse), 249–250
Reading:
- charts, 73–72
- instructions, 67–77
- schematic drawings, 77–79

Relaxation Response, The (Benson), 211, 260
Rep from * to end, 66
Retreats, 182–184
Reverse shaping, 66
Reynolds Yarn, 261
Ribbing, 42, 133
Rib stitch, 41–44
- striping in, 119

Richter, Joan, 233
Righetti, Maggie, 226, 251–253
Robbins, Whit, 225–226
Roberts, Julia, 181
Roberts, Patricia, 178
Roennow, Annette, 192
Rolled edge, 134
Roll-Neck Raglan Pullover with Hat, 84–86
Ronay, Edina, 178
Rosen, Evie, 147
Roving yarn, 24
Row counters, 10, 48
Rutt, Richard, 170–171
Rykiel, Sonia, 178

Safe houses, 148
Saint-Laurent, Yves, 176–177
Salazar, Kim, 189, 197
Salish Indian Sweaters, A Pacific Northwest Tradition (Gibson-Roberts), 172
Sally Melville Styles: A Unique and Elegant Approach for Your Yarn Collection, 254
Scarves:
- Bias Bicolor, 49
- Cabled, 54
- Double Strand, 53
- fringes for, 55
- Lace Rib, 52
- Lengthwise, 50
- Luxury Shawl and Scarf, 246
- Mariner's Scarf, 146, 153
- Seafarer's Scarf, 146, 154
- Tassel, 51
- tassels for, 56

Schaeffer, Michaela, 227
Schematic drawings, reading, 77–79
Schiaparelli, Elsa, 175
Schooley, Ruth, 200
Schrouder, Joan, 201
Scissors, 8–9
Scott, Pat, 230
Scott, Shirley A., 169–170
Seabright, Nyle, 229
Seafarer's Scarf, 146, 154
Seamen's Church Institute, 146, 147
Seaming, 97–100
Seam preparation (blocking), 95–96
Selvage stitches, 71
Selznick, Barbara, 230–231
Set-in pockets, 137–138

Shaping:
armhole, 70
neck, 70
Shetland shawls, 167
Shetland wool, 18
Shoulders measurement, 92
Silk, 20
Single crochet, 111–112
Sizing, 131
adjusting to fit, 93, 95
ease, 90–91
infants' guidelines, 94
kids' guidelines, 94
men's guidelines, 94
taking measurements, 91–92
women's guidelines, 93
Sleeve length from center back neck measurement, 92
Sleeveless T-neck, 82–83
Slipknot, 111
Slipping stitches, 61–62
Slip stitch, 110, 111
Snips, 8
Socknitters, 198
Socks, 112–117
pattern, 127–128
Sock weight yarns, 16
Space-dyed yarn, 24, 25
Sportweight yarns, 16
Ssk (slip, slip, knit), 66
Ssp (slip, slip, purl), 66
Stabolesky, Mary, 187
Standard weight yarns, 16
Stanley, Montse, 249–250
Starmore, Alice, 166, 169, 185
Stitch charts, 73–75
Stitchery, The, 218, 261
Stitches:
cabling, 107–110
crochet, 110
decreasing, 59–61
dropping, 45–46
edge, 47–48
increasing, 57–59
knit stitch, 30–37
purl stitch, 38–40
rib stitch, 41–44
slipping, 61–62
stockinette stitch, 26, 39, 132
unraveling, 46–47
Stitches conventions, 229–231
Stitches Markets, 220
Stitch gauge and needle/hook size tool, 7, 10, 26
Stitch holders, 8, 10
Stitch left (front) cable, 109
Stitch markers, 8, 10
Stitch pattern, 68–69
Stitch right (back) cable, 109–110
Stockinette stitch, 26, 39, 132
invisible seaming on, 98, 99
picking up stitches on, 102–103
striping in, 117
Stocking stitch. *See* Stockinette stitch
Storing knits, 105–106
Straight needles, 3, 4–5
Stranding, 135
Striped Sailor Pullover, 125–126
Striped Stocking Cap, 40
Striping, 117–119
Stuffed animal sweaters, 146
Super bulky or jumbo yarns, 15–16
Swansen, Meg, 142, 201, 248–249
Sweater Design in Plain English (Righetti), 253
Sweaters. *See also* Cardigans
Cabled Pullover, 123–124
Garter Stitch Vest, 80–81
Luskofte ski, 168
Roll-Neck Raglan Pullover with Hat, 84–86
Sleeveless T-neck, 82–83
Striped Sailor Pullover, 125–126
stuffed animal, 146
Sweden, 164, 168
Symbols, 72–73
Synthetic fibers, 21–22, 104

Taos Sheep and Wool Festival, 187, 260
Tape measure, 7–8, 10, 48
Tapestry needles, 9, 10
Tassel Scarf, 51
Tassels for scarves, 56
Tension. *See* Gauge
Terms, glossary of, 64–67
Thick and thin yarn, 25
Thomas, Mary, 164, 171
Thompson, Gladys, 172
Three-needle bind-off, 99–100
Throw, 129
Tie Hat, 37
Tocker, Jennifer, 195
Tools, 3–29
Totes, 10
Tours, 184–186
T-pins, 9
Traditional Knitting (McGregor), 173
Traditional Knitting—Aran, Fair Isle and Fisher Ganseys (Pearson), 172
Traditional Knitting—Patterns of Ireland, Scotland and England (Morgan), 173

Travel, 184–186
Treasury of Knitting Patterns, A (Walker), 256
Treble crochet, 110
Tvåändssticking, 168
Tweed yarn, 25
Twined Knitting (Dandanell and Danielsson), 173

Ultimate Knitters' Guide, The (Buller), 250
Uneven stripes, 118–119
Unraveling stitches, 46–47
Unst region, 167
Upitis, Lizbeth, 171
Ursina, Vita, 232

Valentino, 180
Vardhman Knitting Yarn, 192–193
Variegated yarn, 24, 25
Vass, Joan, 179
Vertical seams, 97
Vertical stitch pickups, 102
Vicuna, 19
Virgin wool, 18
Viscose, 22
Vittadini, Adrienne, 178
V-neck Bicolor Tunic, 241–242
Vogue Knitting, 185, 258
Vogue Knitting: The Ultimate Knitting Book, 250

Waist measurement, 91–92
Walker, Barbara G., 256
Wal-Mart, 214, 216
Ward, Lynda, 151
Warming Families, 148, 224, 259
Warm Up America!, 144, 147–148, 191, 259
  patterns, 155
Washing knits, 103–106
Watch Cap, 153–154
Way, Emily, 196
Weaving in ends, 101
Webs, 217, 261
Weight and yardage, 13
Wise, Cynthia Yanok, 256
wiseNeedle.com, 197
With RS or WS facing, 66
Women's sizing guidelines, 93
Wool, 18, 104, 105, 187
Wool Connection, The, 219, 261
Wool Works, 196–197, 201
Wooly Thoughts (Ashforth and Plummer), 207
Work both sides at once, 66
Work even, 66
Work to end, 67
Worsted weight yarns, 16

Xenakis, David, 201

Yak, 20
Yarn Expressions, 216, 260
Yarn Forward, 194
Yarn-over increase, 58–59
Yarns:
  animal fibers, 18–20
  care instructions, 12
  changing, 131–132
  collecting and storing, 156–163
  color name and number, 13
  company name and yarn name, 11
  fiber content, 13
  joining new strand, 35
  label, 11
  lot, or dye-lot, number, 14
  online purchasing, 190–193, 219
  plant fibers, 20–21
  purchasing, 190–193, 213–220
  reading labels, 11–15
  substitution, 14
  synthetic fibers, 21–22
  terms and treatments, 23–25
  weights, 11, 15–17
Youth movement, 177

Zimmermann, Elizabeth, 249, 253–254